# Seasoned Contentment

# *Seasoned* CONTENTMENT

Musings from the southern she  shed of a life marred by grief, saved by grace, overflowing with gratitude

## *Ecclesiastes 3:1*

# Marti Miller Willoughby

XULON PRESS

Xulon Press
2301 Lucien Way #415
Maitland, FL 32751
407.339.4217
www.xulonpress.com

Unless otherwise indicated, Scripture quotations taken from the New King James Version (NKJV). Copyright © 1982 by Thomas Nelson, Inc. Used by permission. All rights reserved.

Paperback ISBN-13: 978-1-6628-0148-8

Ebook ISBN-13: 978-1-6628-0149-5

# Dedication

For my children, Devin Tara and Nicholas Philip, who always give me reasons to keep breathing. For Lucas and Carrie, who literally helped me breathe through an acute illness. And for their daughter, Alice, who gives me a reason to be called Nana. For Eric and all the Millers who knew me when and continue to remember. For my very last husband, Darrell Willoughby, who encourages me to keep writing and loves unconditionally, especially when I am most unlovable.

# Acknowledgements

So many people have encouraged this book, whether they know it or not—family, friends, faith partners, even a few strangers. They are, in random order: The ministers of faith— Chip and Karen, Charles and Mary Lynn, Sandra, Betsy, Matt, Jim, Dale, Allen, Matthew, Steve, and Darrell; the inspirational worship musicians nearby and around the world; the prayer warrior women at Revelation Church; prayer guides Ashley, Jackie, Laura, Lisa, Sherry, Sue, and Barbara; my first, second, and third families; the Gnomies – Lisa, Mary Lynn, Norma Jean, and Sara. Finally, to the magazine owner/editor, staff, and readers - without you, these essays may never have found a first home away from home. Please know you are loved. As it was in the beginning and will be to the end, it is all for God's glory.

# Table Of Contents

## In Spring
### Beginnings, Birthdays, Bunnies, and Mothers

*Then God said, "Let there be lights in the firmament of the heavens to divide the day from the night; and let them be for signs and seasons, and for days and years."*

—*Genesis* 1:14

**March**

A Wonderful Life, 2007 . . . . . . . . . . . . . . . . . . . . . . . . . . . . . . 1
Marching On, 2009 . . . . . . . . . . . . . . . . . . . . . . . . . . . . . . . . 5
Grief, Grace, and Gratitude, 2012 . . . . . . . . . . . . . . . . . . . . . 8
Coming Unglued, 2014 . . . . . . . . . . . . . . . . . . . . . . . . . . . . 11
Yankernings, 2016 . . . . . . . . . . . . . . . . . . . . . . . . . . . . . . . 15
The Snapdragon Season, 2017 . . . . . . . . . . . . . . . . . . . . . . 19

**April**

When Pigs Fly, 2008 . . . . . . . . . . . . . . . . . . . . . . . . . . . . . . 25
Still, 2010 . . . . . . . . . . . . . . . . . . . . . . . . . . . . . . . . . . . . . 28
Sooner or Later, 2011 . . . . . . . . . . . . . . . . . . . . . . . . . . . . . 31
Little Things, 2012 . . . . . . . . . . . . . . . . . . . . . . . . . . . . . . . 34
Untangled, 2014 . . . . . . . . . . . . . . . . . . . . . . . . . . . . . . . . 38
Little Bunny Foo-Foo, 2015 . . . . . . . . . . . . . . . . . . . . . . . . 42

**May**

Her Secret Hope, 2009 . . . . . . . . . . . . . . . . . . . . . . . . . . . . 49
Pay It Forward, 2010 . . . . . . . . . . . . . . . . . . . . . . . . . . . . . 53
Role Reversal, 2011 . . . . . . . . . . . . . . . . . . . . . . . . . . . . . . 57
Defining Moments, 2013 . . . . . . . . . . . . . . . . . . . . . . . . . . 61

Mine? Mine? Mine? 2014 . . . . . . . . . . . . . . . . . . . . . . . . . . . . . 65

When You Care Enough, 2016 . . . . . . . . . . . . . . . . . . . . . . . 68

## In Summer
### Fathers, Brothers, Friends, and Others
### fig 4

*Now learn this parable from the fig tree: When its branch has already become tender and puts forth leaves, you know that summer is near.*

—Matthew 24:32

### June

Lessons Learned, 2007 . . . . . . . . . . . . . . . . . . . . . . . . . . . . . . . 77

The Daddy Dance, 2008 . . . . . . . . . . . . . . . . . . . . . . . . . . . . . 81

Forecast: Man-Drought, 2009 . . . . . . . . . . . . . . . . . . . . . . . 84

Doodlebugs & Dog Tags, 2010 . . . . . . . . . . . . . . . . . . . . . . 87

The Men Tour, 2014 . . . . . . . . . . . . . . . . . . . . . . . . . . . . . . . 91

Leave It to June, Beaver 2016 . . . . . . . . . . . . . . . . . . . . . . . 95

### July

Oh, Good Grief, 2007 . . . . . . . . . . . . . . . . . . . . . . . . . . . . . 103

Let the River Run, 2008 . . . . . . . . . . . . . . . . . . . . . . . . . . . 106

Sister Acts, 2012 . . . . . . . . . . . . . . . . . . . . . . . . . . . . . . . . . . 109

The Great American Soldier, 2014 . . . . . . . . . . . . . . . . . . 113

Heat and Humility, 2015 . . . . . . . . . . . . . . . . . . . . . . . . . . 116

Reaching Forward: Summer Storms and Horn Worms, 2016 . . 121

### August

Losing the Labels, 2009 . . . . . . . . . . . . . . . . . . . . . . . . . . . 129

Enough, 2011 . . . . . . . . . . . . . . . . . . . . . . . . . . . . . . . . . . . . 132

Green Acres of Gratitude, 2014 . . . . . . . . . . . . . . . . . . . . . 136

Coming Unglued Again, 2015 . . . . . . . . . . . . . . . . . . . . . . 141

The Sticky Wicket, 2016 . . . . . . . . . . . . . . . . . . . . . . . . . . . 144

Liberty & Justice, 2017 . . . . . . . . . . . . . . . . . . . . . . . . . . . 148

## In Fall
### *Makeovers, Survivors, Boos, and Thank-You*
*fig 5*

*When they walk through the Valley of Weeping, it will become a place of refreshing springs. The autumn rains will clothe it with blessings.*

—Psalm 84:6 (NLT)

**September**
Getting the Message, 2008 . . . . . . . . . . . . . . . . . . . . . . . . . 155
Fixing the Focus, 2009 . . . . . . . . . . . . . . . . . . . . . . . . . . . 160
Rules of Engagement, 2010 . . . . . . . . . . . . . . . . . . . . . . . 163
Transitional Lenses, 2014 . . . . . . . . . . . . . . . . . . . . . . . . 166
Refining Moments, 2015 . . . . . . . . . . . . . . . . . . . . . . . . . 170
The Hummingburden, 2016. . . . . . . . . . . . . . . . . . . . . . . 174

**October**
Hidden Treasures, 2008 . . . . . . . . . . . . . . . . . . . . . . . . . . 181
Dancing in the Rain, 2011 . . . . . . . . . . . . . . . . . . . . . . . . 185
Nothing Could Define Her, 2014. . . . . . . . . . . . . . . . . . . 188
Victorious Secrets, 2015 . . . . . . . . . . . . . . . . . . . . . . . . . 191
Pumpkin Chunkin', 2016 . . . . . . . . . . . . . . . . . . . . . . . . 195
Thelma & Louise, 2017 . . . . . . . . . . . . . . . . . . . . . . . . . . 199

**November**
Talking Turkey, 2007 . . . . . . . . . . . . . . . . . . . . . . . . . . . . 207
The Domestic Glitch: And Other Rare Birds, 2010 . . . . . . . . 211
Bibbity Bobbity Boo: The Mess of Magical Thinking, 2011 . . 215
Thanksforgivingness, 2012 . . . . . . . . . . . . . . . . . . . . . . . . 218
Thanksgrieving, 2014. . . . . . . . . . . . . . . . . . . . . . . . . . . . 222
Sparkle & Glow, 2016 . . . . . . . . . . . . . . . . . . . . . . . . . . . 226

# In Winter
## *Gifts Differing, Resolutions, and Love Stories*
## *fig 6*

*She extends a helping hand to the poor and opens her arms to the needy.*

*She has no fear of winter for her household, for everyone has warm clothes.*

—Proverbs 31:20–21 (NLT)

### December
Gifts Differing, 2007 . . . . . . . . . . . . . . . . . . . . . . . . . . . . . . . . . 235
The Christmas Witch, 2008 . . . . . . . . . . . . . . . . . . . . . . . . . . 238
Into the River and Out of the Woods, 2010 . . . . . . . . . . . . . 242
Santa-cipation, 2013 . . . . . . . . . . . . . . . . . . . . . . . . . . . . . . . . 245
A Very Married Christmas, 2014 . . . . . . . . . . . . . . . . . . . . . 248
Gift Wrapped Words, 2017 . . . . . . . . . . . . . . . . . . . . . . . . . . 251

### January
*J* is for Joy, 2008 . . . . . . . . . . . . . . . . . . . . . . . . . . . . . . . . . . . 259
Loading the Resolver, 2013 . . . . . . . . . . . . . . . . . . . . . . . . . . 262
The Biggest Loser, 2014 . . . . . . . . . . . . . . . . . . . . . . . . . . . . . 266
Kicking Against the Pricks, 2015 . . . . . . . . . . . . . . . . . . . . . 269
The Selfie Shirt, 2016 . . . . . . . . . . . . . . . . . . . . . . . . . . . . . . . 273
The Hard Way, 2017 . . . . . . . . . . . . . . . . . . . . . . . . . . . . . . . . 277

### February
One Is Enough, 2008 . . . . . . . . . . . . . . . . . . . . . . . . . . . . . . . . 285
I Do Two, 2014 . . . . . . . . . . . . . . . . . . . . . . . . . . . . . . . . . . . . 288
Tikkun Olam, 2015 . . . . . . . . . . . . . . . . . . . . . . . . . . . . . . . . . 292
Aphids Dingoes and Ostriches, 2016 . . . . . . . . . . . . . . . . . . 296
Let There Be Love, 2017 . . . . . . . . . . . . . . . . . . . . . . . . . . . . 300
Love in the Sixties, 2018 . . . . . . . . . . . . . . . . . . . . . . . . . . . . 303

Afterthoughts . . . . . . . . . . . . . . . . . . . . . . . . . . . . . . . 307

The Age of Contentment . . . . . . . . . . . . . . . . . . . . 309

Power of Writing . . . . . . . . . . . . . . . . . . . . . . . . . . . 313

Milestones for all Seasons of Life . . . . . . . . . . . . . . . 318

# Introduction

Thank you for choosing this collection of essays about one ordinary life wounded by grief, saved by grace, and overflowing with gratitude. It is my greatest hope that, somewhere within, you will find a relatable nugget of hope for your own life—something to hold onto for future reference, or to help in the here and now of difficult times or trying circumstance. I also hope you will find some small bits of humor to encourage you or at least give you a reason to smile.

I spent about thirty years hiding from God. Raised a Catholic, the youngest of five daughters in a home filled with love (though no one dared voice it), there was no choice given about faith. We did church. We did confession, communion, and grace before meals. We learned the rosary and feared nuns with rulers. We had priests over for dinner, hoping their aura of holiness would glow in our hearts.

Then I left home for college, began a career, and ultimately let go of every Sunday obligation. At twenty-eight, and on the rebound from a failed engagement, I met and married a divorced, agnostic firefighter who was thirteen years my senior and the custodial father of a teenaged son. He also happened to be what is often referred to as a functioning alcoholic, much like my dad was in my growing up years (he quit after I left home—hmmm). A baby girl and boy arrived in quick succession, and the closest our children came to religious education was a Lutheran preschool. I was determined, of course, that they would be able to *choose* their own faith. Unfortunately, I gave them little to go on. Love? Sure. Care for others? Absolutely. But church, faith, and Jesus? Not so much. Consequently, they (and we) chose nothing and built our family foundation on some rather shaky ground.

As often happens while busy adulting and parenting, trials and grief arrived in many forms. But the most crushing blow to our family came wrapped in my husband's cancer diagnosis. He was a career firefighter in DC prior to retirement and succumbed to squamous cell carcinoma. It was an eighteen-month battle—including chemo, radiation, loss of nearly 150 pounds, and a very hopeful remission—during which time we opted to move from Maryland to South Carolina and enjoy what we hoped would be a few more years of reasonable health. Though they were invited to join us, our children (then aged twenty-one and twenty-two) chose to remain Marylanders.

Two months after making the move, and just shy of our twenty-fifth wedding anniversary, David Robert Miller died in hospice care, a skin-and-bones version of the hulking man he had been. Less than six months later, my dad passed away in a nursing home, thinking he was a prisoner of war. Just one week after that sadness, my son nearly lost his life in an alcohol-induced vehicular run-in with a telephone pole, thus changing the trajectory of his future for a very long time. I had no hope. Or so I thought. For me, God was nowhere around and certainly not the least bit interested in me, or me in Him. Grief seemed to be my only constant companion. Bystanders were lucky not to choke on the smoke of my raging poor-me fires.

Little did I know that God, Jesus, and the Holy Spirit, the gang of three in one, were near me all the time, patiently waiting for me to stop and turn. The house we had purchased in Marion, South Carolina, after many months of searching, "just happened" to share a backyard with believing neighbors who refused to leave a grieving widow alone with her misery. Nine months later, on March 15, 2007, I would beg His forgiveness and receive His grace. I came to the gifted seed of salvation at fifty-two, ever the late-blooming child.

That very same month also marked the beginning of a ten-year journey writing essays about hope, faith, and love for a regional women's publication, *She Magazine*. Every month I would write out my life, based on the reoccurring themes for each issue. These are the essays I am sharing now, with minor editing to protect the innocent. They chronicle this pilgrim's journey from grief, to grace and gratitude.

Faith remains the center of what has become a most wonderful life—saved by grace, with trials and grief still present, but filled with gratitude for what He has set in motion. I hope you will find these "musings from the she shed" tolerable reading. Each one was lovingly and often painfully written in the continual hope that there will be at least a glimmer of help, hope, and humor for your own experiences with grief and gratitude in this life. The grace is His alone. There will always be joy mixed with sorrow here, while hope breathes deeply through every season and finds contentment:

"Therefore we do not lose heart. Even though our outward man is perishing, yet the inward man is being renewed day by day. For our light affliction, which is but for a moment, is working for us a far more exceeding and eternal weight of glory, while we do not look at the things which are seen, but at the things which are not seen. For the things which are seen are temporary, but the things which are not seen are eternal" (2 Cor. 4:16–18).

# Author's Note

Unlike our calendar year, some beginnings don't happen in January, nor do endings always arrive in December. For me, life began again in March 2007, when I finally stopped running from God and His grace. The ending has not yet arrived, but because *She Magazine* stopped publishing in 2018, that is where the essay musings end for now. Rather than present them chronologically, I have chosen, instead, to use the contributing writers' monthly themes, by season—spring, summer, fall, and winter. Each monthly section is presented chronologically, but as you read from page to page, you will find wide variations in my life circumstance. Depending on the season and year, I may write as a lonely widow, a hopeful engaged person, or a happily remarried one. As it is in this life, grief continues to visit. But grace and gratitude remain always. Thank you for your patience in reading through a somewhat fractured timeline. It's not unlike living in the South, where all four seasons can appear in a single day. I have also opted to share only six stories from each month, instead of the whole batch (you're welcome). And I must confess that I do not own a she shed yet, but my mind conjures one each time I sit down to write. My shed is instead a tiny corner in the smallest room of our humble home, but it transforms into a magical writing shack—on most days. On other days, it's more of a torture chamber. Either way, I am thankful—in spring, summer, fall, and winter. Finding contentment does not often follow a straight line, but joy is ours when we seek the narrow path that follows Christ through hills, valleys, potholes, and fragrant wildflower gardens.

# Spring Season in the She Shed

**Beginnings, Birthdays, Bunnies, and Mothers**

*Then God said, "Let there be lights in the firmament of the heavens to divide the day from the night; and let them be for signs and seasons, and for days and years."*

—Genesis 1:14

March

**A Wonderful Life**
**Carrying On**
**Grief to Grace to Gratitude**
**Coming Unglued**
**Yankernings**
**Snapdragon Season**

*M*arch was always reserved for celebrations of birth and age because the magazine was born in this month. Every year we were called to remember how and why we are grateful to be our current age. The submission of my first article to *She Magazine* initiated what would become a writing journey of over ten years, building new relationships, finding love in the twilight, acceptance of the greatest gift, and learning to find contentment in all things, knowing how the story ends in eternal; peace and joy.

# A Wonderful Life

*March 2007*

*V*ery close to the top of my best-movies-of-all-time list is *It's a Wonderful Life*. No year would be complete without a quiet evening on the couch with Jimmy Stewart, a full bowl of buttery popcorn, and a mug of steaming hot cocoa (and perhaps a few small bags of candy). Each viewing of this classic film and each new birthday cause me to consider what I might have missed had I not been here since 1954. Now that sixty has become the new forty, I am really enjoying my "thirties" again. Here's what I might have otherwise missed:

Had I not been here, I would have missed learning to ride a bike and blow huge gum bubbles, and helping my dad train our bench-leg beagles (and hearing him holler in the middle of the night while spraying said pups with the water hose as they practiced howling at the moon). I would have missed watching my mother masterfully care for five daughters and still find time to sew our clothes and knit our sweaters and cook three full meals a day. I probably should have been taking better notes too, as I have difficulty threading needles and following the simplest of recipes.

I would have missed graduating from high school and college and struggling to find a career by trying on many different ones until I finally looked behind me and discovered that the pathway was there all along—I just couldn't see it clearly. Every job I have ever had—teaching, marketing, advising, even volunteering—has involved writing in some form or other. So now I get it—I write. I don't get paid so much anymore, but at least I get the idea.

I would have missed falling in love, feeling the tearing of my heart and the sadness of bruising another's. I would have missed finding the love of my life and the privilege of caring for him as he valiantly fought and ultimately lost his cancer battle. He spent twenty-seven years fighting fires in Washington, DC, and faced his final fire with the same kind of courage. I celebrated our twenty-fifth wedding anniversary alone, but with the quiet company of memories. I learned many lessons from him; chief among them was the expression of unconditional love. I trust that it is not too late to share those lessons with others, especially our children.

I would not know the honor of friendships, both old and new. I would not be able to say that there are so many blessings in having friends who "knew you when" and know you now, and continue to have a healthy sense of what to remember and what to forget. One friend I have known for fifty years, and our memories are beginning to fade appropriately. We remember our triumphs in great detail, while our failures continue to fade and get fuzzy. One friend I have known for just a few months, and I hope many memories are yet to be made. There are also those friends that appear in between. Here, as in many other things, it's the quality of friendships and not the quantity that truly matters most.

If I were not here now, I would not have known the beautiful bliss of childbirth (and hemorrhoid relief on a donut pillow), the many energies of my children's youthful exuberance, and, yes, the torturous trials of their teendom. It was those very years that caused me to reflect on just why I had waited until thirty to begin the mother thing. The nearly simultaneous arrivals of perimenopause and late-youth rebellion caused a conflagration nearly impossible to squelch. Trials by fire, indeed. We are all still talking to each other, and I count that as a very good sign for our future family togetherness. My children are now cautiously dipping their toes into the pool of adulthood and I, for one, cannot wait to see how they emerge—and with whom. I hear that grandchildren make parenting so worthwhile. No pressure though. I can wait—a little while.

I would have greatly missed the many joys of being the youngest of those five aforementioned daughters my parents produced, in spite of the overload of baby jokes endured over the years. My dad insisted upon introducing me as "The Baby" so often I sometimes wondered if he actually knew my name. Sadly, he left this world last year, just shy of his ninetieth birthday, and I wish I could hear him call me baby one more time. Without this blessing of time, I would not know the joys of sisters becoming friends, despite the fact that they all turned prematurely gray while I continue to rock a lovely shade of our Nana's brown locks (with a little help from the salon).

We all shared the grief of a breast cancer diagnosis and the triumph of watching our oldest sister beautifully and graciously live through it. Then again, being the first family widow, even before our mother, might have hurried along our friendship journey (babies don't get taken too seriously in normal circumstances). Their friendship is still a gift gladly received and worthy of nourishment. We will be taking our first annual sisters' trip to Charleston, SC (yes, the baby gets her way), and are planning next year's adventure in Chicago. It might get a bit tense along the way, as I do harbor just a teeny bit of resentment from all the years of being, well, babied. But this sister-friendship remains a journey well worth taking and cherishing.

While on the subject of travels, I definitely would have missed finding Marion, SC. What turned out to be the final decision of that twenty-five-year marriage involved moving our cancer battle to a warmer, quieter, softer place. We started our search in North Carolina and, thankfully, found this "pretty little town on the way to the beach." Although the battle was ultimately lost, we gained a wonderful victory of time and place and people. Marion is turning out to be one of the best experiences of this life journey. I have reaped the rewards of southern hospitality with neighbors who live in faith and share their blessings with grateful strangers. If not for Marion and her gifts, I would not have discovered the joys (and regular embarrassment) of aerobic exercise in a class filled with welcoming women and very tolerant instructors. I would not be taking baby steps toward the finding of faith with a welcoming church and patient guides. Marion's close proximity to the beach has pretty much guaranteed a steady stream of visiting friends and family, intent on not allowing me to get stuck in my aloneness, and while they are about it, catching a breeze from God's great ocean. It's truly a win-win situation.

All things considered, I'm very glad to be almost fifty-three. I look forward to the gifts of each new day. It is, after all, a most wonderful life. And if you listen very intently, you can almost hear the tinkling of bells as the angels among us earn their wings every day.

# Marching On

*March 2009*

Two years ago this month marked the beginning of a wonderful journey as a contributing writer for *She Magazine*. I submitted an article for the March 2007 anniversary celebration issue. The topic was very similar to this one: tell us why you are glad to be your current age. Well, I'm two years older now and, for the most part, still very glad to be my age—which is currently two months shy of fifty-five.

So, what has happened in these two years to keep me so contented? Three things, really—finding faith, keeping hope, and knowing love. Sounds rather simple though, doesn't it—kind of trite and wishy-washy, like one of those sappy Hallmark cards. It's not, really—not at all. In fact, it has been decidedly difficult and problematic along the way. My natural state, unfortunately, is to spend much energy in the rejection o faith, hope, and even love. I have had an intimate and long-term relationship with depression, melancholy, cynicism, and self-loathing. I tend to think that when I wrote that first article two years ago, I wasn't truly happy to be almost fifty-three—I just desperately *wanted* to be that way. The difference now is that I actually am content to be my age. I am not particularly content to be looking my age, but I guess that's a story for another day.

Things got much worse after March 2007 before they began to get better in the faith, hope, and love areas. Because I was writing an article as a newbie, I had to meet a submission deadline of January (now that I'm a regular, I get to screech in under the wire on the twentieth of the month—great for a procrastinator). Before writing that first article, I had experienced three life-altering events in quick succession: My husband lost his eighteen-month cancer battle on the last day of June; my dad died in a nursing home in mid-December; and my son nearly died in an alcohol-induced truck/telephone-pole collision just one week later. By January 2007, it seemed to me that I had lost or nearly lost all of the significant men in my life.

Then in March 2007, weeks after the article was published, and months after loving care from new neighbors and friends, I came to know the One who would never leave while taking a Beth Moore study. Even then, however, I had quite a bit of work to do in order to get to the contentment of almost fifty-five. Interestingly, God sent the son I had nearly lost to live with me while he began his own journey to a better way of life. You see, I had been so very busy feeling sorry for myself and grieving the loss of husband and father I failed to recognize the very real losses accumulating in our twenty-two-year-old son's life.

From July 2007 to February 2009, my baby boy (and I wonder why our relationship has had its struggles?) lived together—just long enough for me to struggle letting him go again, as he boarded the bus for basic combat training (BCT) at Fort Benning, GA. Our relationship had been fractured at best since his mid-teens. I knew he preferred his father's company to mine; he made that quite clear. He relished, it seemed to me, flunking his eleventh grade English class, mostly because I had been an English teacher. He excelled in history—one of his father's loves. My son had planned to be a GI Joe since he was about eleven years old, while I feverishly insisted that he instead become Joe College. We were like oil and water—I could reference this chemistry all the way back to breastfeeding days, but that might prove to be much too embarrassing for both of us.

The intervening years between graduating high school (a semester late, much to my horror) and the fulfillment of his Army hopes at the age of twenty-four were fraught with problems and sidetracks and heated arguments, frosty silences, and worse. The best we could do was to barely tolerate each other, until I began to learn the true meanings of faith, hope, and love. Certainly, we are both still works of clay in various stages of completion. He has not yet chosen to study under the Great Tutor. It is my hope that he will one day. I have faith that God's grace will be upon him as he begins this long-sought journey of marching on in service to his country.

Now that I have digressed fully from the "happy to be my age" topic, let's see if I can pull myself back together again. To review: The reasons I am happy to be almost fifty-five are faith, hope, and love. I have faith. I see hope. I know love. They are all reflected back to me as I sit here remembering the face of my son as he turned to board that bus in pursuit of his future. I wished that his dad could have been there to see those steps taken, like he was when we filmed those first baby steps over twenty years ago. But it is okay that he is not here. Contentment, after all, doesn't rely on people, places, or things. The storms will continue to come and the peace within them can be found, at least for me, only through faith, hope, and love—whether we are thirteen or thirty-eight or almost fifty-five. I will attempt to remember this before I start whining about not hearing from the aforementioned son for too long a stretch of time. But for today, let me simply march on, content to be two months shy of fifty-five, alone but never lonely.

# Grief, Grace, and Gratitude

*March 2012*

*I*t is said that art imitates life. If we also believe that writing is art, then, indeed, art imitates and reflects this life of mine. Five years ago I wrote to *She Magazine* about why I was happy to be my age for their fifth annual birthday celebration issue. I had moved to Marion, SC, after fifty-two years in more northern zip codes (yes, I would have come much sooner had I known the treasures of southern living) and had enjoyed reading the magazine every month. I also loved driving by the black and pink She office awning as it waved back to me whenever a slight breeze stirred the air. So when I read the editor's invitation for readers to be featured in the magazine's birthday issue, I took a chance and sent in my thoughts. And that's how the journey began.

I cannot believe it has been five years since I sent in that first tentative article. I think maybe the editor just took pity on me. Little did she know that she would not be able to shake me from her inbox every subsequent month? This issue marks my sixtieth attempt to share life and love with *She* readers, and I am beyond grateful for the opportunity. Writing these monthly letters has been the catalyst for righting my life.

Out of grief, I began this journey with *She* readers. My husband of nearly twenty-five years had been diagnosed with throat cancer in December 2004 and we battled that enemy all the way to South Carolina from our home in Maryland in May 2006. It was his make-a-wish come true move. The warmth of a Carolina sun and the state motto, "While I breathe I hope," gave us all the motivation we needed to make that leap south. We searched houses for months before walking through a door in Marion to find our home. Once inside, we just knew it was the right place for us, though we couldn't explain why. We left our children, families, friends, and a career to set off toward that promised hope—much to the dismay of our oncologist, who only reluctantly gave us a Florence medical referral. He knew time was not on our side. We, however, refused to believe it. Unfortunately, he was right. David died just two months after we arrived in South Carolina. My father left this life just six months later, and my son, overtaken by the grief of losing his hero, nearly died in a collision with a telephone pole just one week after my dad was laid to rest. The year 2006 definitely did not end well.

But then came grace. I was in the middle of a powerful Bible study—Beth Moore's "Jesus the One and Only"—led by another *She Magazine* contributor. Mary Lynn Jones and Lisa Campbell had asked me to join them (these were two of my new southern friends that, along with Sara Jones and northern me, made up a fierce friendship foursome). Mary Lynn, by the way, was largely responsible for bringing me back out of the darkness of grief. Though she would take no credit, she was the living, breathing vessel through which the message was received. That woman dogged me until I finally agreed to attend church with her family. Did I mention that the home we "just knew" was right for us happened to share a back yard fence with her family home? Yep. What a coincidence. Not!

It was during that bible study that I quietly and without fanfare, beyond the shedding of a few grateful tears, accepted the gift of salvation so freely offered and so long ignored. It has indeed become the road less traveled by and has made all the difference in this life. It is, after all, the source of endless gratitude.

As surely as I came to know that God had placed us in that home on Oliver Street, I also learned that He was designing a new life for me. He placed a man beside me during a Sunday school class at Mullins First Baptist Church—a mildly annoying, opinionated, and groan-inclined sort of man—who has become, without question and with full clarity of mind and spirit, the only man I will ever need or desire. He gently points me in the direction of Christ by quietly reflecting His traits and loudly, boldly, with sureness of purpose, shows me the true definition of love. So what if he also snores loudly on the Sunday afternoon sofa? So what if he seems to sometimes prefer the company of Italian Cream Cake to me? So what if he prefers jeans to dress pants and ESPN to romantic movies? He is the gift in life I did not even know I desired and surely do not deserve. But he will be the only man for the rest of my life and he is quite enough and surely sent by God.

In the pages of this magazine, I worked through grief and came to grace and now live daily in the gratitude of a life lost to self and gained to Christ—all during these past five years. Some of us work through trials of many kinds and joys of all variety by talking with others or by silently reflecting inward. Others of us write it out—sometimes by gently and tentatively stroking the keyboard and other times pounding out each letter with a knockout punch. We only hope to get it right, this writing of life.

And if we are very, very blessed, we have a forum and an audience—even if only in a crowd of two or three. So, thank you, *She Magazine* and company for the love and hard work that goes into every single page every month. Thank you for the beautiful artwork, gorgeous advertisements, and the inspirational stories of ordinary women (and men) who live through extraordinary moments and excruciating events who are willing to share their stories and their faith so publicly. I have been gifted with the privilege of writing about a few of those amazing people—survivors, artists, godly men and women, entrepreneurs, heroes and she-roes of all kinds.

Amazing stories of love and triumph over seemingly insurmountable obstacles fill nearly every page of every issue. It is most assuredly a wonderful woman thing—and it has helped this one woman right a life broken by grief, lifted by His grace, and now overflowing with love and gratitude. Thank you for the opportunity to write it all out. Thank you for believing that all things work together to paint the portraits of our lives and point us toward eternity.

# Coming Unglued

*March 2014*

For some of us, just hearing the word birthday can be cause enough to come unglued—unhinged from the doorway of reality. Much like all things of this life, birthdays are a matter of perspective. They can either be a blessing or a curse. For example, turning sixty this year is, for me, a great blessing. It means that marriage is on the visible horizon and no longer in the far distant and unseen future. Had circumstances been different, turning sixty might be considered a curse to be dealt with quite severely.

My mother, who will register ninety-five on the birthday scale at the end of this month, looks at each new day as something of a curse—every morning she wakes up with the same thought: "Phooie. Still here." And then she tries not to curse. She'd much prefer to be moving on from this life and settling into her permanent home in God's grace. We try very hard to see it her way, though selfishness prays we can keep her here just a little while longer.

But birthday angst is not really what's on my mind this month. It's something else entirely that is fueling my desire to rant on and on about coming unglued. Literally, it's about coming unglued.

Perhaps I am the only one with this issue, but have you noticed an alarming trend toward excessive gluing on consumer products? It's nearly impossible to actually come unglued without losing at least a few squares of toilet tissue or sheets of paper towels—at both ends. Starting a roll causes loss and ending a roll causes loss. Why? Both ends are glued down with some super substance that won't be easily released. Thus, we must buy more tissue and towels more often because, though there may be a thousand sheets on a roll, we lose quite a few at both start and finish lines.

I think I smell a conspiracy. Yes—that must be it. And it stinks. The manufacturers are conspiring to make us purchase more of their products because we must first waste so much when opening a new batch. And don't even get me started about trying to open up new cereal boxes without first tearing the closing tab ends so the contents cannot be easily reclosed for future consumption Either that or the inner liner bag rips halfway down the side because it's been cunningly superglued at the top making it impossible to open cleanly, thus spilling frosty flakes all over the countertop. Regardless of the outcome, the bag of cereal goes stale too quickly—causing us to buy more cereal more often. Now I love cereal, but very rarely do I eat an entire box in one sitting (unless it's magically delicious). Therefore, the choice is to eat stale honey bunches of oats or toddle off to the grocery for more. Again—conspiracy.

I have also been known to start coming unglued while attempting to remove price stickers from packages or glass items before gifting them. Goo Gone works well, but it stinks and is slimy. Evidently I have enough pioneer spirit remaining in my DNA to do it all by myself. Hot water, fingernails, knife edges, sheer determination and a few choice curse words later, there is still a smudge of residue on the now tarnished gift. Another conspiracy, you ask? Perhaps. This one is a bit more difficult to unravel, but I think I have it figured out. There are also some stickers that come off quite easily—just a slight tug at one edge and off they slide. That's the conspiracy. Get the consumer to hope for a better sticker experience. They'll go out all hopeful-like, in pursuit of more gifts with easily removed stickers. Then zap them again with the gorilla glued stuff.

And, speaking of gifts—ever buy a new roll of wrapping paper, only to lose the first few inches to an uncooperative sticker holding the roll together? Yes—conspiracy once again.

The roll won't wrap as may packages because of that glue loss, so we buy more. And on and on it goes.

This coming unglued thing is a close relative of the pound of coffee that is now a mere thirteen ounces and costs much more. Seen many five-pound bags of sugar lately? No? That's because they now weigh only four pounds and cost the same as their now-extinct predecessors. Frustration mounts just thinking about all this consumer doom and gloom.

I could go on and on about the coming unglued phenomenon, and I had fully planned to do so. Then the dreaded Ice Storm Cometh and stayed too long and when it left, took all electrical power with it, along with the necks and arms of many beautiful old trees. Before the power stayed off too long, there was a certain quiet beauty about all that ice encasing our world. It was so peaceful—not a single hum from any appliance or computer or phone. Unfortunately, the quiet became deafening in direct proportion to how quickly the house temperature dropped.

There's the real story. It's not so much about coming unglued by loss of our modern conveniences—like flushing toilets (who gives a fig about too much glue on a tissue roll when using it at all would be such a great relief) and hot showers and microwaves—it's more about our (okay, my) complacency and take-it-all-for-granted-ness. If all I have to rant about is too much glue on my paper towel roll and hard-to-open cereal boxes, perhaps I am in greater need of a true wake-up call—like an ice storm.

These things have a way of helping us count our blessings more than our paper towel losses. Does it still irritate me, this coming unglued thing? Of course it does. And I came close to coming permanently unglued during three days without power (and email access)—until I took a good look in the mirror (by candlelight—not so bad) and realized it could have been a whole lot worse. It was a whole lot worse for many others.

God gives us the choice to be "blessed or stressed" within our uncertainties in this life. The question of "When will the power come back on?" needs to turn more quickly to: "I will praise Him in this storm" instead (Isa. 4:6). And I will stop looking at my toilet paper and paper towel rolls and cereal boxes as a personal assault on my sanity. Conspiracy? Only in my own mind, that is much too cluttered with other trivial pursuits. It's time for me to come unglued from where I sit and step out on faith, wherever He wants me to go, and in all kinds of weather too.

May your own birthdays this year be overflowing with blessings and goodwill, whether you are thirty-two or sixty-four or a private, unlisted number? And let's all thank the timber wolf for eating that stupid groundhog and his shadow, shall we? Amen.

# Yankernings

*March 2016*

This month marks the beginning of my tenth year writing for She readers. The journey began tentatively, and without any expectation of longevity, when I submitted an article for the 2007 birthday issue. Much to my surprise, it was selected for publication—and thus began an earnest and sometimes painful attempt to embrace the many nuances of becoming a fully transplanted southern Yankee.

It was Melia who first introduced me to the term Yankern—a now delicious and well-seasoned descriptor of my standing (kneeling, sitting, and prone to mistaken word identity position) in the place I lovingly refer to as my home away from home. In fact, when the 2016 calendar flips over to May, I will celebrate a somewhat surprising tenth anniversary of becoming a Yankern.

Home may be where your story begins, but the home you make away from that first home provides almost an endless array of windows and doors and comfy chairs from which to view the world. My story began in Frederick, Maryland—what used to be a rather small town surrounded by dairy farms in northern Maryland, very near the border of Pennsylvania and quite close to the historically significant battles of Antietam and Gettysburg.

Barbara Fritchie lived there and defied the British soldiers to "shoot if they must" her old gray head (though this little piece of Revolutionary history has been debunked, native Fredericktonians still cling to it for dear life, much like Ms.

Fritchie clung to her flag). Francis Scott Key wrote the Star Spangled Banner so near to Frederick that we claim him too.

I grew up surrounded by family and friends in a nearly idyllic setting. Okay, there was the fact that Fort Detrick was doing all kinds of chemical testing and God-only-knows-what behind heavily guarded fencing. But we didn't spend much time worrying about it. We were much too busy practicing how to dive under our desks during air raid drills. We did our school clothes shopping in nearby Baltimore and claimed undying allegiance to the Orioles and even the Colts, before those owner-cowards crept away in the middle of the night and headed to Indiana. Sorry, that just slipped out somehow. Old hurts surface when we least expect it? And, for similar reason, we won't talk much about the Catholic parts of my upbringing either.

West Virginia was the next "home" for me—spent four years there learning to become a teacher (because education was deeply rooted on my dad's side of the family). Then it was back to Maryland for my first grown-up girl job, then about five years in Virginia (the northern part, of course), then back to Maryland for another twenty-plus years. By this time I was married with two small children, a teenaged stepson, and our house was in Southern Maryland. I think it was this part of the "home" journey that ultimately prepared me to become a very contented, if somewhat off-balance Yankern.

Tobacco, corn, and cows surrounded our suburban bedroom community. Amish craftsmen sold their wares at the local farmer's market and lived nearby—not directly among us but very near us. You could tell their farmhouses by two main things—no electric wires attached and plenty of pig manure. My love of all things pig might have begun there, come to think (or stink?) of it.

My daughter played soccer all four years of her high school days—and the playing field shared borders with the cow, tobacco, and corn fields. Chopticon High School was often and not kindly referred to as Cow Pie High by the visiting and usually winning teams.

I guess you could say I cut my Yankern teeth on Southern Maryland surroundings. It shares many similarities to my South Carolina home. Living in Marion, with its proximity to Myrtle Beach and Charleston, reminded me of Charlotte Hall and its convenience to Baltimore and DC.

What I was not prepared for, however, was the far-reaching changes in spirituality, cultural nuances, vocabulary, and vittles. The greatest proportion of Southern Maryland time was spent in Saint Mary's County, founded by Catholics and grounded in that faith from the mid-1600s. A great example of the catholic heritage could be found on the soccer field—where the priest, in his flowing black robe, would plant himself at the private school's goal end and defy the opposing team to score against God. Talk about your guilt-tripping. Finding faith without it has been my saving grace. Literally.

In Maryland and points north, there was seldom a personal question asked, let alone a steady barrage of them. We just didn't "pry." The cold harsh reality is that we probably didn't care to know either. As a Yankern, I have come to understand that a seemingly endless barrage of questioning is not so much about being a Nosey Parker as it is about a genuine desire to know someone better. I have since stopped asking the questioners if they were writing a book, while trying to smooth the shackles that quickly stood up on the back of my neck—yes, I have been known to "snap at my own farts" from time to time. But that dog just won't hunt around these parts.

In Maryland, lunch was at noon, and dinner happened any time after five. I cannot count the number of times over the past decade that someone has had to explain to me the subtle differences in "dinner" and "supper" and why I should not expect to meet someone for dinner on Sunday at any time other than noon. What? Huh?

I have very slowly come to understand the subtle, yet very important north/south differences between "ill" and "sick," "mash" and "push," "clicker" and "remote," etc. I'm still working on the specific times defined by "directly," "before long," "fixing to," and other minute-less terms.

As a Yankee, the faster you could talk the better. Now every vowel and most of the consonants get personal and lengthy attention. My mother never would have been able to make it here, bless her heart. She spoke at the speed of light, even in her very slowed down nineties. And I would love to hear her fast chatter just one more time. My newly slow turn of phrase has been described as both endearing and irritating by my northern family and friends (I suspect that the irritated ones are just plain jealous of the pace of life they cannot achieve up there). The words found in James—"slow to speak, quick to hear, slow to anger"—are taken quite literally and quite seriously here in my home away from home. And I love it, even as I continue to fail at it rather often.

I have come to fully grasp, chew, and swallow what it means to "south your mouth." Unlike the flavors of my first home, I have undying passion for all things butter, mayo, biscuits, fried okra, fig jam, and true grits. I have learned, through much trial and many errors, the blessing of flavor that is fatback or side meat when cooking fresh vegetable dishes (much to my husband's relief).

And, speaking of things like grits, it saddens me to know that I'll never be able to claim a GRITS T-shirt as my own, but at least I can claim ASAP status—as southern as possible, without having been born here. Many thanks for reading and forgiving (?) my learning curve over the past nine years. It is without hesitation that I can share with you that I am now "happy as a dead pig in the sunshine" to be a Yankern—and I'm hankering to stay here as long as our God allows.

# The Snapdragon Season

*March 2017*

What started as an effort to write out an overwhelming grief by convincing myself that I was, all things considered, happy to be in my fifties, has now become an amazing opportunity to share the joys of unmerited favor, overwhelming gratitude, second chance love on Green Acres, and the oddly awkward and rewarding journey of living a transplanted and transformed life.

Ten years ago I was newly widowed yet still determined to begin a new life in South Carolina. Ten years ago I was fifty-two and relatively wrinkle-free. I also had begun a journey of healthier living and regular exercise (thanks, ML), which I was convinced allowed me to brake for all hot donut signs (thanks, Lisa). I had just begun to understand the meaning of southern hospitality and new southern friends who ate dinner at noon and could be ill without getting sick and would rather mash buttons than potatoes. I discovered that steel magnolias are not just found in movies (thanks, Sara).

Also ten years ago, during the very month that first article was in print, I accepted the gift above all gifts and have been working out that transformation of life over the subsequent ten years—the amazing grace of His favor and patience with my learning curve and doubts and confounding pride is nothing short of miraculous. He allowed a new love to bloom, one founded on His definition of the Word. He also granted me, thanks to much fervent prayer, an extension of time here two years ago when it looked like I was, as they say in complicated medical terms, a "goner." But of course He knew all along the outcome. He also knew where I needed to be planted in order to grow in His direction instead of my own.

That brings us to what I like to call (for lack of a better descriptor and in great appreciation of Aunty Acid cartoons) the Snapdragon Season. My mind and memory has begun to snap regularly, causing me to, like a beloved yet annoying old dog, even snap at my own farts (yet another lovely accoutrement of aging). And every other part of this body is draggin' under the weight of overuse, misuse, and sorry lack of use. Thus, we have the snapdragon season of life. I am now ten years older, yet not so equally wiser. In some ways it seems like ten minutes ago, in many other ways it may as well have been a hundred years ago when Melia chose to include my feeble attempts at writing. So much has changed; much is for the better (hopefully including the writing)—and some for the not-so-much-better. Gains and losses can be counted everywhere—as in weight and wrinkles on the gained ground, wallet content and sense of wonder in the minus column.

So, behold the snapdragon, or, in stuffier Latin terms, the antirrhinum majus. I am a cool season annual (yes, I eagerly await the winter season here, all fifteen minutes of it), blooming well in early spring and in late fall. I am low maintenance. Well, sometimes. The snapdragon makes for a stunning display in arranged flowers and is quite colorful—ranging from greens to oranges, to pinks, reds, and whites. Oh, I can make a very stunning display—like when my temper runs away with my better judgement and the subsequent eye rolls and facial expressions are colored in many shades of angry red and/or icky-jealous green.

In the language of flowers, the snapdragon is said to represent grace and strength. It will prosper in rocky ground (ain't that the truth) and stands tall against ill winds (sure, why not?). Snap dragons, or dragon flowers, also can represent deception. Well, I guess two out of three isn't bad. Maybe that has to do with a childhood memory of making the snapdragons talk to each other by squeezing their little blossomy middles, deceiving myself that I had brilliantly become a seasoned puppet master/ mistress. And I have evidently just provided proof of the "snap" part. Yep. Mind snapped. Body draggin'. But still happy to be here, thank you very much.

So in this March season of birthday celebrations for She Magazine, it helps to recognize how far we have each come from our humble beginnings or do-overs—whether that beginning was ten, fifteen or many decades ago. At almost sixty-three, and with so much to be grateful for and so much to have grieved over these years, the bouquet of life has wilted and revived many times over—and will likely continue along that ebb and flow journey until we each come to our personal end points. Flowers wither and die, only to be replaced by new rosebuds and dandelions, lilies and weeds, proud stalks and dainty wispy things along the way. The fragrance of the snapdragon is sharply sweet. Perhaps the next season will bring baby's breath and sunflowers.

One thing I do know for sure. Whether it is snapdragon or sunflower season, there is a Truth that blooms for eternity—if only I would remember it and keep it in focus. It will bring joy in seasons of suffering and has done so much to make this temporary life a bearable journey.

"Therefore we do not lose heart. Even though our outward man is perishing, yet the inward man is being renewed day by day. For our light affliction, which is but for a moment, is working for us a far more exceeding and eternal weight of glory, while we do not look at the things which are seen, but at the things which are not seen. For the things which are seen are temporary, but the things which are not seen are eternal" (2 Cor. 4:16–18).

We are all on a pilgrimage from this life to that which is to come. Surely I can deal with this snapdragon season a while longer, knowing that the best is yet to be. The journey itself anticipates the oncoming fragrance of eternal joy.

April

**When Pigs Fly**
**Still**
**Sooner or Later**
**Little Things**
**Untangled**
**Little Bunny Foo-Foo**

*A*pril's theme varied from year to year but usually included a nod to springtime renewal, the passion of Easter, and all things fresh and new—including precious baby bunny rabbits and spring fashion trends.

# When Pigs Fly

*S*ome people collect beautiful things. Some people collect expensive things. Some people collect rare things. Some people collect compliments. Some people collect debts while others collect dust. Some people come to regret their collections because they always know what kind of gift they will receive for birthdays and Christmas and such. I might be one of those people one day, but for now I have no such regret. There are two things I collect on a fairly regular basis. Okay, three. But the teacups will really come in handy when I open that quaint little tearoom someday, so they fall under the category of business expense (or crazy, hare-brained ideas, take your pick).

The first collection involves anything imprinted with the saying: "Live well. Laugh often. Love much." The shortened version also applies: "Live. Laugh. Love." It has become our family motto. We take turns collecting just about anything emblazoned with those words. Lately there has been no short supply of these collectibles. Evidently we are not the only folks around that find the triple L's words to live by. I even found them imprinted on napkins at Patsy's in Mullins, SC, and promptly purchased a pack for my daughter and one for me. Too bad they are much too cute to use.

The motto was severely tested during my late husband's cancer fight, but the words still found their way onto his memorial program because they accurately defined how he chose to spend his time here. The three sentence collection is beautifully reinforced by taking residence in a state that boasts a similar motto: "While I breathe, I hope." Don't we all? Why else would we be so keen to brush our teeth before sleep? We all believe there's a probability we will wake again and make our dentist smile. If that's not hope, I don't know what else it could be.

I come from a state where the motto is: "Manly deeds; womanly words." Huh? If you want to test that motto though, don't travel on the Capital Beltway around Washington, DC. Manly deeds there include playing bumper cars and king-of-the-exit-ramp at eighty MPH. The womanly words are usually screeched into a cell phone held in one hand while taking slurps from a mocha-berry latte half-caf low foam brew held in the other. Knees are evidently good for steering purposes these days. Sadly, I recognize these creatures of the roadway because I used to be one of them not so very long ago. Don't get me wrong. I love my first state. I just live, laugh, and love that I am here now. The collection is growing in direct proportion to the hope the words bring.

And it is most certainly hope that brings me to the second collected things: flying pigs. Oh, stop laughing. I suppose you think bunnies and froggies are more acceptable. I have happily discovered that my winged porcine creatures are also rather easy to find. For example, I defy anyone to visit a Cracker Barrel store without finding at least one feathery pig. But, if you want to hit the piggy collectors' jackpot, take a trip to Cincinnati, Ohio, where flying pigs are the city mascot and adorn the streets of downtown in large versions and nearly every store within the city limits has variations aplenty. The story goes that it was pigs that were responsible for rejuvenating a dying economy many years ago—sort of like hope wrapped in ham hocks. They make such a convincing argument for hope against all odds. Basically, they represent the sentiment of never say never. Again, words to live by. That's why you'll likely find a veritable herd of flying pigs in and around a certain home in Marion. Some little piggies go to market and some little piggies have flight plans.

So now, what do mottos and flying pigs have to do with springtime and renewal and definitions of beauty as is the theme this month for *She Magazine*? Nothing and everything,

I suppose. Beauty, after all, is truly in the eye of the beholder and our collections are probably proof of that. But there is always hope in spring. Just take a look at all of those beautiful blossoms poking their pretty little heads out of the cold earth this time of year. Even if we have not exactly lived up to our own expectations for ourselves once the blush of a new year has faded, there is always hope found in the promise of spring. We continue to brush our teeth each night and collect our pigs or mottos or arrowheads or pocketbooks. We are all mostly hard-wired for hope, especially in this lovely state of South Carolina. Should you see any particularly handsome winged pigs in your travels, I hope you'll share their locations with me. Meanwhile, I will continue to have faith in their flights, and in the words of Hebrews 11:1 (NKJV) "Now faith is the substance of things hoped for, the evidence of things not seen."

# Still

*A*s four-letter words go, *still* seems rather benign, doesn't it? The reason, upon closer examination, may be that the word actually has five letters; proof positive that math skills were not a gift I received. Words, evidently, are more my thing. And since I'm quite fond of that opening sentence, let's see if we can provide reason for it to stay. How about the fact that there are four different letters? If we agree upon counting only the different letters, we still arrive at a four letter word count. So, it still works—at least for me.

The tiny word also carries an edge to it that bears further investigation—like that very human urge to run one's finger ever-so-gently along the rim of a disposable razor to test if it's still sharp enough to cut through forest-like leg hair growth. Or how about when a bump erupts inside your cheek because you were too busy shoveling in that last bite and you keep running your tongue over the spot to see if it still hurts? Of course it still hurts when we do that but we just can't help ourselves. Curious creatures are we.

*Still* is just one of those amazing words that can be used in so many ways. Artists sing about it all the time. For example, Tim McGraw describes *still* on his album, Southern Voices: "In that quiet place where all of me is exposed—where God dwells and waits for us to come as we are to Him." Love songs from Lionel Ritchie and Reba McIntire have *still* in their titles. The word *still* can be found almost three hundred times in the NIV Bible (look to Psalms, Job, and the gospels). The unassuming, nearly four letter word can be used as an adjective, an adverb, a verb, or a noun. Wow. It can have negative or positive connotations. It can be gentle and quiet or powerful and commanding Oh, be still, my fluttering English major's heart.

First, let's explore the adjective *still*. Sometimes the message of God is described as a still, small voice. We often hear that still waters run deep when a person of quieter qualities is described. *Still* makes for a pretty decent modifier—very, uh, descriptive. Artists paint a still life. Photographers use a still camera.

The adverb *still* can be either negative or positive in usage. For example, a classroom teacher or beleaguered mom might be aggravated enough to say: "I'm still waiting!" A person wishing to convey evidence of a lasting relationship may utter the words "I still love you," even after a perceived slight or wrong is suffered.

The verb form of *still* is probably my favorite though. Consider this: Be still and know that I am God (Ps. 46:10) or The Lord will fight for you; you need only to be still (Exod. 14:14). But how can something not moving be a verb? Doesn't a verb require action? It is an action to be still. Ever try getting a three-year-old to be still in a room filled with toys and puppies? It takes every ounce of strength for that poor child to be still. It is an action of great difficulty sometimes.

Then of course there is that last form of *still*, the noun. The first definition that comes to mind is that contraption sometimes found hidden in woods, far from probing eyes of the law—at least during Prohibition years. A still is just a shortened version of the word distillery, and produces the same liquid refreshments. There are other nouns too. Photographers create stills for movie marketing and promotions. Actors use stills in their portfolios. There is even a Dr. Still, credited with pioneering the field of osteopathy.

In this spring season of new life, when the very nature surrounding us shouts of movement and growth, when our faith can behold anew the fulfillment of the prophesied Messiah, we can get lost in all the excitement and commotion. We just can't be still. There is so much to do—Easter dinners to prepare, dresses and new outfits to be purchased, eggs to dye, baskets to fill, plastic eggs to hide, chocolate bunnies to consume, gardens to plant, homes to be refreshed. Yet we are, perhaps more than any other time of year, called to be still—to remember the greatest sacrifice ever made and the most significant evidence of agape love any of us can ever know. We rejoice in the resurrection, as well we should, but it is in the sacrifice of crucifixion, death, and separation that we know He loves us still. But our sorry little Easter bunny selves want to hop all over the place being busy, busy, and busy. In the words of the great cartoon philosopher, Pogo: "We have met the enemy and he is us." Bingo.

Though we can't seem to be still this time of year, we can know and remember that God so loved the world. He still does. We have only to listen to His still quiet voice beckoning us to live our lives full-out for him—even when the world's music would have us hear a different tune. And if we enjoy a few peanut butter eggs, marshmallow chicks, and jelly beans along the way, we can still be His children—His slightly hyperactive and sugared-up children.

# Sooner or Later

*April 2011*

*A*pril showers may very well bring May flowers but they probably won't get us any closer to circling a specific wedding date on the calendar. Time passes quickly and we continue to put off the selection of a date. We've been engaged seven months now. Emily Post attempts to convince us that it is tacky to be engaged more than a year. What does she know, anyway? It is getting rather cumbersome though, as we are asked the date question by friends, neighbors, family, children, and even total strangers on an embarrassingly regular basis. The time pressure is mounting. Sooner or later, we'll have to choose.

My beloved did come up with one date recently, thinking he was so very clever. "Since April first is on a Friday this year, maybe we should get married next April first, as it will fall on a Saturday. After all, April Fool's Day is a great day for a wedding." Well guess what, Mr. Funny Guy, 2012 is a leap year, so it won't be a Saturday next year. So there.

Not to be left out of the date game, I then suggested it might be helpful to his failing memory if we select February 29, 2012—that way he'd only have to remember it every four years. Too bad it falls on a Wednesday though. We have also tossed about other dates—like December 13, 2014 (12/13/14) or November 12, 2013 (11/12/13). There's always September 10, 2011 (9/10/11), but that's just a wee bit too close. Sooner or later we'll have to decide. Right now, that fork's still stuck in the road.

Time is such a great friend to procrastinators. We bend it and manipulate it and stretch it out of shape or ignore it until its hands reach out and slap us silly. Oddly enough, we both work in deadline driven minefields. Evidently, we can only do so much time minding. Meanwhile, right in the middle of writing this article something of much greater importance happened—out of the blue, and right on time.

I attended the "Just as I Am" bible class at Mullins First Baptist Church expecting to simply hear an introduction to the book of Hebrews. Instead, I heard powerful testimonies. One member of the class had a dream or vision (one might even call it a reckoning). She believed it depicted the end of time—complete with earthquakes, tsunami, and the Church descending to earth to call home believers. This dream came just two days before horrific events in Japan. She shared that it taught her a valuable lesson: the only thing that truly matters is our relationship with our Lord—our homes, our plans, even our children and loved ones must be secondary to our relationship with Christ. And we won't have time to send a text or make a call to anyone when our moment arrives. We don't get to know the day or the hour.

During that same class, another member shared about a frightening close call regarding the health of his mother. This man happens to see health crises and tragic accidents as a regular part of his EMT job, but this time it was his mother in the back of the ambulance. He credited his wife for keeping him steady enough to make it through for his mother. Fortunately, she is resting at home now, the crisis averted. Again, we don't get to know the day or the hour. Might be sooner, might be later.

That same helpful wife also shared how she has so many plans for what she wants to do with and for her children and her church, yet never seems to get it all done—as time goes by so quickly these days. There's simply not enough time, it seems, to accomplish everything on our lists. And still, we don't get to know the day or the hour when our earth time ends.

The class leader was trying to remember an old song about not sending flowers to a funeral but sending them today, so they can be enjoyed by the living, and telling people we love them and are proud of them today. His coleader slyly suggested that he should try to sing a few bars of that song for the class, to help jog his memory. Unfortunately, another class member suggested that his singing might cause the whole class to lose their memory—or worse, to lose the delicious casserole we had just shared.

Needless to say, we never got to the book of Hebrews that morning but we learned so much from each other. God works in amazing ways. I had nearly decided not to join the class that Sunday and would have missed such a great blessing. Just when we think we know exactly what is going to happen, our world turns upside down or sideways and a special gift is received from above—like the perfect timing of a totally unexpected testimony. Time spent in fellowship is so precious—especially when we share faith and fears and laughter and prayers and tasty casseroles. If only we could take more time to do that—share ourselves with each other. Time passes. People change. Lives are lost (and found). It truly doesn't matter what we're wearing or how our house looks—or even the dates we set for weddings.

When all is said and done, what truly matters is the time we spend sharing our faith and building relationships. I let too much time tick away on things that are not as important as I once thought they were and too little time on the greatest matter of all. It's time to remember Hebrews 11:1 and live in it by faith.

As for that wedding date, it will happen. We just haven't been able to figure out a time that works best for all involved. Or perhaps, like some think, we are already married. Either way, we'll be sure to let you know—sooner or later.

# Little Things

*April 2012*

*W*e are reminded almost daily that it's the little things in our lives that carry the biggest impact and/or give us perhaps the most aggravation. We have all kinds of catchphrases about our Little Things. One of the "biggest" ones is this: "Little things mean a lot." Then there's "it's a small world after all" and "big gifts often come in small packages." How could we forget "don't sweat the small stuff, and it's all small stuff"?

Sometimes it's in the littlest of coincidences that we find the biggest gifts—the evidence of things unseen. For example: A friend in great need of something to focus on finds a stray cat on the doorstep in great need of care and attention—and a small furry thing begins to have a huge impact on a lonely life. A frief acknowledging wave of the hand from a dying friend provides comfort and hope for those who must say goodbye. A song plays on the radio at just the right time and brings back a precious memory or offers hope in a time of need.

All too often, the big problems in our lives crowd out the little joys. Simple pleasures often get overlooked in pursuit of big ideas. We each have our own versions of little things that mean a lot, I'm sure. Some we would have in common while others are unique to our own circumstance and experience as our fingerprints. There's a really neat online blog (http:// justlittlethings.net) that simply keeps posting little things that impact our lives to a list that grows bigger all the time. At last check, there were 642 "little things" named there, including the following:

- Successfully untying a difficult knot

- Being able to pull through a parking space

- The sound of raindrops on your umbrella

- Finding a tissue just in time before the sneeze escapes

- Getting a baby to stop crying

- When the phone rings and it's exactly who you hoped it would be

There are hundreds more on the list and we could each name many more of our own. But they are too often overlooked. When we could our blessings, we sometimes want to consider only those great big ones, but it's perhaps the little things that truly color and strengthen the fabric of our lives and our faith. The Bible refers us to the power of little things in Proverbs: "There be four things which are little upon the earth, but they are exceeding wise: The ants are a people not strong, yet they prepare their meat in the summer; the conies are but a feeble folk, yet make they their houses in the rocks; the locusts have no king, yet go they forth all of them by bands; the spider taketh hold with her hands, and is in the kings' palace" (Prov. 30:24–28, KJV).

Indeed, God's Word has much to say about little things—especially about children—our most precious of little things—those tiny seedlings that must be nurtured and well fed with love (and, yes, discipline) in order to grow into beautifully blossomed people with both strong roots and powerful wings. Consider Mark 10:13–15 (KJV):

"And they brought young children to him, that he should touch them: and his disciples rebuked those that brought them. But when Jesus saw it, he was much displeased, and said unto them: Suffer the little children to come unto me, and forbid them not, for of such is the kingdom of God. Verily I say unto you, Whosoever shall not receive the kingdom of God as a little child, he shall not enter therein."

Our "little things" surely mean a lot, as evidenced by God's Word. They desire for them to live out their childhood years unaffected by abuse or neglect. But sometimes they do not. Sometimes they are harmed in the worst of ways. April is National Child Abuse Prevention Month. Unfortunately, the family court system dockets are overloaded with child abuse and neglect cases, juvenile court proceedings and child support hearings.

Fortunately, there are many "little things" we can do to help prevent these cases from coming to court in the first place. We can continue building, brick by brick, communities that support and care for our "little things." There is within each of us opportunity to help prevent them from suffering big hurts. For example, the following list comes from the Child Welfare Information Gateway website at www.childwelfare.gov

Get to know your neighbors. Problems seem less overwhelming when support is nearby.

Help a family under stress. Offer to babysit, help with chores and errands, or suggest resources in the community that can help.

Reach out to children in your community. A smile or a word of encouragement can mean a lot, whether it comes from a parent or a passing stranger.

Be an active community member. Lend a hand at local schools, community or faith-based organizations, children's hospitals, social service agencies, or other places where families and children are supported.

Keep your neighborhood safe. Start a Neighborhood Watch or plan a local "National Night Out" community event. You will get to know your neighbors while helping to keep your neighborhood and children safe.

Learn how to recognize and report signs of child abuse and neglect. Reporting your concerns may protect a child and get help for a family who needs it.

You will probably notice that there is no reference on this list to the greatest of factors in the prevention of child abuse in this country: God's Word. In our separation of church and state endeavors, we have removed the one thing that provides the best assurance against harm for children—following Christ's command to love the Lord our God with all our heart, soul, mind and strength, and love our neighbors as ourselves.

Maybe it's time we stop being so politically correct and start being unconditionally loving and willing to stand up and be counted for something far greater than a census. Maybe during this new planting season we can fertilize it with our active faith. Yes, little things do mean a lot—and they need to grow into big, strong people of faith in love. From the acorn grows the mighty oak tree. With faith a small as a mustard seed we can move mountains. So surely we can notice, nurture, and be grateful for the Little Things too.

*Note: I spent over five years as a volunteer with the South Carolina Guardian ad Litem program, including one year as a stressed out case manager state employee. It was both a most rewarding and most difficult experience, but I met some amazing children, volunteers, social workers, families, and judges. Children deserve a voice, especially when faced with unbearable hardships.*

# Untangled

*April 2014*

*A* few days ago, I found myself seated at the dining room table surrounded by all manner of stressfully unfinished wedded bliss projects. (Have I mentioned lately my uncanny ability to start creative projects and quickly become distracted by another one, leaving the last one abandoned and sadly unfinished?) My focus, however, was on seemingly futile attempts to extract a terminally tangled blob of jewelry consisting of five (yes, five) silver necklaces of varying lengths from one rather sinister, chunky, green-glass beaded stretch bracelet. The task was not unlike that of Sisyphus attempting to roll the proverbial rock up that seemingly endless hill.

Just as soon as I had the end of one chain freed, the bracelet would snatch it again, pulling the helpless silver back into the elasticized blob's belly. In my earlier life, this exercise would have ultimately involved a hammer and strongly worded language spewing out with every blow. But not this time; I found the ridiculous humor in it and used the experience to practice calm, expletive-deleted patience. It actually worked. The chains were freed, one by one, from their green-beaded prison. What a sense of satisfaction—to untangle a mess without taking on casualties. Every part of the blob was still useful for its original purpose, independent once again of each other.

Could this be yet another ah-ha moment for me? A lesson learned in time? Possibly. At the very least, it caused me to consider what else in this life might be in need of freedom from entanglement. Those aforementioned wedding projects might be a good place to start. Perhaps it might be helpful for stress reduction if I would actually finish one or two of them—or maybe simplify the process in some way. The problem with tangled threads or chains or other things is we sometimes can't find the loose end that will begin to free the whole mess. For me it's often in deciding where to start—or deciding anything at all, for that matter. I have laid out the reception floor about 372 times. Round tables? Rectangles? Six or eight seats per table? Flowers at each end or in the middle? Which picnic basket for which table? Who gets to eat inside and who gets stuck outside in the heat of a June afternoon? Will there be enough fun and food for everyone—whether they are six or sixteen or sixty? Exhausting.

And speaking of sixty, this is not your usual age for weddings, is it? I mean, really. Retirement plans? Sure. Getting the children to agree on which nursing home? Yep. But weddings? Not too many of those planned for this stage in life. More logically its things like: should the knee replacement surgery come before or after the nuptials? Do wedding dresses come with elastic stretch panels and/or tummy tucking materials? Haven't seen any—and, believe me, I have been looking—which brings me to the next entanglement.

Try maintaining your nearly-sixty-year-old dignity (or what's left of it) while shopping for a wedding dress with your BFFs in a bridal shop designed for twenty-somethings. The one and only saving grace was having friends who knew better than to snicker when the bride-to-be emerged from behind the dressing room curtain, precariously pinned and stuffed inside a fluffy pink and airy confection, still wearing her sensible brown boots and her many layers of winter fat. To say I looked stunning would be a gross (in all senses of that word) overstatement. Fortunately, these are true friends whose only desire is for me to find *the* dress. They merely indicated their response with duplicate thumbs-down. So, thank you Lisa and Sara (and Mary Lynn for staying in the car—as she surely would not have been able to contain herself—and it's somewhat her fault I'm in this dress-full situation in the first place). Whew, finally untangled those shredded emotions. Feeling much better now, thank you.

Perhaps it's all a matter of proper perspective, after all—sort of like the jewelry problem. Maintain a healthy sense of humor. Live in the moment. Love the outcomes, no matter what. This, of course, reminds me of a familiar motto: Live every day. Laugh with abandon. Love like you mean it. There are, of course, many variations of that triple play. It can be simplified—live, laugh, love. Or it can be built upon and stretched in meaning to fit nearly every moment—whether heavy or light. It helps to remember this saying whenever life gets a bit more tangled than usual—like when you're planning a wedding at sixty, and simultaneously planning a move to the country (well water, septic tanks, and the occasional wild cat or black bear), and suspecting that one or both of these life events will cause irreparable change to current relationships with friends, family, even faith groups.

So, in an effort to follow the untangling of jewelry success, I've adjusted the live/laugh/love thing to the following, with the help of the only thing that never changes: His Word. Now why did it take me nearly a thousand words to get to this point? Tangled thoughts and misplaced perspectives have perhaps clouded my ability to think rationally.

**Live well.**

You shall walk in all the ways which the Lord your God has commanded you, that you may live and *that it may be* well with you, and *that* you may prolong *your* days in the land which you shall possess (Deut. 5:33, NKJV).

**Laugh often.**

A time to weep, And a time to laugh; A time to mourn, And a time to dance (Eccles. 3:4, NKJV).

**Love always.**

Love never gives up, never loses faith, is always hopeful, and endures through every circumstance (1 Cor. 13:7 (NLT).

With these verses in mind, soul, and body, the untangling of current stresses should be a rousing success—one little silver thread of doubt at a time. And you can insert your own verses, too. There are many from which to choose. Surely there will be a few that ring especially true for you. May you enjoy a beautifully blessed April and season of renewal as we joyfully proclaim: We are forever untangled when we are fully bound to Him.

# Little Bunny Foo-Foo

*April 2015*

I used to love Easter dinner—dyed eggs cleverly converted to delicious, yet oddly hued, devilled ones, sugar cured ham (look, it's the flying pigs I love most—they can't make bacon or ham or sausage—they just fly), creamy potato salad, pineapple/pear bunny salads with cream cheese cottontails, homemade yeast rolls, delicious casseroles and scrumptious side dishes provided by friends and family. But the most wonderful part of the meal had to be the bunny cake for dessert

Some years it was a masterpiece of design. And some years it actually tasted good. I don't recall there ever being a year when both design and taste came together though. Sometimes the bunny sat straight up on a bed of green-tinted coconut grass (and tasted much like saw grass). Other years it sort of leaned precariously off the platter like a drunken jack-a-lope, yet had a heavenly taste. No matter. It just wasn't Easter unless the bunny cake was there.

And then my children grew up, and have not yet produced even the flicker of possibility for a grandchild. Alas, no more bunny cakes. Which, given the circumstances of my late-arrived, Christ-following walk, is perhaps perfect timing. Easter bunnies are not exactly what Resurrection Day is all about, huh? Nope, not at all.

But, I digress. It is, after all, April and spring is all around us. What a joyful time of year. Gardens are planted (yes, really—and with a tractor this time). Nature abounds with new life—from birds to tadpoles to bunnies. And this, along with the bunny cake, brings me to remember one of my favorite children's songs (please hum along if you know it):

"Little Bunny Foo-Foo hopping through the forest,

Scooping up the field mice and bopping them on the head.

Then the Good Fairy flew in to say:

Little Bunny Foo-Foo, I'll give you one more chance to be good

If you're not good, I will change you into a goon."

Of course, that's only the second to last verse. There are four. The first two verses gave Bunny Foo-Foo two other chances to be good. He was not. In the last verse, the Good Fairy lowered the boom and turned Bunny Foo-Foo into a goon. I'll save the moral of the story for the end. No. No I can't. I have to share it right now because I just learned it this week. And it's so good. No. Patience is a virtue (there's that, of course, plus I want you to read all the way through).

Oh how great a song, how rich a story. I know. I'm exaggerating just a bit but, really, it does provide wonderful insight into our human nature too, doesn't it? Bunny Foo-Foo obviously had an ax to grind, or he was a bully, or he just didn't believe that fairy. Of course, given a name like Foo-Foo, he probably had good reason to be slightly irritable. But there's never really a good reason to tread (or bop) on someone else's peaceful life.

I never really considered the poor field mice much, until now. They had a defender, but they still kept getting bopped on their little tiny heads, having done absolutely nothing to deserve it. They had every expectation that the bunny would listen to the fairy—at least for the first two warnings she gave. I would think that by the third one though, they may have become rather skeptical, probably expecting a bopping. They had become victims of their own circumstance. I wonder if they ever tried to avoid the rabbit.

Then there's the Good Fairy, flying in and out of the story with her wand, threatening and threatening and threatening. Then finally she followed through. The bopping bunny got bopped. Do you ever wonder why on earth she gave him three chances to be good? Did she just like giving lots of chances or did she have an unspoken dislike for those poor mice? Hmmm.

And where were Bunny Foo-Foo's mama and papa? I suppose they might have been busy making more bunnies or tending to the egg and basket hidings going on that time of year. Who knows? Evidently, he was on his own at a fairly early age. Left to his own devices, he decided to make some bunny else feel bad too. Either that or he though those mice were toys.

Now here comes the bigger (I hope) question. Which of the characters do you most identify with in the Bunny Foo-Foo story? Is it the bunny with the funny name or the defenseless field mice or the fairy with the magic wand? We could have a long discussion on which one is better/worse and why we would choose it and what it says about our characters, but I'm guessing that we might all see a bit of each character in ourselves from time to time—the oppressor, the oppressed, and the defender of the defenseless. Sound familiar? As spring brings forth a new season of life, I hope we'll all lean toward the defender role more often, with a humble heart, and without a magic wand. The power to change things is often hidden within us, if we care enough to find it and use it.

Now, here's the moral of the Bunny Foo-Foo story (at last):

Hare Today. Goon Tomorrow

And, just so you won't be too concerned, dear reader, this article was brought to you by a somewhat delirious writer that spent two and a half days in a fevered stupor, clinging to her stuffed bunny for comfort when her husband had to leave her side. There were also a few odd dreams of bunny cakes.

*Note: This article really was written under duress. Shortly after it was sent to the magazine editor, the writer embarked on a life-altering and death-defying journey with sepsis, including a three-week MUSC hospital stay, dialysis, liver drain tubes, and a huge dose of humility. Never ignore a high fever. Lessons learned. Prayers answered.*

May

**Her Secret Hope**
**Pay it Forward**
**Role Reversal**
**Defining Moments**
**Mine? Mine? Mine?**
**When you Care Enough**

*N*ot surprisingly, the month of May was reserved for celebrations of motherhood—the joys, sorrows, and everything in
between. We celebrated new mothers, grandmothers, adoptive
mothers, stepmothers, being a mother and having one or more.

# Her Secret Hope

*May 2009*

> *Youth fades; love droops, the leaves of friendship fall; a mother's secret hope outlives them all.*
>
> —Oliver Wendell Holmes (1809–1894)

*I* recently had the privilege of spending nearly a week alone with my mother—just the two of us—laughing, talking, sharing memories and opinions (fine, Mom, I'll consider letting my hair go white like my older sisters but it's much more fun to be the youngest when you actually look like the youngest).

Usually, my two oldest sisters share the gentle caring of our mother that allows her to continue living independently. They make a great team, and I am grateful every day for them. Fortunately for me, their calendars got crossed up, allowing another sister and me to each get a week alone with our mother. If you're counting, there are five sisters in our family sharing one mother. Cozy isn't exactly the first word that comes to mind when describing our growing up years—but the relationships have become increasingly warm as we age (and live in separate homes in separate states).

I've been my mother's youngest daughter for fifty-five years now, but I'm still not sure I know her all that well. One would think I might understand her a little better now that I have had almost twenty-six years to practice my own motherhood, but I never lived through the Depression or World War II rationing with a husband serving in the Navy and two daughters at home under the age of five. Nor did I move in with my in-laws right after the wedding to care for a dying mother-in-law, without knowing the first thing about cooking or housekeeping. The reason she didn't know those things is due to the fact that she grew up in hotels. Her parents managed or owned hotels, from wedding to deaths. She even survived a devastating hotel fire when she was a young girl, and the memories remain fresh in her mind. I didn't spend a year in New York City studying fashion design fresh out of high school either. She made all of our clothes (even my Barbie fashions). I never learned to sew, knit or crochet like she did. Frankly, I was relieved to squeak by with a *D* in high school home economics. We are mostly similar in looks alone (thanks so much for the freckles and pear-shaped body, Mom).

The amazing number of relationships accumulated in her life is much more than I could ever imagine. Evidently, being a late bloomer does have its downside. She has twenty-one great-grandchildren (with three more on the way this summer), twenty-one grandchildren (with thirteen spouses among them), five daughters, four living sons-in-law, one lifetime marriage, and, as of this year, ninety birthdays celebrated. We celebrate those birthdays while she mostly just endures them.

Like the words of Oliver Wendell Holmes suggest, her youth faded long ago, but definitely not her mind. Her one love has left this world behind, and we still miss him dearly. Most of her friends are gone, too—and she laughs about her habit of reading the obituaries every day, knowing she has pretty much run out of familiar names. But the big question mark for me comes at the end of that Holmes quote. What is my mother's secret hope, after all?

For as long as I can remember, when asked what she might like for a birthday or Christmas or Mother's Day celebration, her only stated hope was for "peace and quiet." Try being a ten year old, riding her bike downtown to search for and purchase that little gift. But that couldn't possibly have been her secret hope, could it? Certainly not—it was definitely no secret, as she begged for it at every opportunity.

Perhaps if I rewind some of the family history tapes I'll be able to find the right clues to unlocking her secret hope mystery. One of my earliest memories of my mother was watching her cut out sewing patterns on our dining room table, with straight pins tucked between her lips. I can still hear the sound of pinking shears cutting through pinned tissue paper and fabric. This, unfortunately, conjures up yet another memory—the one where I shamefully whine for just one dress from an actual shop, one with a price tag attached, and one that six other girls would likely be wearing too. What a brat I was. Maybe her secret hope was to have a more appreciative child.

Another vivid memory is from November 1963. I was nine years old, watching a little boy on TV salute his father's flag-draped coffin, and noticed that my mother was sitting very still while quiet tears fell from her cheeks to her lap where her hands were clasped together tightly in prayer. I had seen the praying hands often, but never before had I seen my mother crying so openly. Her tears, I suspect, were shed mostly in private moments away from her children. I'm still not sure if she was crying for the child, his father, our country, or maybe all three. I'm sure she cried when my sister shared her breast cancer diagnosis, and again when the treatments saved her life, but I never actually saw it.

One other memory of my mother is rather recent. It happened nearly three years ago at the McLeod Hospice House, shortly after the nurses confirmed that my husband had died. The only person I wanted to talk with then was my mother, and as quickly as possible. Thank God for cell phones and quiet corners. When I heard her voice, somehow I knew that life would still go on. After telling her that her son-in-law was gone, I remember thanking her for the example she had always set—the one that allowed me to breathe again because I had children to consider. Maybe this memory holds the answer to her secret hope.

I'm guessing that every mother's secret hope is pretty much the same. It's the one where we hope for our children to grow into life and become who they are meant to be. We hope that they will remember us and think fondly over their memories, even as youth fades and love droops and the leaves of friendships fall away. We can't protect our children from every bump in the road, nor should we, but we can secretly hope that they survive the journey.

# Pay It Forward

*May 2010*

*L*ast month I once again had the privilege of visiting in Maryland with my still independently living ninety-one-year-old mother. Her independence is possible due to the daily help of my two oldest sisters living nearby. Another sister and I shared the "mom watch" duties while the older sisters were out of town. Fortunately for me, a close friend encouraged me to listen very carefully to everything my mother had to say (something I have not always done well). In that listening time I began to see a much clearer picture of who my mother truly is, and how she came to be the kind of mother she has been and continues to be for me. She happily filled in many gaps in our family story—including the fact that she never wished to do anything other than what she had spent most of her adult life doing—being a wife and mother to five stunningly wonderful daughters (I may have embellished just a tad there).

I am grateful every day that our mother is still among us, but she grows increasingly weary of this world and is rather anxious to be called home. When her eyes open each new morning, she fights the urge to let unpleasant words escape her lips. If she were to leave us tomorrow, there would be a wonderfully rich legacy remaining in her place. She has been our strongest advocate, even when we wished she would not be. For example, it took me too many years to realize that she was absolutely right in her assessment regarding the wrongness of miniskirts and bellbottom jeans on her rather hippy daughter. Truth hurts.

She has given us a fine picture of motherhood and we, for the most part, have followed her lead. We each have our own spin on it, but we have tried to pay forward her dedication with our own children. My sisters' children have, in turn, done the same for their own children. Mine have not yet had the chance, but they are showing me that they will by the lives they are choosing to lead now. Although, my daughter recently sent a picture message entitled "new boyfriend." It was a Mr. Potato Head, and the caption read "He's perfect. Anytime he gets sassy, I just pull his lips off." Oh dear.

The friend whose advice was to listen intently to my mother knew what she was giving me, as her own mother was called home over a year ago. She had been given the gift of some quality time with her, to mend broken fences, to truly hear her mother's words and to be sure her mother knew how grateful she was for the love she had shared. She paid that advice forward to me. I am grateful for the encouragement (though it came across more like a command, the results were wonderful). I have other friends who will be missing their own mothers this month too, especially as we approach Mother's Day. Some have a rich and beautiful storehouse of memories, while others endured losing their mothers to that horrible thief of life, Alzheimer's disease. Some of our mothers, unfortunately, leave us long before they die—some to illness and some to choices made or not made well.

Some mothers, either by choice or circumstance or misunderstanding or addiction or lack of faith or even in tremendous acts of love (think adoption), are not able to be the mothers they hoped to be. Some mothers let varying priorities take the place their children should hold. Some have not had the opportunity themselves to know the benefits of positive mothering and cannot pass it on.

Unfortunately, the impact is felt most strongly and directly by their children. Sometimes very negative things are paid forward. Every day in our country, children are under threat of harm or neglect, or have already been made victims. Our family courts and social service systems are overburdened with cases, especially in difficult economic times. Perhaps it is unkind to approach this topic during a month in which we celebrate mothers, but there is such an overwhelming need for advocacy for these children. They are our children—in our schools and neighborhoods and around the next corner. These children need someone to stand up for them when their own families cannot or will not or do not know how. These children need to be seen and they definitely need to be heard.

To pay it forward in society is to take a kindness or helping hand or generous gift and, instead of returning it to the giver, extend it to someone else in need and ask that they too "pay it forward." Anyone who has had the benefit of loving, marvelous, maddening, mediocre, miraculous, or even terribly unloving parents can pay it forward by becoming an advocate for children. One way to do that is by volunteering with your county Guardian ad Litem (GAL) or Court Appointed Special Advocate (CASA) program.

Any time a family enters the court system, a guardian is assigned to advocate for the child or children in each case. The guardian attempts to see through the eyes of the child during independent investigation and paints that portrait for the family court judge. It is not the easiest of volunteer choices, certainly, but it can be a most richly rewarding one. Just ask current volunteers who have held infants suffering drug withdrawal and were able to comfort them, or played on the floor with a toddler covered in bruises and were rewarded with a shy smile from a frightened child. Children can and do recover from harm. They can and do need help to do so, though. Even the most defiant of young teenagers can see light in a dark world when an advocate breaks through that brick wall of defenses. Just consider Luke 1:37. Truly, all things are possible with God.

A child may be waiting just for you to pay it forward. Your mama would be so proud. In the movie *Pay It Forward* (1980), the soundtrack includes the song "Calling All Angels."

This is probably not a mere coincidence. Please consider yourself called or, at least, consider calling on someone you know who may be ready, willing, and able to advocate for a child. If each of us can pay it forward in some fashion, we all will benefit from the change it will surely make.

# Role Reversal
# My Daughter, the Mother

*May 2011*

Having just spent a wonderful Sunday morning swimming spiritually through the Book of Esther, it seems only fitting to talk about daughters this month, instead of mothers. As far as we know, Esther had no children, but she was one awesome mother. When a potential reversal of fortune threatened her people, she responded in true mama fashion. She loved without ceasing and protected like a champion warrior. The spirit of God is written all over her story, though His name is never mentioned—not even once. Her ability to save her people was not a coincidence. She was Spirit led and God ordained. And she was a Jew—a chosen one of God. Yet, she was not a mother. Her own mother had died when she was very young (we are lead to assume).

Like Esther, my daughter often takes on the mother role, though she remains childless. She has loved without ceasing and has protected like a champion. During her father's illness and death, she was my rock (at the very time she needed one of her own—hideously bad mothering on my part, I know). Two months earlier, when her father and I decided to fly away south, far from cancer, she was there, along with her older brother (my stepson, Eric) to unpack boxes and provide comic relieve by diving into the early May pool water—fully clothed. Even when her heart was breaking at the thought of losing both her parents—one to cancer and one to distance—she still made us laugh. She, in motherly fashion, put our needs ahead of her own.

Devin Tara Miller was named for her mother's Irish roots, although we spelled it incorrectly. According to the sticklers, Devon is the correct female spelling of the name. Fine, blame the mother again. I thought it would be easier for her to learn to spell it with an "I" instead—you know, like Kevin, only with a "D."

Alas, every other Devin she knows is male. I know this because she feels compelled to contact me each and every time she meets a new one. Sassy pants.

When she was in high school and early college and her mother (me, again) was suffering through the beginnings of menopause and personal summer syndrome at the exact same time her younger brother was busy sowing some very wild oats, she was there—like a wise mother, offering little tidbits of fun family history and acting as mediator, so mother and son would not leave each other with permanent scars.

When her cousin needed help with a newborn third child, she packed her bags and headed across the ocean for six months—leaving behind a steady boyfriend and a just-started college major. When she returned, the boyfriend was history and she was a semester behind her peers. But, she gained so much in that experience, she still says it was all worth it. I hope so. She called home regularly so that her parents (okay, mother) would not suffer too much separation anxiety (thanks to cheap calling cards).

My niece still tells anyone who will listen that she would not have survived those days without my daughter—even though I'm sure there were times when Devin was more like a fourth child than a second pair of hands. She has also comforted my niece in later times. Her eldest child and only daughter is now fifteen and Devin has comforted my niece by telling her that it will all be okay through the trying teenage years. She knows this because she could barely stand the sound of her mother's voice as a teenager (whaaaat?) but lives to hear it now that she is beyond her teen years and separated by so many miles. She gives both of us much hope for the future of mother-daughter relations. I will forgive the snarky comment about my voice.

Devin mothers her friends (and is mothered by them as needed) and serves as chief liaison and mediator for the ongoing dramas and traumas of life in the twenties and thirties. She has comforted broken hearts and listened to difficult life problems and even wrestled pills from the hands of a particularly desperate friend in great need of a particularly loyal friend. She suffers their losses and celebrates their joys. It's good practice for her future, but gives her own mother (again, me) cause for much concern that she is too busy nurturing and friending to be nurtured and befriended and/or found by her own true love (the one that will help provide the grandchildren her mother so selfishly hopes to meet).

This daughter of mine is a treasure beyond words. She lives her life in the present—right smack dab in the middle of today. She also remembers the past with frightening accuracy—even down to the very words spoken, or screeched, on ill-fated family car trips—things the rest of us had hoped to forget. She recalls her father's every mannerism—and he had them aplenty. We giggle and cry together over some of the more revealing ones. She knows how to treat each member of our extended family— on all sides of the tree—and can be counted on to always gather us to the laughing places of our shared memories.

She has the ability to calm both young children and older patients in her work at the hospital (or at least get them to think about something silly). From the time she was herself a rather young person, she has attracted children and seniors to her, like bees to honey. There is something in her nature that draws young and old alike. It's just hard to say if it's her humor , nurturing, or pure goofiness that attracts them.

Maybe it's best not to dwell on the why.

She has worked in the Rehabilitation Department of Saint Mary's Hospital since she was a junior in high school and will receive her ten year service award this summer. Loyalty is yet another trait she owns—perhaps to a fault. Case in point:

because she knows her mother worries about bathroom habits, she happily sends detailed description messages on a very, uh, regular basis. Sometimes these messages are even accompanied by a photo. What a joy she is to me!

Even though she has had no child of her own, she is so often a most wonderful mother. Perhaps she was born for just this kind of work. Wishing you a Happy Mother's Day, daughter. May God hold you in the palm of his might hands and continue to bless you and keep you all the days of your life. I am so grateful He has loaned you to me, for the good times and bad, but especially for such a time as this (Esther 4:14).

*Note: My daughter is now working on her twentieth year with the same hospital. She continues to mother her mother from time to time and I continue to be grateful beyond measure.*

# Defining Moments

*May 2013*

I t was probably the lack of sleep resulting from the recently dreaded "spring forward" event that caused me to focus on the subject of time—or lack thereof. This in turn led me to consider those little moments along our life journeys that tend to define us. Sometimes they come in a whisper and sometimes in a roar—sort of like the season that comes in like a lion and goes out like a lamb. Wait a second—that's March, isn't it? Well, phooey. I'd switch to the subject of April showers or May flowers, but since we had plenty of showers in March (weather-wise and wedding-wise) and early April froze the flowers, the theme doesn't work so well, except where it involves defining moments. And, as luck would have it, it does. Oddly enough, I can't recall too many defining moments pre parenthood. I'm sure there have been quite a few, but it appears that my memory is attached mostly to defining mom moments.

My future husband's only son is getting married in May and each of his parent's families hosted a shower for the happy couple one weekend in March. The bride's parents came all the way from Texas to join in the celebrations. Both were wonderful events. Plenty of delicious food, lots of fun, and love all around—or at least some intense liking. Okay, so maybe tolerating is another possible choice. As usual, I hid behind my trusty camera and busied myself with capturing the moments, so I would not have to talk too much (it also ensures that I am not captured in any photos either). There were many great moments on both days.

But the truly defining moment for me was in the discovery that I have gained a friend in someone I classified much too early and incorrectly as a foe. What a gift—a showering, if you will, of blessings for a peaceful and laughter-filled future (until we start fighting over the grandchildren). The defining moment happens when you choose to not let the past disrupt your present or intercept your future. When you start fresh and seek common ground, the resulting treasures are easily mined. And those Texans enjoyed themselves in little old Marion and Ketchup Town and on Reedy Branch Road, too. Just don't give one of them any coconut-laced morsels.

The eight of us shared a meal together after the second shower that included a bean-filled Santa Fe soup. I will assume that the evening concluded right after dessert, not because they were bored but because they desired not to relieve any resulting gas attacks in mixed company. And that brings me to another defining moment. I knew for sure that love was here to stay when I could relieve the aforementioned attacks in front of my future husband without concern for his leaving me in a cloud of disgust. He, of course, had felt comfortable in front of me much earlier in our relationship. The defining moment arrived as we decided to take each other just as we are. We don't always like it, but we choose to take it on in love—so there's that, and we try to space out our bean- eating adventures.

Unfortunately, our defining moments are not always positive ones. They change us and make us who we are, but they are not ones we would choose to experience. Sometimes these defining moments are hurled at us in words as deadly as machine gun fire: Cancer—Stage IV—Metastasized—Terminal. These are words we do not want spoken around anyone, least of all those we love. But it happens. And those bullet-like words can define all of our remaining moments—if we let them. The cancer word is enough, but when coupled with the others, it can drop even the strongest of human spirits right in their tracks.

Two wonderful people I have the privilege to call friends are dealing with these defining moments right now. They each have suffered the loss of a spouse already and had begun to know love again with each other—a gift not always given in the evening of our lives. They have strength though, and will find an endless supply of it in their mutual love for our Lord. They know where true hope resides, even as they pray for a miracle. And we pray they receive one from the Great Physician.

Sometimes defining moments come as we sit and wait in cold rooms for a test result that will tell us our immediate futures. The waiting can be its own defining moment as we see in real time exactly how it feels to be suspended in a living purgatory, not knowing whether the door that opens next will bring a good or bad report. It is a wonderfully defining moment when we learn that negative is not always a bad word. Sometimes that waiting on the edge of uncertainty can give us more clarity of purpose than we ever imagined possible.

There are times in our lives when two separate defining moments can be wrapped in eerily similar surroundings. I vividly remember standing in BWI airport one very cold December morning giving my son one last hug before he boarded a plane that would ultimately take his unit to Afghanistan for a year. I promised him I would not cry. I did not—at least not in front of him. When your baby boy turns to leave and you don't know if you'll ever see him walking toward you again, it is a crucially defining moment. But the joy found in the next airport scene returned the breath to my soul as he walked through the gate in Florence the following December—much thinner and much quieter—but very much alive. Fortunately, this time I did not promise to remain tearless. Unfortunately, my son believes his mother's only defining moments are her tears—the ones that fall for any reason at all—happy, sad, funny, silly, devastating and delirious moments. And he may be right, as the tears are falling as I type.

I had one of those oddly defining tears sessions not too long ago. After chasing the new puppy (the one that is now quite large and a defining moment all by himself) around the yard and back through the living room in an attempt to get him bedded for the night, I sank to the floor in a puddle of uncontrollable sobbing as Mr. Willoughby looked on in shock and disbelief (and very poorly timed amusement). I may have mentioned this episode in an earlier article. It defined for me the need to seek medical opinion on the state of my menopausal well-being. Will keep you posted on which state I end up in residence. Right now it's looking like the state of confusion in crazy town.

According to my trusty online dictionary, a defining moment is "a point at which the essential nature or character of a person, group, etc., is revealed or identified." They say it originated in the early eighties. And since I became a mother in those years, I can without any hesitation heartily agree with the description.

I witnessed my daughter's transformation from child to woman as she sat in her dad's hospice room, talking softly to him, playing his favorite Celtic Women cd, and dabbing his lips with glycerin swabs. This was the same child who took great delight in making the veins in his neck pop out when she dumped the kitty litter tray right outside the basement door instead of walking it to the woods. Perhaps this was a defining moment for all three of us. I hope so. I trust he knew she was there. She misses him so much and yet has found room to love the man I will marry next year. On Valentine's Day she told me she was very grateful for him because he takes such good care of her mom's heart. And again the tears fall.

But perhaps the greatest defining moment of all came six years ago when I finally stopped running from the love of Christ, turned, and accepted the gift of salvation through faith in Him alone. If all of our defining moments are wrapped first in the choice to stand and believe and follow His lead toward home, we will all come to know the peace that passes all understanding. No words or events or choices outside of that gift can bring us to any better definition. I will travel the road He has laid out for me, and (pardon me Robert Frost) it will made all the difference. It is my hope that my children will choose it to define their own paths in this life even though their mother did not draw them to it as they grew.

# Mine? Mine? Mine?

*May 2014*

*I*f you or your children or grandchildren are fans of Finding Nemo, reading the title of this article has already conjured up an image of selfish little beady-eyed seagulls attempting to make a snack out of a poor helpless fishy. Fortunately, he escaped their obnoxious cawing and clawing grip just in the nick of time. This is not so for others of us, who, like myself, find the word "mine" to be a rather common part of daily vocabulary. We may not have an overpowering taste for fishies, but we flap our possessive wings over many other things, don't we?

Believe it or not, the famous seagulls clip was played during a recent morning worship service at Revelation Ministries in Marion. (Yes, I even have the handout to prove it.) We were studying the Book of James in the fifth chapter and the clip set the stage beautifully, and humorously, for our serious lesson on riches, possessions, and worldly endeavors. Are we continually so preoccupied by our stuff-gatherings and personal collections that we neglect to recognize where real need exists or, worse still, where our hands are too tightly gripped around certain things or people? Mine? Mine? Mine?

In this month when we celebrate mothers and mothering and all things maternal, I find myself referring to the remaining female parental unit in our family as mine—as in, my mama, my mother, my mom, my mommy. She just turned ninety in March and appears to be on her way to the one hundred mark—her mind is still pretty sharp and she still bounces pretty well when she falls. This, unfortunately, happens on a fairly regular basis, but she has had so much practice at it that she has yet to break anything major. But she loves where she spends her time now—a great assisted living home in Frederick, MD. We think maybe it reminds her of growing up in a hotel. Plus she gets daily visits from at least two of her daughters and an assortment of grands and great-grands.

She never complains, except to say that there is way too much food to eat and they eat "three times a day, for heaven's sake." Mary Frances has also confessed to feigning sleep on some mornings or afternoons when she's just not ready to make the trek to the dining room and line up her walker with fifty others. She also recognized my (see?) voice when I called her on her recent birthday and abruptly woke her from one of those naps. This was a great gift—that my (see, again—mine, mine, mine) mother would still know my voice. After all, there are five daughters in the family and many, many grands and great-grands to remember. But she does very well for ninety-five and I'm so glad she's mine, mine, and mine.

But my mother is also very much her own person. After all, I have been told that she was a whole and fully functioning person long before she was my very own mother. The same holds true for all the other possessions I love to claim—my daughter, my son, my soon-to-be husband, my friends, my family, my life, and on and on ad nausea. Not one of them is truly mine, mine, and mine. And this is actually a wonderful thing, once one can get over the initial shock of such a brutal truth.

I become particularly aware of my self-centered mother-possessiveness during the month of May. There is, of course, the Mother's Day thing to be blamed for much of this mine/mine/mine mindset. For pity's sake, I can't blame myself for anything, now can I? May is also my birth month, at which time I took full possession of the "mine" thing. Are you my mother? Why, yes, you are, you lucky girl. It has taken me nearly all of my sixty years to fully grasp the reality that we really don't possess anything or any being. Not really, and not ever.

This was brought home to me fairly succinctly when I read a little story that was circulating online (yes, I do glance there from time to time). Seems a very sad and lonely woman decided to ask God one day why He is called "I Am." Gently He responded, by telling her this:

"I Am Love. I Am Peace. I Am Grace. I Am Joy. I Am Safety. I Am Strength. I Am Shelter. I Am Power. I Am The Beginning and The End. I Am The Way, The Truth, and The Life."

With a slow realization and through silent tears of understanding the woman looked toward Heaven and quietly asked, "Then, Lord, who am I?" He tenderly wiped her tears by saying:

"You are Mine."

That one word is all that matters when its source is the Great I Am—so very deep the meaning and so very sheltering the sound, to be called His alone. It is, after all, the only possession there can be. When The Great I Am calls us His own, there is no other word through which joy can be experienced.

The seagulls can continue to squawk and flap in pursuit of Nemo. And I can, unfortunately, keep insisting that my mother, daughter, son, siblings, friends, family, and almost-husband (and his family) are mine, mine, and mine. But we know the truth. None of us really owns anything or can lay claim to any possession—not even to the things we think we make ourselves. All things, great and small, He owns them all, even those annoying seagulls.

# When You Care Enough

*May 2016*

The very best thing I can say about this Mother's Day is I will not be attacking Hallmark stores frantically searching for a card that does not use the word *mom*, does use the word "Mother," and also manages to omit flowery, sweet-as-honey words that she would find ridiculous. I can tell you it is nearly impossible to find a card like that—one that hits all three criteria. I should know. I've looked for said Mother's Day cards for over fifty years (it was temporarily okay to use "Mommy" up until I was about ten—but never "Mom").

This year, sadly, I'll not need to search or send. Our mother passed on peacefully the day after Christmas, at the blessedly advanced age of ninety-six. She would have been ninety-seven in March, a milestone she did not wish to see. According to her, she had been ready for at least seven years and was quite tired of waking up every morning—if not for that one cup of coffee, the effort for her was not particularly worth the trouble.

When one's life spans almost ten decades, it includes an awesome set of experiences. Hers was no exception. She grew up in hotels, the firstborn daughter of an Irish Catholic immigrant and a Methodist school teacher turned business partners, experienced the Great Depression as a young girl, spent a year in New York City attending design school, married a bit earlier than anticipated so she could care for her dying mother-in-law, endured WWII with her husband in the Navy and two tiny daughters at home, ultimately had five daughters as a work-at-home mom, saw presidents shot, a moon landing, and twin towers fall on TV, grieved both her youngest daughter's widowhood and her own in just a six-month span, and tallied six sons-in-law, twenty-one grandchildren and thirty-one great-grandchildren before she left the shackles of this world behind.

Because both our parents had requested no funeral services of any kind—mostly, I think, because they had no desire to attend them, alive or deceased—the sisters, four out of five, decided to get together in Maryland to share memories of our mother and bid her farewell. The Chicago sister couldn't make it, so we just talked about her the entire weekend.

The overachieving sister decided (we call her that because it makes us all feel a little less inadequate about ourselves—labeling her gives us permission to just watch and roll our eyes as she twirls happily around us, accomplishing things in hours that would take an army of us a week to complete, if at all) it would be wonderful to draft a list of questions for each of us to answer about life with our mother. Out loud and in person.

She presented the questions in a deceivingly adorable little basket, along with detailed verbal instructions on how we were to proceed. Oh yes. We had to answer in age order, youngest to oldest, and then advance the order for each subsequent question. Did I mention that the overachiever is also a bit of a control freak? I'm including her questions here, but will not bore you with our answers because they are only interesting to us, and thus not fair to you. I am also including them because, if she ever reads this article, she'll wonder why they weren't included. Plus I have an overwhelming desire to be her favorite. Or anybody's favorite. Never mind. Here are those questions:

What is your favorite memory involving your mother?

What is a memory you would like to forget involving your mother?

What was your favorite childhood dinner your mother made?

What do you think is the most important thing you learned from your mother?

What do you think was your mother's most outstanding quality?

Name three things about yourself that you believe are a direct result of having the mother you had.

Do you discipline your children the way your mother disciplined you?

Name something you had to do growing up that you really did not want to do.

Name something you really liked to do with your mother.

If you could change one thing about what it was like growing up with your mother, what would it be?

I will tell you that our answers brought out both our shared and differing experiences of growing up with our mother. Something that is worth noting here—our ages span a twelve-year gap from oldest to youngest. The first four came within five years of each other, like peas in a pod. Then I arrived seven years later, like a rogue weed in the family garden. I am still a bit surprised that my nickname isn't Boo-Boo or Oopsie Doodle.

The growing up years were quite different from the oldest to the youngest. There were wins and losses at both ends of our stories. In fact, my oldest sister shared that she used to cry about how different our growing up years were, hers and mine. I got the alcohol-induced discord years but had the less strict and more indulgent ride. My sisters got the sweeter, more joyful years but they were so bunched together, always enduring shared space and attention. Through it all, our mother always cared enough.

If your own mother has passed, I encourage you to consider these questions this Mother's Day or draft some of your own. And, if you are still blessed to have her in your life, ask her the same questions about her own mother. I promise it will be a most enlightening experience, especially if you have sibling answers in the mix too.

All things considered, our mother always cared enough. I hope when I die my children will say the same about me, that I cared enough as their mother. They know I love them, just as my mother loved us, though she was a bit more distant in her approach—she was of the generation that did not request or desire displays of affection or verbal confessions of love. I guess I craved it so much that I found it necessary to smother my children with those displays and words of love (or to hopefully counteract my angry side). They are much more tolerant of it as they get older. Perhaps the therapy is helping.

I know for sure that our mother cared enough to give her very best effort for each of us in her very own way. Maybe she wasn't a walking Hallmark card, but she cared enough to deliver the very best she could. She even managed to surprise each of us with a check that sisters weekend—the remaining balance of her life, divided by five. This was accomplished, in large measure, by our oldest sister who has always quietly and completely cared enough for those around her, most assuredly our mother. She and the Overachiever became quite a team in caring for our mother, especially in her last years. The rest of us will always be grateful for that care.

Happy Mother's Day to all who have been blessed with the gift of a mother (biological or otherwise) who cared enough to give her very best. And to each of my sisters, thank you for sharing her with me.

# Summer Season in the She Shed

Fathers, Brothers, Friends, and Others

*Now learn this parable from the fig tree: When its branch has already become tender and puts forth leaves, you know that summer is near.*

—*Matthew 24:32*

June

**Lessons Learned**
**The Daddy Dance**
**Forecast: Man-Drought**
**Doodle Bugs & Dog Tags**
**The Men-tour**
**Leave it to Cleaver, June**

*T*he month of June was reserved for all things male. It was usually a very popular issue for a women's magazine, and included profiles of men in and around the Pee Dee region of South Carolina and beyond. Most of my earlier writings included whining about a lack of male companionship. That changed.

# Lessons Learned

*June 2007*

$S$ ince this month's issue is dedicated to men and makeovers, I began to consider what I might share about the man I married twenty-five years ago and it occurred to me that perhaps it would be best to share instead the many things he taught me over the years. It wasn't until he was no longer with me that I realized how very much wiser he was than I will ever hope to be. And, more to the point, I discovered that he was just fine exactly the way he was. I spent so much wasted effort trying to transform him into "Mr. Perfect." Had I just been a little bit more keenly observant, I might have spared myself all that stress of begging and pleading for more coordinated clothing, less belly, better manners, and quieter sleep, to name a few.

I guess I shouldn't have been so surprised about his wisdoms though. He was thirteen years my senior. So, without further ado, here are twenty of the lessons my late husband taught me.

He taught me how to hug. It wasn't so much that I didn't know how, I just didn't give them out or seek them very often. He changed all that. I learned what it feels like to both give and receive them. Now I know how it feels when they are missing.

He taught me what it is to be loved unconditionally. He knew how to love and he showed it every day, even when I didn't deserve it, even when I was having a nasty little shit or being an evil shrew. He loved his children the same way. Even when we made that big vein pop out on his forehead, he still loved us.

Real men do eat quiche. And they go to the grocery store, cook meals, change diapers, clean toilets, wear pink shirts, pass gas, have ear hairs, and are fearless in their protection of home and family.

Real men can have weird wardrobes. They wear funky sweat pants and torn T-shirts and Chuck Taylors without socks because it's not the wrapper that's important. It's what's inside that count. It is also not important where that wrapper came from—a thrift store, a giveaway pile, or even the side of a road.

He taught me the meaning of many nautical terms, like port, starboard, rudder, jib, and of course, *mayday*. He also taught me that when you name your boats *Water Witch*, *Miss Wide Water Beach*, and *Tinkerbelle*, you can pretty much expect that you are going to make the gods of the seas angry (and he did—often).

Any mess can be cleaned up, even the dead fish your long-haired dog rolls around in. All you need is to slather enough Vicks VapoRub under your nose. The retching and dry heaves are just a side feature.

Heroes sometimes wear uniforms and rush into burning buildings when others are running out, but they also face unseen fires with the same kind of courage and bravery. They wake up each morning believing that life will get better, even when it doesn't. My husband, the career firefighter also taught me not to unpack on vacation until the entire family has walked the hotel hallway, counting the number of doors to the stair-well. Just in case a fire ignites.

Turn up the volume on a car radio if said vehicle develops troublesome noises, until the sound goes away. The same goes for a dad voice to be heard over any other noise, like loud children or squealing girls during a slumber party.

Christmas trees are supposed to be crooked and hollering at the tangled sets of tree lights is a cherished family tradition not to be skipped or avoided.

Handkerchiefs are not dirty until you fold them over for a fourth time and wearing underwear is only necessary if one is not careful with zippering. He wasn't always, but underwear remained optional.

Moustaches are handsome things and to be treasured, at least until the wearer catches a bad cold or eats spaghetti with meatballs and extra sauce.

Work is just work and your real life happens outside of it. But, lifelong friends can come from your work, making your life richer by far than any paycheck ever earned.

Wives can gain fifty pounds when pregnant and they still get to enjoy a pint of cherry vanilla ice cream every night and not a single word is spoken about how the same wife (me) plans to fit back in her prepregnancy jeans.

A father's greatest revenge on children who won't clean their rooms properly or often enough is to time the mowing of grass on a hot day, without benefit of belly or man-boob shirt cover, just as a packed school bus is depositing said children at the top of the driveway. Waving frantically to get their attention, as they step from the bus, is icing on the revenge cake.

Life is not meant to be perfectly manicured and tied in a pretty bow for all to see. It is meant to be lived with all its attending wrinkles, warts, and boo-boos.

Suspenders are necessities. They are not simply accessories, but mandatory items of clothing for those who wear nonelastic waist pants and suffer from large bellies and no backside.

He (and his mother) taught me the joys of butter and mayonnaise and grits. I had grown up surrounded only be Miracle Whip, margarine, and oatmeal (also cream of wheat). Fortunately this lesson was learned before moving southward. I can't be a G.R.I.T.S. but at least I know what they are.

It was perfectly okay that he and his mother (and mine) would always be much better cooks, but I learned that I was loved for trying anyway.

Always be careful what you wish for, because you just might get it. I always wished to have my alone time and I always wished he'd stop snoring. If I could get a do-over, I'd gladly take back both of those wishes. I'm alone way too often now, and the silence at night is deafening.

In the end my husband taught me that the true measure of a man is not in how much he weighs or how tall he stands or how large his shoes. The true measure of a man is found in the breadth of his heart and in the depth of his hope. My husband's heart and hope were immeasurable, as is the space now left by his absence from our lives. I've learned this last lesson all too well and much too soon. But, there is still some joy to be found in this month we celebrate fathers. The Father to whom we pray each day holds the hands of the husbands and fathers we miss so dearly. In that thought, there is comfort, grace, and peace.

# The Daddy Dance

*I* recently had the great pleasure of attending the spring wedding of an old friend near Charlottesville, VA. Well, she's not old, but I'm old enough to be her mother and she already has a lovely mother, so we are simply friends. Since my invitation said "and guest," my daughter graciously agreed to be my date, thus saving me the embarrassment of a solo trip. And, should anyone be brave enough to step forward, my dance card still has plenty of room. Sadly, the usual April showers had advanced into May and threatened to wash away the ceremony and reception, both of which were planned for outdoor enjoyment.

Fortunately, the rain held off just long enough for the happy couple to exchange vows before family and friends on a lush green hillside with a gently rolling river as backdrop, and an occasional songbird for accompaniment. During the ceremony the minister suggested that it is not the couple gazing lovingly at each other that will enjoy a lifetime marriage, but it is instead the couple that passionately looks in the same direction toward God's love that will find the peace and joy of a lifelong commitment. Thankfully, these two nearly-weds appeared to clearly grasp the concept of directing their gaze upward.

The Mexican-themed reception, chosen partly because the honeymoon would be spent south of the border, included a tasty taco buffet, salsa music, and even a piñata for the youngest attendees. But before the festivities and feastings began, my friend's father led the gathering in a prayer of thanksgiving and a request for the support of this new marriage. Standing before him was his only daughter, and the last of his three children to marry. What a beautiful blessing for this child to hear her daddy's prayer as she began a new life with her husband.

Later, we witnessed the traditional first dance for the newlyweds, followed closely by the requisite father-daughter dance. It was during this moment that I glanced at my daughter-date, who was sitting quietly beside me, watching the pair twirl around the dance floor. She wore a wistful smile, but that did not hide the tears rimming her lashes. I knew what she was thinking and quietly patted her leg a few times under the table. As is her way, she was happy for the love being shared by this family, but it was a heart-stabbing reminder that she would never have this same moment to share with her own father. The tears then came to my own eyes as we both looked quickly upward in hopes of averting the waterfall about to cascade down our cheeks. Thankfully, the move was successful. Nobody likes to see sobbing faces at their wedding reception.

The wedding continued to its beautiful conclusion and we drove back to our hotel, having a nostalgic conversation about her dad and my husband. Fortunately, we laughed quite a bit. He was, after all, a funny guy. And he loved his daughter. He did not always understand her, or appreciate her own sense of humor, but he did love her. I know he would have been overjoyed to dance with her at her wedding, even though dancing was not one of his favorite activities. Just the mention of the word could set his trick back into horrible spasms. His daughter is particularly good at remembering the tiniest of details and quirks about her father—little things that I had forgotten about him are permanently imbedded in her memory and she is always good at foraging for them, as needed.

They didn't always see eye to eye, and not just because he towered over her at six foot three. My husband had never been around little girls before, having had only one brother, a batch of nephews, and two sons—one older and one younger than his daughter. He was simply ill-prepared for all the joys of squealing slumber parties and stinky soccer practice carpools and the surprises of stepping on spiked heel Barbie shoes in his bare feet in the middle of the night. But he did it all. He changed her diapers, introduced her to popsicles and vanilla ice cream, tried to protect her from sadness, and vainly attempted to chase her down for punishments. She might have been much shorter, but she was always much faster. He laughed about that last one later in life, but definitely not during the actual chases. She however could laugh and run at the same time. Our daughter has a powerful storehouse of memories to sustain her for the rest of her life. She has his gift of fun and ability to relate to people of all ages. She just won't get to have that dance at her wedding.

My own father is no longer with us either (why they both had to leave within six months of each other is something I keep in my "not fair" box). I did get the chance to dance with him at our wedding though. It was the first and last time we ever danced together, which is probably a good thing since we marched to the beat of very different drums. He was an accountant. I hate numbers. He loved to garden. I do not by any stretch of the imagination enjoy a green thumb. He loved sarcasm. I hated being the recipient of it—though I did learn to make use of it later myself. He loved to watch his four older daughters play basketball in high school. The only thing I can dribble is icing. He could get chickadees to eat birdseed out of his hand (I have the pictures to prove it.) I have a cat that keeps most birds out of my yard by staring out the window while licking her lips. I do love birds though—maybe we did have a few things in common. The music we danced to in life is of a different measure but the memories still make for a beautiful song.

Maybe my daughter won't be deprived of the wedding dance with her dad after all. Maybe she will know that he'll be there dancing around in her memory of him—the foxtrot, twist, boogaloo, and chicken dance too. Meanwhile, we'll both continue to look up when the tears of loss begin to fall. It is, after all, the only direction that leads to joy.

# Forecast: Man-Drought

*June 2009*

From where I'm sitting (and watching and waiting), the sky is not exactly pouring out men all over the place. It's not even drizzling over here on Oliver Street—nary a sprinkle, or even the promise of one. No happy little man puddle to jump in with both feet. At last check, there was a big fat zero chance of rain in the man forecast.

The husband of twenty-five years will be missed for three whole years this month. The daddy left here shortly after the husband, with nearly ninety years of living behind him. The son is off "soldiering" his responsibilities and, hopefully, learning to survive them—from Fort Benning to Fort Drum and now in Afghanistan. Yep, it's rather a bit of a man drought for this old Marion maid (it is not exactly kind to snicker at that last phrase, ladies and gentlemen—and I know who you are).

Certainly, there are men all around, everywhere. Just look at the pages of this magazine (June is the Man issue, after all). They are on the streets where we live and work and play and worship. Unfortunately, they seem to all have a bad case of too—as in too young, too old, too fussy, too fierce, too humorless, too dull, too weird, and most importantly, too married.

When you haven't dated in a very, very long time, you begin to wonder if it's really even worth the effort anymore. But, attempting eternal optimism, I've embarked on a widow's makeover, thanks to the enthusiasms of my new southern friends. I now wear make-up, even to exercise class. I sport bigger earrings and a new bra (quite the uplifting experience, by the way), and a more up-to-date hairstyle, one that takes much more finesse to style than my old pal, the ponytail. For what it's worth, I'm very busy working out the many kinks in my physical appearance department (uh-oh, better get Maaco).

For added inspiration, I decided to troll about for more man information and searched the Internet (no, not the dating sites—I may be somewhat concerned about this man-drought, but I'm not yet desperate). Lo and behold, I tripped upon a website called The Art of Manliness. It offered great tidbits for men on how to remain or become a real one—complete with a daily email service entitled "The Toilet Paper—Daily News for the Thinking Man." Maybe if I can grasp some better understanding of them, I might be able to actually locate another real one. As luck would have it, I hit pay dirt on this site.

One of the website articles was about Benjamin Franklin's thirteen virtues, and how they remain words to live by for manly men. Evidently, when he was a young man of about twenty years, Franklin decided to draft his plan for living. His guiding light was Philippians 4:8. These virtues pretty much describe the man of my dreams. Who knew that the man who lobbied for the turkey to be our national bird would come up with such an eagle-eyed view of what is so beautifully attractive? Here they are, along with his brief descriptions:

Temperance—Eat not to dullness or drink not to elevation

Silence—Speak not but what may benefit others or yourself. Avoid trifling conversation.

Order—Let all things have their places. Let each part of your business have its time.

Resolution—Resolve to perform what you ought. Perform without fail what you resolve.

Frugality—Make no expense but to do good to others or yourself. Waste nothing.

Industry—Lose no time. Be always employed in something useful. Cut off all unnecessary action.

Sincerity—Use no hurtful deceit. Think innocently and justly; and, if you speak, speak accordingly.

Justice—Wrong none, by doing injuries or omitting the benefits that are your duty.

Moderation—Avoid extremes. Forebear resenting injuries so much as you think they deserve.

Cleanliness—Tolerate no uncleanness in body, clothes, or habitation.

Chastity—Rarely use venery but for health or offspring; never to dullness, weakness, or the injury of your own or another's peace or reputation.

Tranquility—Be not disturbed at trifles, or at accidents common or unavoidable.

Humility—Imitate Jesus and Socrates.

Now here's the plan: wait for God to send him my way—the one that practices the thirteen virtues penned by Benjamin Franklin, with divine inspiration from Philippians 4:8. Meanwhile, I'll practice patience and perspective and peace while I'm waiting for that new man to show up on my doorstep. Did I mention that one of my favorite pastimes lately is gazing out the front window, watching for his arrival? I'm not kidding. Yes, it is sad—but hopeful. And if it's not too much to ask, I'd also like him to have a moustache and chest hair, stand about six feet tall, and weigh more than I do. He'll be comfortable in jeans and T-shirt or suit and tie. And he'll know how to fix things.

Oh, who am I kidding? Please Lord, just let him stand upright, breathe fairly regularly, and have some of his own teeth. But if that new man doesn't come my way, at least I'll remember with joy the one I had (and failed to adequately appreciate). I'll be grateful for the memory and content in the present, knowing what eternity holds. For now, I'll be optimistic and keep my umbrella handy. Either that or I'll just keep rewinding the bathtub scene from The Bridges of Madison County. It adds a whole new meaning to the Eastwood phrase, "Go ahead; make my day."

# Doodlebugs and Dog Tags

*June 2010*

What a difference twelve months can make. Last year, the magazine theme was "It's Raining Men" and I, sadly, filled my contribution with whining and complaining about the nearly intolerable man-drought season of my life. Husband? Dead. Dad? Dead. Son? Combat soldier heading to Afghanistan.

Significant other was just a ghostly figment of an overactive imagination. And that's what caused most of the obnoxious whining and complaining in the first place.

So, what has changed? If you endured reading my love-struck February article this year, you already know that there is indeed a very significant other in my life now. But what you may not know is just how significant he has become. This man who follows Christ has captured this whining and complaining woman's heart completely. He is patient and kind and not arrogant and seeks not his own and bears all things and hopes all things and endures all things—even my northern attempts at southern cooking. I can do grits and even shrimp and grits, but biscuits still elude me, unless my steel magnolia friend is hovering over me in the process. I don't own a respectable frying pan. Banana pudding? Sorry, no. A thousand times no. Fortunately, he has a healthy sense of humor and uses it freely when reminding me of those times when I am less than pleasant (northern?) to be around. I don't really enjoy tallying my faults, but fair is fair. But, while we're on the subject of faults, I'm not really crazy about his habit of whistling Dixie every chance he gets to remind me of where I now live. I did rather enjoy my recent Confederate Memorial Day holiday as a South Carolina state employee.

He is a fine southern gentleman—a true farm-raised catch-fish who can fix almost anything and does not shy away from hard work. He reminds me always where to find the source of all strength (and it's not in coffee or chocolate—a real surprise for me). When he returns thanks before meals, it is always inclusive of those we both love. He blends our families in prayer like his mother used to thread quilts. I will overlook that he seems to be especially prayerful before northern-themed dishes. When my friends up north ask how I got so lucky, it's difficult to answer. I don't think luck had anything to do with it. I believe it is only by God's design and by our mutual choice to follow His plan. I'm not sure why He tossed together two people from such diverse backgrounds. Perhaps it is proof of an almighty sense of humor. But I'm pretty sure it had little to do with all my whining and complaining last year.

This godsent man did an especially wonderful thing recently. It was beyond any romantic notion I might have ever had about dating—even beyond the dancing in the driveway under the stars to "Unchained Melody." (Yes, that really happened. Who needs chick flicks when you have the live version?) He went way out on a dating limb and introduced me to doodlebugs. In fifty-five years of life, I had never heard of a doodlebug—ladybugs, sure, but not doodlebugs. And not only did he find one for me, he actually sang the Doodlebug Song while hunting it down. It takes a very strong man, grounded in faith, to sing a little child's song while twirling a bit of string between his fingers, squatting over a tiny hole in the sandy soil, waiting patiently for a doodlebug to respond by kicking up little puffs of soil, followed very shortly by the appearance of said bug, in search of tasty little ant snacks. I was so sure he was taking me on a snipe hunt that it took me a while to actually see it.

Once I laid eyes on that doodlebug I was pretty sure this man was a keeper. Anybody can do the romantic stuff, but where else am I going to find the kind of man who will hunt such amazing treasures for me? He may not have had me at "hello," but he has me now for sure, after singing "doodlebug, doodlebug, come out of your hole." Be still my tiny northern cynical lovelorn-no-more heart.

As if that was not enough of a change from the past year's storyline, my son contributed yet another. He recently visited during his midtour leave from Afghanistan duty. Last year he was just graduating from boot camp and heading to his first assignment at Fort Drum, NY. Now he's had three months in "the Stan," as they call it, and just returned for at least another eight months. Contrary to his requests otherwise, he will always be my baby—but I got a full introduction to the man he has now become during that visit.

Because he was so appreciative of a group of fourth graders who had written to him during the beginning of his tour, he visited their classroom while he was on leave. I had the privilege of making that visit with him (after promising to sit quietly in the back and not take too many pictures or cry too loudly). It was during his discussion with those children that I saw the man in my "baby." He spoke enthusiastically of his mission as a US soldier and how he hoped to do more. But it was his ability to speak to their interests and needs that truly struck me. He understood (remembered?) what it was like to be a fourth grader and didn't overstate the dangers of his mission or use inappropriate word bombs. He made sure he answered all of their questions and called on each child at least once. The class asked wonderful questions and he gave great answers. What I thought would be just a fifteen minute howdy-do and thank you turned into an hour long adventure, with children still asking questions after the bus bell rang.

It was a beautiful opportunity for a mother to witness a son's transformation to manhood. Then he pulled out his dog tags and described their use. Until that moment, I had forgotten what would likely be attached to those tags. I had given my son his dad's wedding ring at Christmas, right before he left for Afghanistan. His dad had always been his hero and it seemed fitting to pass his wedding band on to the son who would now take on that family role. But when he described for the children why he kept his dad's ring on his dog tags, I had to break that earlier promise not to cry. Thank you, Mrs. Campbell and Mrs. Beeson for your fourth graders at Pee Dee Academy. You helped me see the man my baby had become, all in one amazing afternoon. The weekly Bible verse on the chalkboard was Psalm 56:11. I treasure the photo of my son reading it while waiting to speak to your classes that day. I hope he will remember it too.

A year really can make a huge difference in our lives. Sometimes it takes only a week or day or moment, but change is always a gift that God gives us. Whether it's doodlebugs or dog tags or something else entirely, I pray I will always find the joy within the change that is inevitable in this life. It builds character. Character builds perseverance. Perseverance builds hope. And hope, well, that's just what we do while we breathe through the changes that will come our way until we meet eternity.

# The Men Tour

*June 2014*

*A*h, yes. June is the month we celebrate the men. I am particularly excited to celebrate them this month as I will be marrying one really great one on the 22nd (more on that in August issue, I suspect—you've been warned). And since the old wedding bells (and I do mean old) are about to ring, it seemed like a good time to take a little trip down memory lane—on last men tour, if you will. Of course that phrase rather quickly led me to think about actual men-tors—those amazing people in our lives that wisely advise us, sometimes without realizing what they are truly doing for us. Come to find out, the men tour is a pretty effective mentor trip as well.

I guess that makes sense. The word men-tor does have a lot of testosterone in it. Many ascribe its origin to the Greeks. Mentor was a character in the *Odyssey*—a friend of Odysseus and advisor to his son, Telemachus. He was the first known literary "wise advisor." How could it take me this long (age sixty) to realize that male mentors have been threaded throughout most of my life? I've always attributed good advice to the women I knew/know—who knew the men could contribute too. Man, what a surprising development.

Without further ado, and in order of appearance, the men tour looks like this for me:

The Daddy/Father/Dad—He was the first man in my life. And because I was the ninth girl in his (one mother, two sisters, one wife, five daughters), my entrance was not exactly newsworthy or special. But we developed a relationship over time that helped me determine that only certain men make great daddies. He was already pushing forty when I arrived, so our bonding took on much more meaning as we both grew older. He was of the generation that lived through the Depression, wore a uniform in World War II, and worked steadfastly to provide for a family while his wife maintained the home front. Being surrounded by women most of his life, he was, in a word, spoiled. He was also very well versed in playing the "oh, poor me—I have no sons—how terribly awful for me" game, while secretly basking in the glory of being waited on rather consistently and most contentedly. He was not quick with the "I love you" phrase—at least not until he was closer to the end of his life—and then he said it often, with powerful and effective meaning until he escaped this world just a few weeks short of ninety years. I do miss him, but he left behind some great counsel.

The brother(s)—if you're lucky enough to have any. I didn't. Not a single one. I'm clueless on what it means to have a brother mentor. But I have gathered a basketball team of brothers-in-law (five so far—and will add a few more on June 22). They have each offered their own forms of mentoring, from teaching me to be a better swimmer to providing lessons in humor and exactly what to look for in a husband. I still wish I had a brother though—maybe a younger one I could boss around. Being the baby is not all it's cracked up to be.

The first crush (and second, and possibly third)—we learn a great deal about ourselves by discovering who we are attracted to and who is attracted to us. My very first one delivered our newspaper on his bicycle—in sixth grade. Turns out we dated off and on through college and beyond, never quite making it to the altar. He was the first to prick my heart and the first to break it. We took turns doing that—he taught me all about bad and good timing. He was also the first "date" after my husband died—if you count attending a high school reunion a year later as a date. It wasn't. But he helped me determine that there could be some life remaining after all the grief and sadness of terminal cancer. It wouldn't happen with him, of course, but he helped me see some light at the end of a very dark tunnel.

The first husband—Although he left much earlier than expected, it wasn't his choice to go. He fought and fought, up to the very end of his life, to stay. He taught me that hugs and loudness and boldness are not such bad things. He taught me that it's not necessarily how you start out in life that matters. It's how you finish. He finished well, and left a legacy of love for his children. For me, he left the advice to seek a full life—one centered on hope and edged in laughter.

The son and bonus sons—I have one biological son, one bonus son from first marriage and another bonus son from this new and final one. They have mentored me in many ways (and will continue to, I hope, for years to come). My son has just completed a five year Army tour and is ready to fully engage in civilian life once again. He has showered me with unbelievable life lessons, this "child-man" that I have loved from before his birth. He also showered me right after his birth—which is not surprising considering my lack of male baby parts experience. Fortunately, I learned quickly not to yawn while diapering, no matter how tired.

My bonus sons—one forty-five and one thirty, both married, have taught me what it is to choose to love another woman's son and be permitted to do so without conditions or limits. It is a privilege to be "related" to them, no matter how distant that connection may be.

The final husband—I cannot begin to describe all of the mentoring this man has done with me. All I know is he must be fairly exhausted by the efforts. Every day he shows me what it is to be a godly person (and an occasional pain in the neck with a dry, tart wit and low tolerance for my sometimes northward attitude). Life is filled with joy, even within the low points and storms, as long as he is with me. He has loved me through our differences and without hesitation. There will be no other for me. I will love him all the remaining days of my life.

There is one, however, that mentors like no other I have mentioned. He is the first, last, and only one that truly matters in and beyond this world—He is mentor, father, brother, and groom. He is salt, light, spirit, soul, and body—our Savior and soon-coming King, Jesus Christ.

The prophet Isaiah said it best: "For a child is born to us, a son is given to us. The government will rest on his shoulders. And he will be called: Wonderful Counselor, Mighty God, Everlasting Father, Prince of Peace" (Isa. 9:6, NLT).

And on that glorious verse, dear reader, the June 2014 Men Tour has ended. They have mentored well and I have learned much. God willing, there will be many more lessons ahead on this journey.

# Leave It to June, Beaver

June 2016

Where I come from school doesn't let out until June—usually the middle of June and high school seniors don't graduate until the calendar flips past May, which means that I am not ready for summer until at least June 20. This is problematic when one resides in the South and the summer season seems to begin much earlier—sometimes in February. The month of June causes us to involuntarily cling to our clothes while simultaneously desiring to be unhitched from our winter clothing choices in favor of shorts, flip-flops, and bikinis.

That used to be true, anyway, back when wearing a bathing suit did not conjure up horrific nightmares. Nowadays the cavernous loss of enjoyment in swimming attire is wide (quite literally) and deep. I have been searching unsuccessfully for a ¾ sleeved, capris version of a bathing suit for a few years now. Probably time to give up on that one and just say yes to the moo-moo dress. Or I'll just plant myself under the ceiling fan and spend the summer watching marathon screenings of old TV shows and wishing I could be more like high-heeled, pearl-wearing June Cleaver.

If you are anywhere near my age bracket, you probably enjoyed watching Leave it to Beaver (first-run versions, not the syndicated ones—really, I'm that old—it ran from October 1957 to June 1963). Perhaps you had/have a mother or grandmother very much like good old June Cleaver. Maybe she didn't wear pearls to vacuum, but she did have a strong sense of family duty, coupled with a good mind and heart—not too sweet but oh-so savvy. No wonder Ward and the boys appreciated her. By the way, do you know the reason June wore those pearls? Well, I didn't either until I began researching this article.

June Cleaver wore pearls because back in the day the cameras and lighting were not as technically terrific as they are today. The natural contours of her face evidently cast an unflattering shadow on her neck—thus the pearls. Who knew? I learned this little gem via a You Tube video interview with Barbara Billingsley, the actor who portrayed Beaver's mom. She was a young widow and mother of two sons in real life while filming the show. Didn't know that either. She said it informed her portrayal of June Cleaver. I didn't even notice. She and Ward Cleaver just seemed to have it all together.

June 30 marks ten years since my late husband lost his cancer battle and left a huge hole in our family tree. Some days it seems like it happened a lifetime ago, and other days the weight of it can nearly drop me to my knees, as I observe my adult children muddle through every Father's Day, birthday, and anniversary of loss day without him. It can be painful to watch, as they attempt to soldier on for my sake and with respect for the new man that we all agree is my last husband. June Cleaver would have known what to do for my children. She would have been a great help, with all her pearls of 1950–60s wisdom.

But grief can be a funny thing. And by that I mean odd, strange, and unusual—not the more amusing definition of the word. Although, if truth be told, most grief survivors can remember some weirdly amusing things happening in the depths of our griefs—as sorrow and laughter are like Siamese twins, the ying and yang of our everyday lives. We can't seem to do one without the other showing up, usually uninvited. We marry. We cleave. One leaves. We grieve. We cleave to our wagon of loss. We unhitch that wagon. We have a good giggle. We survive, with or without June Cleaver's help.

While concentrating mightily on the Cleavers this month—June, Ward, Wally, Theodore—I couldn't help but take notice of the word cleave. The bible is full of references to leaving and cleaving.

The King James Version offers forty-five verse references to the word *cleave* or *cleaveth*—forty in the OT and five in the NT. Here are just two:

"And every beast that parteth the hoof, and cleaveth the cleft into two claws, and cheweth the cud among the beasts, that ye shall eat" (Deut. 14:6, KJV).

"For this cause shall a man leave his father and mother, and cleave to his wife; And they twain shall be one flesh: so then they are no more twain, but one flesh" (Mark 10:7–8, KJV).

Well, no wonder we are somewhat confused by our grief. In the midst of it, it feels as if we are being cleaved in two, yet we cleave to our memories, as do a husband and wife to each other. It tears us apart, yet the process of it brings us back to a new kind of wholeness. Just like when we die to self and live for Christ, we cleave to Him as we continually attempt to cleave our sins from our imperfect selves.

How, then, do we process it? I do not have an answer for that one. It is different for each of us. No two grieve alike. And no two recover from grief in the exact same way. God gives us light in the darkness. And joy in our sadness. May we cleave to love as we cleave the sorrow from our souls? Evidently, it is so. Consider Romans 12:9 (KJV): "Let love be without dissimulation. Abhor that which is evil; cleave to that which is good."

In a more hopeful sense, the month of June also remains the most popular wedding month, the one in which we are biblically instructed to cleave unto our mate while simultaneously being parted from our parents. It is fascinating to me that the word "cleave" has such directly opposing definitions. Depending on intention, the very same word that means to split, separate, loosen, disjoin, unfasten, rend, or rip can just as easily mean to unite, to join, to hold together and not let go. One cleave defines attachment while the other cleave describes separation, and usually with a sharply wielded instrument, like an ax or, well, a cleaver.

Two years ago this month, I was fortunate enough to marry for the last time. June is, at least for me, the month of sad endings and beautiful new beginnings. In the span of ten years

I have been cleaved from and grieved one husband and now cleave to and love another. And all the while I can't seem to get to the June Cleaver level of wifedom. I will, however, continue to try, minus the pearls. She is perhaps the TV version of the Proverbs 31 woman. I am more often the female embodiment of the characters Eddie Haskell and Lumpy. With that said, let's just leave it to Beaver, June.

July

**Oh, Good Grief**
**Let the River Run**
**Sister Act**
**Great American Soldier**
**Heat & Humility**
**Summer Storms & Hornworms**

*J*uly was an interesting month, topically. Summer was in full sweaty swing in the South, and we were called to write about a wide range of topics—from summer outings to patriotism to time with family and friends as the season slowed to a graceful crawl and gardens produced a bountiful harvest.

# Oh, Good Grief

*C*harlie Brown's world aside, is there really any such thing as good grief? After a year of attempting to live and breathe in its grasp, I still can't exactly describe grief as being anything even remotely close to good. Maybe the good happens when the grief subsides. But that is perhaps when the fear begins. Will it ever be over? Will life ever be really good again? Oh, if wishes could make it so. And therein may be the answer to these questions. Life probably will be good again, but I suspect we must first of all choose to make it so. It has been a year now and it's time, at least for me, to stop being defined by widowhood and partnering only with memories. Every person grieves in his own way and on his own time, or so I have read. For me, it's time to start letting go. And now I wonder if Linus will let go of his security blanket long enough for me to borrow it for a while.

Last month I shared some of the many things that my husband taught me before and after he died. This month will be the time for marking down the things that I still wish to learn in this life. It's time for me to get on with it. We are here for such a very short time. It only makes sense to squeeze as much as possible from the fruits of our days—be they sour lemons or sweet peaches or juicy watermelons.

I will learn how to be single again. Not just a widow. Not just a mother or a daughter. Right now, I don't seem to remember how *not* to be part of a set—like salt and pepper or cream and sugar or Laurel and Hardy or even oil and water. It's time now for being just one of a kind. Maybe it won't be such a lonely number after all—who knows? Are you there, God? It's me, your little slow learner and late bloomer. I might be in need of a few extra lessons on this subject.

I will learn to go kayaking, and live to tell about it. It's time to think very small when it comes to watercrafts—something that can be hoisted onto the roof of a car and toted to the river without fear of losing anchor lines or tempers or small children. Hey, if I can learn to keep in step with my aerobics classmates, anything is possible.

I will learn to fiddle. There's just something about that music that moves me. I mean really, can you hear "The Devil Went Down to Georgia" without tapping your toes just a little? Besides, that fiddle will help hold up at least one side of my saggy neck skin. I can make a joyful noise and get a partial chin lift, all at the same time.

I will learn to create with clay. My daughter recently gave me a child-sized pottery wheel and encouraged me to get in touch again with my artsy side. I will worry later about why she was laughing so much that tears flowed freely when she presented it. Maybe I should also learn to develop her wacky sense of humor. Creating things with words is great fun, but it is also how I earn a living. Having another outlet will be wonderful (she says hopefully). If I can get the little wheel to turn fast enough, I might just be able to craft a tiny teapot short and stout. Then I can have a proper tea party.

I will learn to develop a broader social life. My neighbors and family are very gracious with their time, but I know it has to be a drag to tote me, the fifth wheel, around everywhere. I don't expect or even desire to fall in love again, but I do expect not to be alone in the world for the rest of my days. Not that alone is a bad thing, mind you. It's really not. Honest.

I will learn to spend more time with God—in prayer, in devotion, in gratitude, in conversation. And not just on Sunday mornings. I have been too long gone from Him and I wish to make amends. He's already helping me learn to pluck the log from my own eye before inspecting the speck in someone else's eye.

I will learn to be a better friend. In this year of grief and sadness, there have come my way some wonderful blessings of friendship. One friend sent a Maya Angelou card every month—for inspiration, and to remind me that I was not forgotten. One made sure to call at just the right time, to take a verbal "okay-ness" temperature and offered much pain relief in the form of quiet listening and gentle laughter. Another kept right on offering a shoulder and an ear and various enticements to leave the safety of home to venture out among the living again, until I reluctantly said yes. She may be regretting her earlier persistence, as I seem to be hanging around most of the time now. They have each given me great examples of how to be "a friend indeed to a friend in need." I will do my very best to return their favors whenever needed and to pay them forward to others.

I will learn to accept that my children will make their own lives and trust that they find their ways, even if those lives and ways are not what I might choose for them. They do stay in our hearts always, but they do not reside under our roof or rules forever. If I remain quiet and patient, they may even provide grandchildren later for blissful spoiling purposes.

There truly is a time for every purpose under Heaven. Now is the time to laugh and to dance and to heal and to plant and to build up. The time to mourn is gone for the moment. As I look over the list of things yet to learn, it's probably a good time to stop writing and start learning. Should I begin with the kayak or the fiddle? Time will tell.

# Let the River Run

*July 2008*

On a beautiful Saturday morning in late May, a merry little band of travelers set out on the Lumber River for a leisurely paddle in the direction of the Little Pee Dee. We meant to bond with nature and each other and our Creator (Ps. 118:24) and hopefully not with alligators or snakes or big creepy bugs. Some were experienced paddlers; others might be described more accurately as piddlers or maybe puddlers, and no amount of coaxing will make me reveal the name(s) of either type. It was, all things considered, a wonderful experience. We won't discuss the attack of the shoreline trees or the 360 degree turns unintentionally and repeatedly made in the middle of the river or even the colossal blister that erupted between the thumb and forefinger on paddle hand. Those things were easily erased by the triple joys of pleasant conversation, a beautiful sunny day, and the discovery of turkey, deer and bear tracks during a sandy-shored pit stop.

We ranged in ages from not-quite-teenaged to beyond the half-century mark and, as usual, the not-quite one had the most energy and sustained enthusiasm during the trip. Perhaps it was that little motor attached to the back of his boat. More likely it was his ability to create fun wherever he could find it. Surrounded by adults and near-adults, this young person found a way to enjoy himself, whether it was letting his paddle fishtail the river water into the boat behind him or finding a fishing hole while waiting patiently for the last meandering canoe to catch up. Ah, youth—so very wasted on the young. Maybe not.

Perhaps we can find ways to let our creative rivers run for many years if we can just remember how to paddle and navigate them successfully. Some among us do it every day. I am not yet one of those some.

It seems that the problems and trials of our everyday lives work to erode our youthful creativity and simple joy for living. Does the ability to transform an empty box into a pirate ship, or two chairs and a sheet into a safari tent run off to never-never land as we grow older? When was the last time we cracked open a brand new sixty-four-count crayon box to run your finger over the pointy-ended colors before they were dulled to stubs by active use? Or let muddy puddle water ooze through our bare toes? Or trapped fireflies in a mason jar on a summer night? Some of us are lucky enough to find little trickles of imaginative thinking return when we have children or grandchildren to entertain. Others of us must dig a little deeper to tap into the long-buried creative waters of memory.

We all know people that make beautiful things with clay or paint or wood or fabric or even flour, eggs, and sugar. They each tap into that flowing river of creativity that seems to escape others. Perhaps we were standing behind the door when God handed out those traits or perhaps God gave it to all of us equally, but we have not allowed it to grow and flow. We may have squandered it in front of a TV set or let stress and worries dam it upstream. It might just be stuck somewhere in our childhood, waiting for a chance to reemerge in our older ages. Sometimes the very act of living day to day draws away our creative ability and keeps us from seeing the inspiration lurking just beneath the weight of our responsibilities. But like pebbles tossed and drifting slowly downward to rest in the rich riverbeds of our memories, they are just waiting for something or someone to stir things up and churn them back to the surface.

Teachers and mentors, for example, have learned to churn those pebbles up quite well—in both classrooms and life rooms. Some may disagree with this assessment, but Herculean efforts spew forth every day from people whose task it is to educate, whether paid, underpaid, or unpaid. Bible and Sunday school teachers use the same book year after year after year and find creative ways to bring the lessons to life, offering practical applications for daily walks of faith. Of course, they do have the Master Teacher's example to follow, don't they?

Speaking of faith and trials and errors, children, teachers, and others, we may discover how to let our own creative rivers run long after our youth leaves us parched and dry. It's in the same place we find the answers to all of life's questions. Instead of lamenting what may have been lost, creativity can be rekindled in the midst of our trials. Surely the God of all creation expects us to find the peace that He offers within the trials of life. Consider the lesson of Romans 5:3–5. Trials create endurance. Endurance creates character. Character creates hope. And hope floats. We just sometimes need to do a little bit more creative paddling while we let the river run.

# *Sister Acts*

*July 2012*

When you come from a family of five sisters, one might expect never to lack for friends—unless of course one is the youngest, in which case it gets a little bit tricky navigating on the friend ship. The oldest ones never seem to fully embrace the concept that babies become adults while the ones closer in age (even though the gap is still seven years) can't quite get past their resentment of your birth and survival of their childhood taunts and pranks. Being the youngest of five is rather difficult regarding the cultivation of sister-friends. The first act was the toughest.

I remember many things about the sisters of my childhood—like when they would chase me around the house with our Dad's prized stuffed pheasant (the one with beady glass eyes and sharp beak). Oddly, they never attempted this "game" when said parent was around to defend his treasure (not me, the dang bird). I also vividly recall being called upstairs to play by my meanest sister, only to have the giant box window fan turn on just as I passed it at the top of the stairs. My breathless anticipation of acceptance by her was immediately replaced by breathless fear of being sucked out the window or chopped up by the blades. But any attention was preferable to being invisible. Almost.

When I started first grade and couldn't stop crying, the twinned-sisters were summoned by the nuns from their lofty eighth grade classroom to comfort me. As they descended the stairs, the looks on their faces immediately told me that comfort was the last thing on their minds—murder perhaps, but surely not comfort. Oddly enough it was the same expression I saw on their faces when an opponent dared to elbow them on the high school basketball court. Nightmares could be more pleasant.

Then, one by one, they began to marry and have families of their own, leaving me to fend for myself while wishing I had gotten to know them a little better before they left home for good. They did ask me to be in their weddings though, so that was pretty friendly. And eventually I followed in their marriage paths, much later than each of them and much to their relief, I later learned. Evidently they had been concerned that I would never settle down as they had and that all I would ever produce would be four-legged, tail wagging children. Thus the second act of sister-friendship began without much fanfare. It lasted for too many years. We moved away from each other geographically and emotionally. Fortunately, the bloodlines remained intact. I guess it really is thicker than water in many ways.

Something amazing begins to happen though, as the baby moves into the maturity of her fifties and the sisters lean into their sixties and seventies. Even though we begin to teeter on the brink of dementia, something approaching actual acceptance begins to emerge, followed closely and rather precariously by, dare I dream it, sister-friendship. Now the curtain rises slowly on Sister Act III. It was unfortunately motivated to some degree by the death of my husband. I suspect they thought I might regress to that long-ago first grader crybaby routine and didn't want history repeated. I don't think I could have survived seeing those same looks on their faces again.

Just last week I ventured back home to "help" my two oldest sisters (one of whom, by the way, decided it would be fun to teach me how to smoke at age five—and she's considered the sweetest one) orchestrate our mother's move to assisted living at the age of ninety-three. Because they are just fourteen months apart, they have spent many, many years in each other's company and both live in our hometown of Frederick, MD. They are, however, about as different in temperament as two sisters can be. The oldest is very steady and cautious, with a quick and biting wit and steely determination that helped her survive a breast cancer diagnosis. The second in command is the family super achiever. She gets more accomplished in fifteen minutes than the rest of us can do together in three hours. They care for our mother with a synchronized beauty that defies sisterly explanation. Between them they have contributed eighteen great-grandchildren to our mother's current total of thirty.

Evidently we have all dipped our toes far enough into our mother's gene pool to emerge with some commonality of purpose and poise and, hopefully, longevity. She remains with us in large measure because of my older sisters' great care and attention, coupled with her own good habits. They have learned to play to each other's strength. I especially love to watch my older, quieter sister boss around the super achiever. She actually listens to her elder. I also enjoyed watching our mother gracefully enter this next phase of her life with determination and even a little humor, as she shared her first group meal with a deaf man and found joy in not having to make idle conversation. She is now enjoying her meals in the company of three gentlemen at their table of four, much to the consternation of the other women residents. My only concern is that she will end up marrying again before I do. Oh well, such is life. Maybe I'll get to be a bridesmaid one more time.

I am reminded of several verses that seem appropriate for this Sister Act III we find ourselves in these days. Romans 12:18 comes to mind. "If at all possible, insofar as it has to do with you, be at peace with all men." And that means sisters too, I'm sure. Mine are a hard act to follow, but follow them I will—even if it means I have to run as fast as my short, chubby legs will go. A little chafing is worth the journey toward becoming true sister-friends.

Because we grew up Catholic, the Bible was not something we studied verse by verse, but we have learned much by following its example. Consider these words: "Do nothing from rivalry or conceit, but in humility count others more significant than yourselves. Let each of you look not only to his own interests, but also to the interests of others" (Phil. 2:3–4). Maybe not always have we done so, but now that we are all AARP eligible, I think we may have it worked out. We have survived (and enjoyed) sisters' trips—coming together from Chicago, New England, South Carolina and Maryland. As for me, I'm hoping the curtain stays up on our Sister Act III for a very long time. After all, a sister-friend is someone who knows your faults and loves you anyway. In my case, they even changed my diapers, endured my tears, and love me anyway. I'm pretty sure of it. When the last curtain falls on our Sister Act, I hope I'm the last one standing. Selfishly, I don't want to say goodbye to any of them.

# The Great American Soldier

*July 2014*

I should have known when he started making army soldiers out of backyard sticks as a wobbly toddler, that one day he would choose the same fate for himself. I just wasn't prepared for it, didn't want it for him. I couldn't stand the thought of losing him. But since my opinion never carried very much weight with him, he insisted on enlistment despite the mommy-whines. Perhaps I should have rethought the decision to clothe him in his sister's handed down pink onesies long ago. It evidently had a far-reaching and detrimental effect on our relationship.

After a few side trips along the way, my son enlisted in the United States Army and began basic training in 2009 at Fort Benning, Georgia. I remember my fear turning to mama pride as I tearfully pinned on his blue braid at graduation. Not only did he choose to Go Army, he also insisted on the infantry. He could have chosen many different paths, but no, not him—he had to be "in the fight."

And rather quickly his wish was granted. He deployed to Afghanistan in January 2010 for a year tour. Much to his dismay and my relief he was stationed at Kabul, doing some "missions" but mostly training Afghan soldiers. I do remember the horror of his first call home once he arrived there. We were having a rather pleasant "how are you" conversation when a loud boom was heard on my end and the line quickly went dead. This was one time when a vivid imagination is not a good thing. I feared the worst and nearly threw up breakfast (Lucky Charms are not nearly as tasty on the reverse trip.)

Fortunately he was able to quickly call back, as it was only a dropped line and not the deadly attack my mommy-mind had conjured. This scene repeated itself on nearly every call he made. It only took me about six months to get used to it. (Oh, who am I kidding? I never really got used to it.) But, he was finally doing what he had always wanted to do. He was a soldier, and he was serving his country. Many prayers later from many sources, God's will brought him back home safely. Well, not exactly "home." He was stationed at Fort Drum, New York (aka the frozen tundra) for the rest of his enlistment.

Because he thought there might be a chance to deploy again (this I will never quite understand), he chose to extend his contract an extra year—serving five years instead of the original four. However, there was to be no further deployment and he was honorably discharged in May as a sergeant. He is now living temporarily in South Carolina (he emphasizes the temporary status at every opportunity, by the way), with plans to use the GI Bill to further his education and begin a new career path.

I am so grateful for his service to country and for his willingness to now help his mama transition from widow to country-fried bride. He has bonded well with Mr. Willoughby—they share a very sarcastic sense of humor, facial hair growth, and farting contests. They also have worked well together in transforming our "new" house into a home—power-washing, wood floor finishing, etc. And both have the hammer scars to prove it.

An American soldier, especially a combat infantryman, is willing to give the ultimate sacrifice for our freedom. My son has also given his mother the gift of coming home and letting go of the past in order to build a future. It remains to be seen what that future will hold for all of us and I hope that one day he will find the only source of true hope—the greatest gift in life. And he'll know that he shares with Him the willingness to lay down his life for others so undeserving of the sacrifice. But for now I love the man he has become and I'm thankful for the memories he cherishes of his father and for his ability to allow space for another wonderful man to enter our lives. Putting up with the gas-passing and sarcasm is just a small price to pay for such peace of mind. Or so I'm told.

# Heat and Humility

*July 2015*

*I*t seems I have missed two whole months of writing opportunity deadlines: May and June. I could blame it on the heat, but some of you already know that I had a rather extended lapse in health lately, made worse by a refusal to believe there was anything really wrong with me (like a fever of 104 and uncontrollable fits of shaking are no more dangerous than the sniffles. Duh.)

In May I missed the opportunity to share happy thoughts about my mother, who turned ninety-six in March, had a life-threatening bout with her very tired heart, and yet still managed to return to her assisted living home relatively unscathed. I also missed the chance to share how my daughter became the mother figure while I was struggling to regain my sense of self, which had been nearly obliterated by tubes and drains and twice-daily shots of Heparin in the tummy. She also took on middle-of-the-night potty duty at the hospital—a task not for the faint of heart. Suffice it to say that intravenous antibiotics wreak havoc on the digestive system. She also spent two weeks with us at home and I was awed by her take-charge abilities as a temporary domestic engineer. This, after all, was the child who never met a mess she didn't enjoy.

I also missed the chance to share how three beautiful friends were determined that I return to them so we can all grow old together (some of us are way ahead of some others of us) and continue to laugh and cry and goof our way through all of the life-bumps that bombard us. And my relatively new (pardon the pun) sisters-in-law kept watch and shared updates with the rest of the family like I had been a member for much longer than the actual nine months of marriage. Part of this new extended family also includes my husband's ex-wife who kept in constant contact through their son, giving him the encouragement to put up with me. Oh the gifts God provides us in the most unexpected of places. If only she would stop looking younger every time I see her.

I discovered more sides to my stepson's wife—a professionally trained eye for knowing exactly what is happening medically and sharing it in layman's terms; a sweet and caring side that brought occupational therapy (crayons, markers, play clay, blank paper, stress balls, crosswords, Sudoku puzzles, and two little piggies—one stuffed and one clay), among other treats. She also peeked in on me at the hospital whenever her schedule allowed and made room for us in their home like it was the most natural thing to do. She will make a most wonderful mother when the time comes for them.

My sister and her husband arrived in Charleston from Maryland, just to make sure I was really alive—not well, but at least alive. This is the sister who takes on all family concerns as her own responsibility and does not rest until she sees for herself what is happening. She has probably an overdose of mothering genes, but I am thankful for her and humbled by her strengths.

The women (and men) of Revelation Ministries spent much time in prayer over my "situation" and sent so many messages of inspiration and encouragement. They collectively banged on God's front door and I believe He heard them loud and clear. Several years ago we studied Psalm 23 in a women's group so it was a perfect choice to send a fluffy stuffed lamb my way as a reminder that "the Lord is my shepherd; I shall not want." What they didn't know is that the words of that psalm were repeated in my head many, many times during that long hospital stay.

It seems I am surrounded by a wide variety of strong, beautiful, mothering women and I missed the chance to share the joy I have in knowing them because my dum-dum fingers and brain could not take the heat of a May issue deadline. I hope they will still know how much they mean to me.

As if this May faux pas was not enough, I also failed to meet the June Man-ual issue deadline as well. This would have been the perfect opportunity to share exactly what some of the men in my life have meant to me, especially during the past few "sick girl" months.

First, of course, is the husband of now just one year (boy, did he ever sign up for a mess) who overnight became my chief caretaker and overseer of all things nutritional and medicinal. The man of my dreams quickly turned into a rather hairy yet very capable Florence Nightingale. When my daughter had to leave Charleston to return to work, he even took over the potty duties like it was the most natural thing in the world to do. I can assure you it was not. But I was given great lessons in humility and gratitude during those days—ones that neither of us will soon forget (no matter how hard we try). Caretakers have the most difficult duty in times of stress, but he handled it all with a calm, firm assurance that helped my children see God's Hand at work. What I did not know until much later is that he prayed boldly to Him that first night in expectation of a miracle. And it was ultimately received. I'll leave out the parts when he tried to force-feed me protein-rich foods and I wanted to sucker punch him. This, after all, is a testimony to answered prayers, not a rant session.

His son became an instant hero to me as he navigated the medical waters for us and let his father lean on him for guidance and reassurance that the right course was being taken. This same son (my bonus child) always knew how to irritate me into submission when I was going down a wrong road emotionally or physically (I did wander off a few times too many). I will forever be grateful to him for his strength and knowledge and annoying sense of humor. He is a wonderful combination of his parents, though he is truly his own person. If only he had been able to see the flying pig sculpture I insisted was hanging in the hallway outside my room when I was moved from ICU to a "regular" bed.

Then there were the EMTs in Conway that promised my husband that they would get me to Charleston, even though my blood pressure had bottomed out at 50/30 and they had to pump five liters of fluid in me to keep me with them. They also assured him that they were believers and they knew we were too. A nurse indicated that "these guys are the best of the best." Evidently they were, because they were true to their word. We know one EMT in particular that would have promised the same thing. He's the one that called my husband regularly to get updates and to let us know we were in their prayers. I'm just sorry I missed all the excitement (no, not really—I think that might have been God's "hedge of protection" around me).

When we were finally able to return to church in early June, we chose to begin by attending a Sunday evening bible study. One of the ministry team was filling in for the pastor (who, by the way, visited the hospital several times—a six hour roundtrip), which was fine with us, as we loved him too (sorry, getting a little mushy here). Guess what the chosen study was for the night? Give up? It was the 23rd Psalm. Well, of course it was. So God provided yet another chance to provide testimony of His miracle works.

We have so many people and churches to thank for their prayers of hope and healing—men, women, and children from many different places who took the time to call out to the Great Physician on our behalf—Iron Hill Baptist Church, Mount Pisgah Baptist Church, churches in Mullins and Marion, and others in Maryland, Texas, Alabama, Illinois, New Hampshire, and even Puerto Rico.

The reality of life, whether it be in the sizzle of summer or the dead calm of winter, is that there will always be some sort of heat (problems, illnesses, crisis, loss, sadness) and accompanying humility opportunities, if only we can recognize them. The "trick" is to find the gratitude in each one. It is always there, just waiting to be discovered, if we'll only see it. For example, our families have drawn closer together—my children have come to know their new sibling and wife on a whole new level which would not have happened except for this close encounter.

I did not have a direct meeting with Jesus "while I was sleeping." He did not show Himself to me. I saw no bright light. But what I did experience was the profound power of prayer, of miracles, and of relationship with brothers and sisters of faith. My husband and I now have another testimony to share—each a bit different because of our perspectives and experience—but one that we believe may bring hope and assurance in some way to someone in need.

All I know for sure is that the power of prayer still produces miracles. We were surrounded by loving care and earnest prayer over many long, hard weeks. I am humbled by being a tiny part of God's great miracle works. Because, after all, I don't really think it was for me. It was a reminder for all who believe and even those who are skeptics that God is who He says He is and He can do what He says He can do.

# Reaching Forward
## Summer Storms and Horn Worms

*July 2016*

*A*h, summer! For many it is the most delightful season. It's a break from school schedules and stresses. It's homemade ice cream and refreshing trips to the beach, family reunion adventures and sand-laced suntan lotion. It's stars and stripes and fireworks. It's juicy peaches and hot buttery corn on the cob and thick-sliced tomato sandwiches slathered in mayo (no, hold the mayo). It's time to grill out and jump in the pool—or the river or the hammock or the ice cream bowl.

As for me, however, I'm more of a fall and winter kind of gal. Give me cool breezes and crisp mountain air. And long pants and sweaters. And Halloween and Thanksgiving and Christmas and jumping in leaf piles and snow drifts. This appears to be especially true for the summer of 2016—at least so far, anyway. Please allow me to share with you the following early summer adventures.

I was reaching forward to select the ripest of garden peas one recent toasty morning when my dear, sweet husband simultaneously reached forward to introduce me to my first ever horn worm. Now, I have been around the garden, so to speak, in my sixty-two years. I've learned a thing or three about what vegetable is what and when it needs to be picked. But I have never, ever in my life seen, up close and personal, mind you—a ginormous horn worm.

If you have never had the joy, let me attempt to describe him (I guess) for you. He was undulating along an innocent pea pod, heavy-laden with previously consumed pea leaves. If you are a fan of Star Wars, my best descriptor is this: he looked just like Jabba the Hut, only skinned in a bright Kelly green shade—not unlike the pea leaf he was undulating upon. Clever worm. And of course there was that horn thing protruding from his body like a weapon of mass vegetation destruction.

As if this were not enough, Mr. Willoughby decided to give me a lesson in how to rid the garden of this disgusting, grossly overweight blob of a pest by hurling him forcefully to the ground beside me. Old Horny literally exploded before my eyes as dark green innards spewed forth like earthy fireworks—all over Mr. Willoughby's uncovered, hairy calves. Yes, there is justice in this garden world. And it was the only positive portion of that chance encounter with my first ever and hopefully last horn worm.

But wait. There's more.

I was reaching forward toward the kitchen one bleary-eyed morning in anticipation of my first cup of life boosting hot java nectar when my not-so-keen-yet eyes glanced at something in the corner of the kitchen. Keep in mind that I was still in my nightie and barefoot. I heard a slight thumping sound too. What could that be? Auuuugggggghhhh! It was a very large snake, in my *kitchen*, just two feet from my bare tootsies. I ran. And I screamed. And screamed some more.

Waking a man who sleeps soundly without his hearing aids is not an easy task. That morning was the exception. Perhaps it was the running and screaming in his direction. He shot out of bed like a rocket (not like the usual bear waking from winter hibernation). He made it to the kitchen in record time, only to discover to our mutual horror that the snake had disappeared. Again, perhaps it was all the running and screaming.

Upon this discovery, my husband wrongly decided to share his golden rule about snake sightings: Never take your eyes off the snake. Oh, right. Sorry. Guess I forgot about that while I was busy running and screaming. Fortunately, he redeemed himself later in the day by successfully extracting said snake from the dining room as it slithered up beside him while he sat quietly at the table contemplating his game plan. Evidently, he followed the rule of snake sightings because, when I was calm enough to return to the house, the snake (a five foot long corn snake) was lying outside, dead as a doorknob. So I forgave him for repeating the snake sighting rule to me while I was gasping for breath during my early morning pre-coffee panic attack.

Summer fun, you say? Well, you can have it, horn worms, snakes and all. I can't wait for fall. But there's really much more to this story, all of our stories, than just the occasional pest or critter in our lives. A horn worm and a snake are but minor annoyances compared to the actual problems we all face daily, regardless of the season.

How do we continue to reach forward in this life, given the incredibly difficult news of our times? We are all accosted by widely varying problems and heartaches. Summer just seems to bring out the heat and humidity and storms of this life into a harsh and unrelenting sunlit view. If we were to share with each other the deeply personal issues that face our families, the history that keeps repeating itself, we would probably agree that snakes and hornworms are nothing. And we would be right.

I've discovered a bit late in life that the same approach to getting over the varmints is also quite effective in weathering the larger storms and villains. And it comes from the only source that can be trusted not to change with the winds of time. Our only hope is to continue reaching forward, steadfast in faith, for the prize that awaits us on the other side. For me, the secret can be found, among many other passages, in Philippians 3:12–16—verse markers removed, emphasis mine.

"Not that I have already attained, or am already perfected; but I press on, that I may lay hold of that for which Christ Jesus has also laid hold of me. Brethren, I do not count myself to have apprehended; but one thing I do, forgetting those things which are behind and *reaching forward* to those things which are ahead, I press toward the goal for the prize of the upward call of God in Christ Jesus. Therefore let us, as many as are mature, have this mind; and if in anything you think otherwise, God will reveal even this to you. Nevertheless, to the degree that we have already attained, let us walk by the same rule, let us be of the same mind."

And of course there's the added joy in believing that horn worms and snakes will not be waiting there for us. In other words, "Darling I love you, but give me Park Avenue." Do-do-dee-do-do. Do-do!

August

Losing the Labels
Enough
Green Acres of Gratitude
Coming Unglued Again
The Sticky Wicket
Liberty & Justice

The month of August, similar to July, included a smorgasbord of topics. Teachers were often celebrated as school returned to session by mid-month in most areas. It was still at time for some relaxation and reflection as the beach still beckoned (especially as the vacationers returned to their home territories).

# Losing the Labels

*August 2009*

There's really no easy way to jump into the description of a recent unusual event than to simply tell you exactly what happened. But first you will need some important background information. My husband lost his cancer battle at 1:15 p.m. on June 30, 2006. He was at the Florence Hospice House— the place where angels gather, disguised as healthcare workers. After that fateful day, one of the things I did to keep his memory close to me was to wear his wristwatch every day. Fortunately it resembled the trending boyfriend-watch-wearing fad, so I didn't look too very crazy. Every time I looked at that watch face, I thought of him and was oddly comforted by the memory of that same watch on his wrist and how he often glared at it as he waited—the Navy guy, the firefighter, ever ready, always on time, usually early—for the wife who wasn't.

Long before daylight on the third anniversary of his death, my precious little four-legged family members decided to start whining for their morning pee break way too early (in my not-so-humble night owl opinion). I glanced at David's watch with the help of its nightlight feature to determine exactly how irritated I should be about the early whining and tail thumping. I immediately noticed that the watch had stopped keeping time— the sweeping second hand was no longer sweeping. This was not a great big deal until I also noticed the time it had stopped. Cue the creepy background music. It took its last licking and quit ticking at exactly 1:15 a.m. on June 30, 2009. Oh, have I ever mentioned that he was definitely a morning person, completely opposed to my midnight oil burring tendencies? Coincidence? I think not.

After recovering from the initial shock, I decided I had two simple choices. I could either throw the covers back over my head and sob uncontrollably (a very tempting choice) or I could simply consider it a gentle nudge , perhaps from above, that it was truly time to move on. Choosing the second option, I gently removed the watch from my wrist, kissed its face, and put it away in a memory drawer. Three years, evidently, is long enough to labor under the burdens of the widow label, at least for me. God doesn't always send us the messages we want—He instead sends the ones we need. His timing is perfect.

So I am officially declaring the removal of my widow label. It is the beginning again of a singular life. Certainly, I will always love my late husband. He was the father of my children. But the "widow" sticker is being removed along with its entire messy residue so that a new life can begin. God gives us an endless capacity to love others. It isn't a finite resource unless we choose it to be. We simply have to choose to do so. The widow window has closed and a new door is opening (pardon the mixed metaphors).

While declaring the removal of this one label, I began to consider all the labels I have worn and removed or continue to wear in this life—from baby sister (that one I'm keeping) to friend, from girlfriend to wife, from daughter to mommy, from student to teacher—the list is long and sometimes heavy. Each one carries with it so much definition, so much description But sometimes the labels can carry the burden of confinement and pigeon holes—those labels that do not allow us to move about freely in this life. We can feel stuck under their heavily glued weight.

How do we deal with those types of labels? I've spent a good portion of my later career years working with students as they determine who and what and where they will be in their lives. I've been trained to interpret personality type (MBTI) instruments. Are you an extravert or an introvert—gaining energy from others or from within? Do you make decisions by feeling (considering others, for example) or by thinking (just the facts, please)? According to this tool, there are sixteen different personality types, and we each fall into one of them primarily. Based on the MBTI label, career choices and college majors can be presented as potentially good fits. So, is that helpful or limiting? Sometimes it can be a little of both. If there were a strictly held formula for life paths, someone would have made a great deal of money by placing labels without error—and we would all be a little worse for the wearing.

When children are diagnosed with learning disabilities, or given names for their various behaviors, does the label sometimes become a sort of academic prison sentence, or does it allow them to better understand their differences and work with them? Again, it can sometimes go either way. It's not unlike labeling pathways differently for boys and for girls—like toys and colors and books. Some boys can sew and some girls can hammer nails. Some labels need to be removed on both sides of the equation.

Do we label our friends and family members to their benefit or to their detriment? Is the firstborn in a family always a leader? Is the youngest always an independent yet whiny brat? Do we give our friends labels much like the seven dwarfs—happy, grumpy, sneezy, bashful, dopey? Labels tend to be difficult to remove when they are placed inaccurately or are no longer valid. Goo Gone does not work very well on people labels of any kind.

There is, however, one label I am happy to slap up there on my forehead. Sometimes it gets a little crooked and wrinkly or hangs by a thread, but I know it will stay. It's the one that allows me to take control by letting all else go: I am a child of God; I am believing. Present, Active. Here and now. Always. Yep, that's a label worth wearing—it goes with everything and nothing can remove it. I will press on and remind myself daily to be inspired by following the path of Philippians 3:12–14 (NIV). Evidently, He plans for the label to stick. I only need look to the end of Matthew 28:20 (NIV): "And surely I am with you always, even to the end of the age." Amen to that.

# Enough

*August 2011*

*F*unny how that word has bubbled to the surface so often in recent weeks. It started innocently enough (see?) with a forwarded email from a long-distance friend. The subject line was "I Pray You Enough." It contained a beautiful prayer within a moral storyline and touched a deep inner chord, so I sent it on its way to friends and relations. Some of you received it too, I'm sure, as it continues to make its way through cyberspace I had seen it before but on this recent reading circumstance and attitude conspired to give it significantly more meaning. This should have been my first clue—God was about to open my eyes once again. He evidently has had just about enough of my shenanigans.

How much is enough? It's an age-old question, isn't it? Have you had enough? Do you know when enough is enough? Oh, enough already. But what does it truly mean, this word *enough*? It is defined in an online dictionary as "adequate for the want or need, sufficient for the purpose or to satisfy desire." But is enough ever really enough? Sometimes we know exactly when it is enough, other times we can't for the life of us figure it out.

It filters through our lives in interesting ways. For the alcoholic, one drink is too many while a thousand is not enough to satisfy the beast within. The frustrated worker/parent/teacher determines to have had "just about enough" of something before totally losing an otherwise cool-as-a-cucumber composure. Families trying to budget within their means wonder if they will have enough funds to survive until the next paycheck

132

arrives. Anyone who has enjoyed a sumptuous southern buffet (Webster's, O'Hara's, Magnolia's, Garden Alley, Dry Dock, Woodhaven, etc. in Marion County SC alone) wonders when enough is enough. It usually happens too late, after that second trip to the dessert bar.

When it comes to education/schooling, how much is enough? And how do we know when we have it? We're often encouraged to never stop learning, even long after our formal education ends. All of us have special teachers we remember— some for the good and some reserved for those educational nightmares—like the one where we are giving a required speech, naked, in the front of a classroom filled with adequately attired peers while Ms. Gulch, the speech teacher, shakes her head, tsk-tsks, wets her number two pencil with the tip of her snake-like tongue and jots down the giant *F* beside your name in her little black grade book. No? Well, some of us have this one regularly and, yes, therapy might be a good idea. I can't thank *you enough* for the suggestion.

And what is the measure of enough faith? A mustard seed-sized version is biblically enough, but sometimes we question if we truly have enough to claim or maintain our salvation. Another answer to that can be found in the lyrics of Chris Tomlin's Enough lyrics: "All of You is more than enough for all of me, for every trust and every need; You satisfy me with Your love, and all I have in You is more than enough." That's pretty good stuff. Not enough? Spend some time with 2 Corinthians 12:8–10, Philippians 1:19–21, Matthew 6:33–34, and probably all of Job, or seek out all ninety-nine references in the NIV for *enough*—as in Genesis 24 and Rachel at the well. Surely Christ is enough, but can we ever say it or live it enough?

Sometimes people can be victimized enough to turn the tables on their villains and take a stand against injustices, real or imagined—and sometimes they simply never find that moment when enough is truly enough and so continue being victims forever. Young women like Jaycee Dugard and Elizabeth Smart found they had enough in them to move from victimization to victory. They've had more than enough to deal with yet are reaching out and speaking out to help others. They could have remained captive to loss and lived a defeated life, yet they managed to have enough faith to forgive and enough love to find victory. I know of at least several young women one in particular, who, if they could find enough strength of faith to make the same choices toward victory, would create pathways to finding more than enough joy in their lives. I hope and pray that one day she/they will choose to say "enough" and cast off the victim robes once and for all.

And that brings us back, as usual, to me. What and where and how much is enough for me? In the midst of writing this article, I had anticipated that it might be the last one written for a while—that y'all may indeed have quite enough of me already. After fifty-four articles offered in varying degrees of doneness, it might just be more than enough to endure or skip over (yes, I understand if you flip to the pretty ads). God has granted such blessings in this life. Quitting does not make one a very effective laborer for His kingdom. I have done quite enough of that already. It is better to keep on stepping out on faith to do His bidding, instead of seeking only my own. There are many lessons left to be learned—like how to make edible figgy muffins and piggy cakes, how to properly pronounce Horry and pecan and live more contentedly as a Yankern, how to return thanks effectively for gifts received, when to marry again (the who and the why being fully established) and how to do the work that makes it work, perhaps even how to make and—gulp–consume banana pudding.

There are indeed so many lessons yet to be learned and, judging from the diminishing time between hair color appointments, so very little time remaining. Fortunately, God is sufficient for every need—and there is so much more to share with you about how He has made and will continue to make lessons available to learn. So, until next time, here is a portion of that forwarded email prayer:

"I pray you enough sun to keep your attitude bright, no matter how gray the day may be.

I pray you enough rain to appreciate the sun even more.

I pray you enough happiness to keep your spirit alive and everlasting.

I pray you enough pain so that even the smallest of joys in life may appear bigger.

I pray you enough gain to satisfy your wanting.

I pray you enough loss to appreciate all that you possess.

I pray you enough hellos to get you through the final good-bye."

For every day and in all ways, I pray you enough.

# Green Acres of Gratitude

*August 2014*

Remember I warned you ahead of time about what would be the topic for August. Since the wedding took place as planned (well, mostly), it is now my great pleasure and honor to thank all those who made it so wonderfully memorable for us. There are so many who went above and beyond our wildest expectations—from pre-planners to post-dancers, from family to friends and back again, both old and new. What to do?

We'll borrow a suggestion from *The Sound of Music* and "start at the very beginning, a very fine place to start. When you read you begin with ABC." So when you wed, you must begin with the One that made us into we. Left to our own devices, the new Mr. and Mrs. Willoughby would not have even glanced in each other's direction. More likely we would have made every effort to steer clear of each other—a slightly liberal-leaning northern widow with a Catholic background and a strongly conservative divorced Southern Baptist—a "city girl" and a country-fried guy. But God, in His mercy, chose to heal us by bringing us together—and we tolerated each other's differences long enough to discover a lasting love and a very healthy, yet sarcastic, sense of humor. We hope our gratitude for His love was evident in our ceremony and will continue to be evidenced by the central place He will retain in our married life.

Speaking of tolerance, our children come first to mind. Not only did they tolerate the embarrassment of having old parents enjoying new love, they stepped right in and stood with us as we wed—and shoved us out of the reception so they could take care of all the after-party take-downs and returns. We love and appreciate them so much. If Carrie ever tires of pediatrics, she'll have a future in old lady hair design. Devin will always know exactly what her mother needs, when she needs it—from hot donuts to a cold, lifted eyebrow when I'm about to step out of line. Lucas can keep a secret like no other (honeymoon location and flower fiascos) and Nick knows how to irritate his mother into submission when nerves are on the fray. They are each and all loved beyond measure.

This brings us to gratitude for friends, old and new. Sara Jones offered, in what must have been a very weak moment, to be our wedding coordinator. This role grew to include cake orders and deliveries, flower orders and near-disasters, and the tying of tags on what must have felt like thousands of mason jars. Since the wedding took place on a Sunday, we were lucky enough to gain access to the venue for a few hours on Saturday for set-ups and flower arranging.

Connie, the original and replaced flowers were beautiful. Thank you so much for your help. Jim, Jody, and Whitney. Thank you for your great assistance and design help. The barn was transformed. And there's another transformation that took place there too—Gayle Ham Hayes, the dreaded ex-wife turned great friend, stayed late and added her touches while we rehearsed. She also gifted us with a perfect *W* metal sign, lavender flower, and much appreciated road snacks bag. God continues to make miracles from our messes.

But I digress. Back to the original mess now. When Sara arrived Sunday morning to begin cutting up strawberries for the reception with the help of Mary Lynn Jones (more on her later), she expected to simply open the venue refrigerator doors and retrieve the flower arrangements and bouquets. I can't even begin to imagine what went through her mind when she opened those doors to find frozen vases holding blackened stems and blossoms instead. Nothing but the three bouton-nieres survived. Being the steel magnolia that she is, she quickly (?) recovered and began calling in the troops. Whitney Cooper, with the kindness of her grandmother Judy Baker and Sterling's offer of garden flowers at the venue, saved much of the day. And if Whitney ever tires of hair design, she has a great future in flower design. Wonder where she learned it.

Sara then returned to Connie's shop for help with redos. Remember, this was a Sunday, and Connie is also choir director at her church. She met Sara at the shop and rebuilt bouquets that were just as beautiful as the first ones, even offering some of her own garden flowers.

This bride had no idea what was going on behind the scenes that day. Lisa Campbell was enlisted to help with the strawberry slicing and she quickly came, without concern for her own preparations. She also visited with the bride before returning home to get ready and was bombarded with nervous bride questions. But she never gave away the secrets. Lisa had also made the bride take a shoe and undergarments trip to Florence the week before she left for vacation because she knew the bride would procrastinate herself into wearing old flip-flops.

Kindness, and Girl Scout-like preparedness, evidently runs in Lisa's family. Lisa's sister Cindy McMillan offered some of her daughter's wedding items for our use—easels, signs, benches, buckets, fans, and George McMillan even made delivery and pickup runs.

Several weeks before the wedding, the women of Revelation Ministries succeeded in providing a surprise bridal shower— complete with all kinds of amazing country themed gifts (think mason jars, bandanas, and hilarious starter baskets) for the happy old couple. Rob and Donna Bacon, another happy old couple, created an American gothic wedding portrait that both stunned and delighted all who saw it. Karen Scruggs and company truly outdid themselves and gave this old broad a shockingly good time in the company of her faith sisters.

Mary Lynn is also a member of that RevWoW group and is largely responsible for the wedding taking place, if you consider that she's the one who would *not* leave a grieving widow alone and helped turn her toward His word and His salvation. Later I discovered that she also spoke with Mr. Willoughby about six years ago, asking if he would be interested in dating "a friend of hers" (who had threatened to return to Maryland), and he said a kind but quick no. Evidently, he changed his mind somewhere along the way. God and his miracles are evidenced once again.

The one and only Melia Flowers is also a responsible party here. It was her encouragement that led me to become a contributing writer and allowed me to work out my grief to grace to gratitude journey. She also insisted upon providing a photographer for the wedding—Mr. Jonathan Boatwright. He was perfectly suited for us and we can't wait to see the rest of his work. But my favorite shot, so far, is the one he took right after the ceremony—after we exited to Morris Ward's great rendition of "Green Acres." It truly captured our joy—and it also captured Ms. Flowers and her beau behind us in the chapel doorway. I hope she'll allow Marti Willoughby to contribute to her magazine too, as Marti Miller has retired. Surely there will be some wonderful stories about life out on the farm.

I know for sure my new sister-in-law and next-field neighbor, Mary Willoughby Joyner, will provide some useful topics. She has already provided much love and laughter—and she'll keep the bride grounded when she starts itching to take flight from the dirt road and head toward town. Or maybe she'll come with me. We'll go visit her sisters (and now mine), Linda and Wanda.

Thank you to all who came and shared the day with us, especially those who travelled so far and endured the blazing heat and stifling humidity of a southern summer day in June: My sisters and their husbands from Maryland, New Hampshire and Illinois; my first sister-in-law and David's brother/family from Alabama; my first stepson Eric and his wife Rosa and precious Sebastian from Washington, DC; Amanda our great helper, popcorn server and cake cutter from Iowa by way of Maryland; Jackie, Megan, and Paige, our friends of long-standing and Marion visits, my high school pal Marcia and her husband from North Carolina; Carrie's parents from Houston, Brian and Diane Busch; Melissa and Madeline, Tom and Christian; Wanda and Troy; Stacey, my niece and talented crafter of our wedding rings, and her boys from Maryland.

Thank you for the example of enduring marriages from Linda and Wayne, Nicky and Larry, Sandy and Denny—each will be married fifty years in 2014. Wow—and they're still sitting beside each other and smiling.

To our church families in Marion and Mullins—who says southern Christians can't cut a rug and have fun? Y'all showed us love in so many ways. From the clown-nosed photos to the line dances, from the wedding bingo players to the hugs and heartfelt prayers, we are grateful to be counted in your presence, no matter where we stand. To our pastor, Chip Scruggs—thanks for the freedom to worship Him in a marriage ceremony filled with laughter, praise and tears of joy. And to Rev. Dale Willoughby for offering a return of thanks after the ceremony that left my sisters (and others) in happy tears—we only wish we could have heard your words too.

All this gratitude brings me again to the realization that God grows some pretty amazing people. I was somewhat aware of that early on, but after many Maryland years, eight years here, and a beautifully memorable second-chance wedding day, I am certain of it. Thanks goes to God for blessings undeserved, for your Son and Savior, and for providing the path that lead us to step out on faith and dance again as Mr. and Mrs. Leland Darrell Willoughby.

# Coming Unglued Again

*August 2015*

*A*h, sultry and sweaty August is upon us—the month of last-chance sultry summer road trips and sweaty back-to-school nightmares (for some of us, anyway). But neither of these topics is on my mind right now. Oh, no. I have much bigger and stickier fish to fry.

I just finished tussling with a new box of cereal. And the box won. Again. Have you ever noticed how much glue is attached to those boxes? It is nearly impossible to open one without tearing the top clean off—or at the very least messing up the tab closure so it will never, ever close again, leaving a nearly full box of cereal to go stale in the cupboard, especially in summer. Yes, I have heard of those convenient plastic containers for storing cereal and other dry goods. I don't like them much. I prefer, instead, to drone on and on about the doggone glue globs.

And another thing, it seems to me that the bag inside the cereal box used to be glued in at the bottom, to keep the whole bag from launching itself into your cereal bowl. Not anymore. They have unglued the bag and glued up the box top with the leftover glue. Why? My theory is that it will cause the unsuspecting consumer to buy more cereal more quickly. If shredded cheese can come in a zip lock bag, why can't cereal? Ah-ha! I smell a conspiracy—and it's not just the cereal boxes either. Oh no. Just about every dry good in a box has the same sticky and stuck-up problem.

Have you noticed how much glue is slathered on a new roll of paper towels or toilet tissue? I have. Quite a few towels/

tissues are sacrificed in order to unglue the rolls. It's annoying and time-consuming to pick at the roll with your fingertips, hoping not to rip more than one or two sheets. No such luck. And it happens at the other end too—lots of glue to keep the rolls in place. The consumer loses at both ends. All this getting unglued is causing this consumer to come unglued, as I seem to shop much more often for these glued up paper products and boxed up dry goods. Yep, a conspiracy is afoot.

I've become quite a fan of popsicles and straws this summer—both of which require an engineering degree to gain access to the wrapped contents. And don't even get me started about the hermetically sealed bottled beverages. From water to sweet tea to the forbidden diet sodas, all take the strength of Samson and the patience of Job to open without spilling the contents or the wordy derds that long to escape the lips. Is it just me? Am I coming unglued all alone here? Perhaps so.

I have noticed a trend in my summer season—coming unglued in all this sticky and drought-prone weather. Maybe it's the dirt road. Maybe it's the residual effects of that septic shock adventure. I am, after all, losing my hair—and it's not from pulling it out at the roots, honest.

There comes a time or season or chapter in our lives when coming unglued seems to be an almost daily occurrence and the best response to unbelievable, unreasonable or unfair situations. Some days are better than others and some are nearly unbearable. And we are none of us immune from them.

How does a young mother cope with the sudden loss of her spouse? How do parents breathe after losing a child (no matter the age)? How do friends deal with difficult misunderstandings? How does anyone handle a diagnosis of Stage IV cancer? How does a child deal with relentless bullying? How do veterans cope with their memories of war? The list could go on and on—these and many other problems of life are an integral part of an otherwise wonder-filled existence.

I suppose we all come unglued at least initially or privately, but then for people of faith it quickly becomes a matter of prayer, hope, and love. We have to look upon the life of Christ and attempt to respond to "coming unglued" moments as He did—in love. But it's not always an easy task. It is especially difficult in those days—the unbelievable, unreasonable, unfair, hurtful ones—that we have to find a way to get glued up again before we stray into a dangerous reactionary walk.

Whether we use white school glue or rubber cement or a hot glue gun, we have to apply our faith with copious globs of stick-um. We must use those guns (glue guns, glue guns) to fasten ourselves back to the Way, the Truth, and the Life. Maybe we talk with a faithful friend or pastor. Maybe we dig deep into His Word. Maybe we get busy in praise and worship instead of shrieking and gnashing of teeth. Maybe we pray more fervently. Maybe we look around to see all of those situations that are far worse than our own. And maybe we do all of the above.

Meanwhile, back at the cereal box carton. Sigh. No more coming unglued over these minor irritations. I will grin and bear it. And I will write a scathing letter to the manufacturer. Oops. That just slipped out. Now, where did I put that glue gun?

# The Sticky Wicket

*August 2016*

We're all a bit sticky these days, what with it being August in the South and all. Bless its heart. And given the headlines bombarding our hearts and minds with terrible heat of a different kind, we are experiencing a conflagration, a heat-generating inferno of near biblical proportion. I used to think I knew everything I needed to know about heat, humidity, and difficult predicaments just by sheer proximity of living in the suburbs of Washington, DC—arguably the literal home of partisanship inspired problems. Evidently I was wrong. Sticky wickets are everywhere.

What, after all, is a sticky wicket, anyway? It's defined by Merriam Webster as "a difficult or delicate problem or situation." Synonyms include a bind, a box, a catch-22, a dilemma, a fix, a jam, a pickle, a quagmire, a rabbit hole, a rattrap, a swamp. It seems like these words rather accurately define the state of our nation and the world. We are definitely in a big old pickle. There is unrest all around—from our choices for presidential candidates to whose lives matter, from civil unrest to entanglements of our soul choices.

Defining the "problem" is one thing, but coming to solutions seems to escape our collective grasp. We talk about our forefathers and our lack of fathers and even our heavenly Father without much agreement. In light of this continuing sticky wicket, I've been reading up on some fathers—those who shepherd flocks in this life. I came across one in particular who seems to have somewhat of a firmer grasp on what ails us. As evidence, here are just a few quotes from some of his sermons and written works:

"I believe that one reason why the church of God at this present moment has so little influence over the world is because the world has so much influence over the church."

"A time will come when, instead of shepherds feeding the sheep, the church will have clowns entertaining the goats."

"Right is right, though all condemn;
Wrong is wrong, though all approve."

"The word of God is like a lion. You don't have to defend a lion. All you have to do is let the lion loose, and the lion will defend itself."

Great words, yes? Too bad he's no longer with us. Charles Haddon Spurgeon lived on this earth from 1834 to 1892. He was a British Reformed/Particular Baptist preacher. His words echo evidence that the more things change, the more they stay the same. There is nothing new under the sun. Nothing. (See Ecclesiastes 1:9). But the beautiful thing about it is we cannot stop believing it will change for the good of all. Hope is ever present. Perhaps that's why Song of Solomon follows Ecclesiastes. It was present in Charles Spurgeon's messages to thousands during his lifetime. It is present today. It just gets buried under piles of perceived wrongs and misunderstandings.

Christianity has struggled across time and space in reaching souls for Christ—even those who have received the gift of salvation continue to struggle with much the same questions as did our forefathers and mothers. Doubt plagues us. We hope to love our neighbors as ourselves, but we continually miss the mark. It is yet another continually sticky wicket.

Many stand "Around the Wicket Gate" (a work by Mr. Spurgeon that references the wicket gate of The Pilgrim's Progress) believing we are already there, or at least close enough to grasp the handle and open heaven's gate when our time comes. We play at church. We are oh-so-close, but we fail to truly go all in. And I wonder which is more frightening—those who are as far from faith as possible, fighting it always, or those who are within a hand's stretch of salvation but believe they are already there. One of my greatest doubts involves being aligned in the wrong group—am I saved? Am I not still a sinner? Even if, like some believe, faith is a myth, are we not better off to follow it to our dying breath? We will either live eternally for Christ or we will be eternally separated. I hope to err on the side of life.

And what, you might ask quite appropriately, did I consume the night before writing this to you that has made my mind so muddled and my conscience so cloudy? Could it have been the refried beans and spicy salsa, perhaps? God only knows.

I have also recently become reacquainted with a surprisingly timeless Cherokee story about our good and evil natures. It's the one where a wizened grandfather chieftain shares with his curious young grandson the picture of our greatest and most hard-fought inward battle. There is the evil wolf within us that craves only anger, envy, sorrow, regret, greed, guilt, and hatred. And there is the good wolf that lives on nothing but love, joy, peace, kindness, hope, and truth. These two wolves war inside us constantly (much like the aforementioned beans). When the boy asks which wolf is stronger and will win the battle, the old warrior replies: "It will be the one you feed." Indeed.

Lately, my evil wolf has been fed much more regularly than the good one. This must stop. It is a sticky wicket for August and for all the days of this life. It's a rabbit hole with no clear exit that burrows deeper with each new headline. Am I prejudiced in some ways toward what is familiar to me? Yes, I believe I am. I believe we all are. I do not understand what I do not know firsthand. Does this excuse evil thoughts, words, and actions—just because we have them and choose to act on them? No, it doesn't. The natural effect of beans on the body is nothing compared to the unfortunately natural effect of evil continually fed and allowed to grow stronger.

By our very fallen natures, we are good wolf/bad wolf. It is the one we choose to feed that will grow stronger and ultimately kill the other. Now is the time to choose which it will be, because our time here is running short. It is past time to "let loose the Lion" and unhinge ourselves from these very sticky wickets. Thanks for the inspiration, Charles Haddon Spurgeon, Cherokee chief, and all the true ministers of His Word.

# Liberty & Justice

*August 2017*

*I* remember reciting the Pledge of Allegiance many, many times in my life; so many, in fact, that memorization of the words was a fairly easy accomplishment, even for a first grader without the advantage of a kindergarten education. I was thrust directly into first grade wearing an itchy white-collared shirt and blue jumper uniform that, by the way, did absolutely nothing for my already fluffy figure. I remember staring down at my desktop (scratched wood surface attached to dinged-up metal frame, with ABC gum lurking underneath) in hopes of not making eye contact with the large and decidedly unhappy-footed penguin-like creature-teacher at the front of the room.

We were instructed to stand beside our desks with our chubby little right hands over our hearts (which I discovered much later was not, after all, located way over by my left shoulder—and not all of us had chubby little hands either), face the American flag in the front right corner of our classroom (just above the beady-eyed penguin, tapping her unhappy feet with impatience). We then recited, in very solemn, squeaky and somewhat breathless voices:

> I pledge allegiance to the Flag
> of the United States of America,
> And to the Republic for which it stands,
> One Nation, under God, indivisible, with liberty and
> justice for all.

That scene played out every single morning of elementary school—even after I was snatched from the jaws of Catholic school and placed in a neighborhood public school for sixth grade and beyond. Honestly, I don't remember if we did any pledging after sixth grade. I'm thinking we didn't. It was 1967 when I transitioned to junior high. There were other things happening in our country by then that took us away from the flag allegiance activity. I missed it. (But I did not miss the penguins. After fifth grade, they only appeared on Sunday mornings and, thankfully, kept their distance in faraway pews, not wanting to mingle with the riffraff of standard variety, unveiled worshippers.)

Nowadays I don't recite it much, except maybe for solemn occasions like graduations or Veterans Day activities. Kind of a shame, don't you think? What a waste of good memorization. But, then again, maybe we aren't really meant to pledge our allegiance to a red, white, and blue cloth. And, just maybe, liberty and justice isn't for all, after all. Kind of seems that way these days. Does it to you?

Given the state of our rebellions and disagreements and wanton disregard for anyone or anything that does not follow the same path we are on (politically, morally, socially, emotionally, etc.); we are in what I remember the penguins calling "the devil's playground." There is still liberty and there is still justice—but they both seem to be frayed around the edges, very much like our flag symbol. It has been trampled, burned, spit upon, yet it still waves at us, a constant reminder that liberty and justice are to be represented by stars and stripes, not earned by a pugilistic nature that results in getting one's clock rung by a verbally abusive beating. Evidently, kindness can no longer make a home with liberty or justice.

I learned a tiny little bit about this liberty and justice for all, when my son took up an Army uniform and pledged to fight for just those things we take for granted. The motto of the company he served was "Deeds, not words." Combat veterans have always put their feet to their words of allegiance, for one and for all. If only we could take a hint from them and the sacrifices they have willingly made for us. They volunteer for this duty, and it is most assuredly not for the pay.

But what is liberty, after all? That word is difficult to define. Some would say it is a freedom—like the freedom to choose or the freedom to be whomever and however we choose. Unfortunately, we tend to forget that our liberty extends only to the point it does not affect another negatively—and that line is exceedingly difficult to find or define. If our liberty causes a brother or sister to stumble, is it still a liberty? From a biblical viewpoint, the answer to that question would be no. Others would argue that we are not our brother's keeper. And on and on the conflict continues, because we ultimately have the liberty to define the word for ourselves. Sigh. And humbug. And please pass the headache medicine.

The justice we pledge along with liberty is also a word that nearly defies definition—as it seems that justice, like beauty, is in the eye of the beholder these days. One's perception becomes one's reality. Wikipedia defines the word as "the legal or philosophical theory by which fairness is administered." Justice, then, is only best served when it personally serves each of us? Ho boy? This is getting wackier by the minute. Also, I don't know anyone that thinks life is necessarily fair. I begin to long for the stiflingly chalky classrooms and the fierce penguin gazes, those sweet days when reciting the Pledge of Allegiance was just a well-loved and comforting memorization activity—at least until the air raid drills and under-desk diving brought us face to face with the potential loss of the very liberty and justice we pledged.

Maybe that's why we seem to have collectively and individually lost sight of the liberty and justice ideals. Each generation has its own set of fears and anxieties. Baby boomers remember the air raid practices and the threat of what lived behind the Iron Curtain. The previous generation knew all too well the sacrifices and mortal wounds of World Wars I and II. The threats facing the current generations seem to fluctuate in a constant nightmare of terrorist acts, offset by a virtual reality of technological advances and the cocoon of "safe spaces."

Though penned many years earlier, the title "Pledge of Allegiance" was adopted by Congress in 1945. The words "under God" were officially added on Flag Day in 1954, when Dwight Eisenhower was President (and just after my joyous birth; yay me). Our flag, our pledge, and I, have seen better days. We seem to have lost significance all over the place. But we're not done yet. Oh no. Not us. Not by the old, gray hairs of our double-chinned chins.

I can't help but wonder, though, what our Pledge of Allegiance would have sounded like had Benjamin Franklin gotten his way and we had the wild turkey as our national bird instead of the bald eagle. I'm guessing we'd be eating a lot more chicken at Thanksgiving. But considering our cultural, political, and moral struggles these days with liberty and justice, the turkey somehow seems much more representative of us. Then again, maybe that's just me. When all this deep thinking becomes too much for me, I rely instead on the liberty and justice of His Word, especially 2 Corinthians 4:16–18.

"Therefore we do not lose heart. Even though our outward man is perishing, yet the inward man is being renewed day by day. For our light affliction, which is but for a moment, is working for us a far more exceeding and eternal weight of glory, while we do not look at the things which are seen, but at the things which are not seen. For the things which are seen are temporary, but the things which are not seen are eternal."

The Pledge of Allegiance, memorized years ago, is awesome, but it can't even hold a candle to those verses. Perhaps these words need to be memorized with even greater intention of purpose.

# Fall Season in the She Shed

Makeovers, Survivors, Boos, & Thank-Yous

*When they walk through the valley of weeping, it will become a place of refreshing springs. The autumn rains will clothe it with blessings.*

—Psalm 84:6 (NLT)

September

**Getting the Message**
**Fixing the Focus**
**Rules of Engagement**
**Transitional Lenses**
**Refining Moments**
**The Hummingburden**

*F*all fashion news was the hallmark of the September issue. It also included a special feature on makeovers for a group of readers each year and was nearly as popular as the "man" issue in June. Instead, I usually chose to focus on internal moments and makeovers.

# Getting the Message

*September 2008*

Because I am an ASAP (not from the South but arrived As Soon As Possible), I tend to rely heavily on various communication devices to stay in touch with non-ASAP family and friends—from emails to text messages, from voicemails to snail mails. The messages sent and received range from heart-wrenching to hilarious and just about everything in between. One such message recently received could likely be placed at either end of the emotional spectrum, depending on how it is interpreted. It came in the form of a forwarded email prayer and I received it from several different sources. It was called "The Powerful Woman's Prayer," and read something like this: "Dear Lord, please make me the kind of woman that causes Satan to respond with, 'Oh, no. She's awake' when my feet hit the floor each morning."

Unfortunately there are many mornings that I am fairly certain his response is more like: "Yes, let the games begin." On those mornings, the daily devotional gets grabbed up even before the coffee is poured. The day just seems to work out much better when it begins (middles and ends) with prayers.

I received another interesting message from a childhood friend that also grabbed my undivided attention. His wife is about to undergo bilateral mastectomy surgery in the hopes of remaining in this life long enough to meet her grandchildren and watch them grow. His older brother is fighting a losing battle with lung cancer. My old friend is now an ER physician by profession and a master gardener, fly fisherman, talented teller of tales, and an all-around good guy by choice. However, it was a remark he made in passing that caused me to prick up my ears to full listener level. He mentioned that he and his wife were greatly enjoying watching Olympic sporting events that they ordinarily don't give two hoots about during the four-year intervals between torch ceremonies, and wondered why they cared. For them, I suspect it is simply welcomed relief from the medical and emotional stresses they are facing.

But what's my excuse? I too had been cheering from my easy chair for the young, and not so young, American swimmers and gymnasts and sport teams. I wanted them to win big for the good old Team USA. Why? Not sure. Am I looking for excitement, diversion, or patriotic opportunities? I don't know.

I also confess to spending a little time watching American Idol and Dancing with the Stars competitions. And I can't wait until Grey's Anatomy returns to the air this fall. I read the headlines on Brangelina and Brittany as I'm standing in line at the grocery store, too. These things are not the center of my life, but I don't exactly ignore the stuff either. What message am I sending and receiving by spending any time at all engrossed in these things? Probably not a good one, I'll venture.

I don't worry so much about watching the Olympic hopefuls or even Dancing with the Stars. They are, mostly, practicing and polishing their talents to pursue a goal or gold. But what about how much emphasis we as a society place on all of our public figures? Does it really matter how many gold medals a person wins or which celebrity is voting for which candidate this November? I'm sure Oprah and George Clooney have excellent reasons for their choices. I just need to make my own, without their help or influence. Fame is so fleeting. Just ask John Edwards or Michael Vick or even Taylor Hicks. There is just no benefit in idolizing anything or anyone other than The One what brung us. Consider Isaiah 46:5–7.

We spend so much time and energy fanning the flames of fame in our culture. It may not be idolatry, but it certainly comes too close way too often. I even read recently that Madonna just turned fifty and is expected to be the new face of her generation.

Excuse me? Not for this fifty-something is she the face. I'll pass. Thanks anyway. I'd rather spend my time learning more about the faith that allows a woman to continue breathing through a life-altering surgery, or a mother learning to live without a child lost to illness or accident, or finding grace and peace with a child's serious disability. I'd rather know more about the family that practices forgiveness even in the most difficult of circumstances, or the young person who bravely faces adversities knowing that the full armor protects him/her from worldly harm. Ordinary people do extraordinary things every single day. We really don't have to look that far outside our own windows. Perhaps, just maybe, we can simply catch a glimpse of them in our own kitchens or living rooms, or in our electronic message boxes.

So this ASAP will continue to enjoy receiving the messages from computer and cell phone and mailbox. They inspire and enlighten and entertain, and remind me to have faith in God and everyday people and ordinary heroes. Might just spend a little less time in front of the idiot box and a little more time dancing with The One what brung me. I think that's called getting the message. Look to 1 John 1:5 and 3:11 for inspiration and reminders.

"This is the message which we have heard from Him and declare to you, that God is light and in Him is no darkness at all" (John 1:5).

For this is the message that you heard from the beginning, that we should love one another (1 John 3:11)

Just one more thing, though. What do you think it means when your daughter sends you a picture message early one morning from many miles away that shows her happily sitting in the hospital cafeteria with a plastic spoon dangling from the tip of her nose? Some messages are more difficult to receive than others, I guess. I'm hoping that message is simply: "Oh no. She's awake." But that message most likely is coming from her coworkers.

# Fixing the Focus

*September 2009*

*D*o you ever answer those little quiz questions about the one thing you would change about yourself if you could? I do—all the time. And the answer changes on a regular basis, depending on which part of me seems to need the most attention at any given time. Sometimes it's all about the personality flaws—too tentative, too short-fused, and too weird. The "too weird" part actually caused me to purchase a sign that hangs in my kitchen. It reads: "Pretending to be a normal person day after day is exhausting." Of course the sign was not really necessary. The flying pigs, silly rabbits and summer snowmen sitting all over the place and on the porch are likely enough of a hint for any visitor to conclude that things are often weird around here.

Sometimes the answer is another ridiculous wish for physical changes—like being taller or slimmer (yes, I do have control over that one, but did I not mention earlier that procrastination is a personality trait in need of overhaul?). I'd also like to be a natural blonde. The nose could definitely use a trim and if the legs were more elongated I could fix both the taller and slimmer simultaneously. Surely it's not too late for braces that would straighten my teeth and some kind of color-correcting bleach, while we're at it. I love my Irish heritage, but the freckles are quite disturbing, especially when surrounded by many porcelain-skinned southern beauties. It would be great to lose the bifocals and contacts too, if it's not too much to ask. I'd be such a happy, focused girl if I could only see the alarm clock instead of blindly slapping at its snooze button each morning.

It's no wonder I spend so much time answering those quiz questions—I have such an endless list of suitable answers. The question should read how many things you would change instead of just one thing. Evidently I'm not the only one who enjoys asking "what would you change?" A 2008 global survey on beauty conducted by Synovate (an international market research company) found that over 40 percent of respondents would change their looks if they could, even though over 60 percent of the same group indicated that true beauty is about nonphysical attributes. Rather schizophrenic of us, yes? Here's another little gem: According to a recent *Fitness Magazine* survey, 64 percent of respondents indicated that trying on clothes lowers their self-esteem. The same survey found that 88 percent of respondents said a clothes buying trip inspired them to reevaluate their bodies. Whether it's our hips or our feet or our boobs or our upper-arm wing flaps, we tend to wish for changes. We focus on what's wrong with us so much that we forget to notice what is so very right with us. It's exhausting.

One of my favorite desires for change is that loved ones wouldn't ever leave us behind. But they do. Everybody does, eventually. But grief does not need to be endless, unless we choose to remain focused there, wallowing in its muddy puddle. If we stay there, all else will be washed away and we will be left only with sadness for companionship. The "woe is me" tune doesn't serve to move us along, stepping to the music of life. We become little Johnny or Jenny One Notes until we hear a new song and choose to change our focus. Fortunately, I have another little sign at home that reminds me to fix my focus:

"Life is not about waiting for the sadness to end;

It's about learning to dance in the rain."

Because of the nature of freelance work, I have regular deadlines to meet each month. Procrastinators and dreamers really, really need deadlines. We tend to shift our focus away from the work at hand to follow something—anything—but the work required of us. We tend to have the attention span of a gnat—a very indecisive, unfocused gnat. With that in mind, I found a smooth rock that rests on my desk, engraved with the single word: *focus.* It seems to help most of the time. However, a very dear friend suggested a slight modification. She encouraged me to add the words "on the Lord." She's certainly correct—annoyingly so sometimes in her correctness—but she is correct and most often clearly focused.

Maybe that's where my September makeover needs to begin. With all my focus on changing myself physically and emotionally, I tend to forget that God sees me as I am where I am. Trying to adjust the attributes and characteristics of the clay might just be a bit of an affront to the Potter. Though He certainly expects us to care kindly for our vessels, He doesn't likely want us to poke around with it too much or allow our focus to rest only there. Instead, I could serve Him better by focusing on living my life for Him first and letting the rest of this life fall into place, behind His purpose for me.

This place we dwell temporarily, in a mere breath of time, doesn't justify the focus we tend to put on it. We gather lovely things around us. We place our needs above others. We claw and scrape our way to prizes we think we deserve. We continually attempt to make ourselves over. We are simply humans, being human. But the life that awaits us on the other side of this one is the place where true beauty dwells. Yes, I will still apply lotions and potions and attempt to exercise against gravitational pulls and wear colors and clothing that bring out the best of my features while hiding the others. But the focus of my life must ultimately turn toward Him. I need to remember to "dance in the rain," and always to the music of His purpose instead of my own.

# *Rules of Engagement*

*H*ope you're relaxing in a comfy chair or lounging on the sofa right now, or maybe even killing time while waiting for your name to be called for your medical appointment. If you are seated elsewhere, please wait until you've finished your business before reading this one. I just can't stand the thought of anyone reading what comes next while being otherwise engaged.

Yes, dear reader, "engaged" is indeed the operative word here. It's in the title and again in the first paragraph, and already in this one, and is about to be fully revealed during the next rather lengthy sentence. On the one year anniversary of our first "date," and with a Cool Whip-topped, freshly fried donut as a presentation pillow, my beloved deliverer of packages bent to one knee (an exceptionally loving act all by itself, given the aging and long-suffering condition of said knee) and asked me to be his wife while a sparklingly beautiful diamond ring sank ever-so-slowly into the whipped topping.

For the first time in my life I encountered two rather strange sensations simultaneously. First, I literally could not speak, and, second, I gave not one fleeting thought as to when my mouth might encounter that homemade deliciousness he offered. The speechless thing is a bit more common for me, but the lack of donut grabbing desire was very, very unlike me. I have developed a tremendous appetite for fried dough—especially freshly fried dough traveling down a conveyor belt while the "hot sign" blazes in a window. I had never even heard of hot donuts before moving to South Carolina. We had Krispy Kreme donuts in Maryland, but they came in cold boxes of twelve, usually by way of sport team fundraising efforts.

The fact that tears welled up quickly is a rather common situation for me—happy, sad, frustrated, angry, scared, and laughing hysterically—tears seem always at the ready. It's a bit of a family tradition. We leak at the slightest provocation, which is really great fun for the teenagers in our lives. Can you imagine the shock and horrible embarrassment for a fifteen-year-old son showing his mom (me) his freshly acquired learner's permit in a public place as she (me again) spontaneously bursts into happy/terrified tears? Just imagine the scene that developed when the same son said goodbye to same mom at an airport in Baltimore as he boarded a flight that would take his uniformed self to fight in Afghanistan.

Back to the rules of engagement: as I sat and stared alternately at the sinking ring and at the man I love without hesitation, the silence was broken by that man inquiring if I planned to answer his proposal before that ring completely disappeared into the Cool Whip or if I'd rather wait until sometime later in the evening as we attempt to fish the drowned bauble from the whipped goo. Fortunately, I was able to muster a sniffled "yes" before completely losing sight of the ring that now rests comfortably on the third finger of my left hand.

When my precious daughter later heard our news she said, without missing a beat, that she knew we would be happy together and quickly added that she would be exercising her precious (and only) daughter rights by calling dibs on the maid of honor title. My sister, in true family form, proceeded to sob loudly into her Maryland end of the phone until I could almost feel the wet in my South Carolina ear when I told her the rules of engagement. Friends (both north and south) are busy gathering weird thoughts on the mature wedding attire and giggling to themselves something about fluffy-sleeved tangerine dresses. I sure hope they are enjoying their tiny little amusements.

Meanwhile, the rules of this engagement are truly very simple. We know that God has a plan for us. We know that He made our connection possible. And we know He will be the center of our lives together. Beyond that, we have no real clue at the moment about when, where, or even how this engagement will transform into marriage. But we do know for sure that it isn't about a wedding ceremony or tangerine dresses or decorations or menus (except for the obligatory donuts). It will be about blending two lives and several families and giving our grown children space and time to know each other and consider how much or how little they will be together with us. We will accept and respect our pasts and honor and cherish our present and pray that we have a long, contented, and donut-laced future together.

As luck would have it, we each have a reunion coming up soon on our family calendars. This will give both of us a wonderful opportunity to check out the swimmers, floaters, and sinkers in our respective gene pools and determine if we are prepared to take a dip. I have four older sisters and he has four older siblings, each with sets of children and grandchildren among them. Neither of us has met all of them, but each of us knows already that we will love who the other loves. We already do.

A little over a year ago, I received a lovely letter from a She reader who encouraged me to be open to finding love again after I had written a rather droopy article about remaining in widow world. Thank you for your kind words of encouragement, Ms. Bell. I kept your letter as a reminder that there are those who believe that love does return. I will surely continue to cherish it, knowing how very true your words have been for me. The choice to love has been made and will continue to be made every day God grants me life. His rules of engagement, after all, remain blissfully unchanged.

# Transitional Lenses

*September 2014*

Wearing glasses is nothing new for me. I've been pushing them up the bridge of my nose with a perturbed fore-finger for many years now. That same forefinger was strate-gically employed when I switched to contact lenses and was only perturbed when the flimsy little things wouldn't align on my eyeballs fast enough. I've lived through the forty-year-old stage of needing reading glasses over contacts in order to see just about anything in print. The fine dance of shopping and checking price tags while juggling reading glasses between nose and purse was only offset by the wonderfully fashionable choices available in said reading spectacles and their accompa-nying cases.

At fifty, I reluctantly transitioned to wearing one contact for distance and one for close-up work. Once my brain adjusted and was able to let me walk again with some steadiness of purpose, I must confess that I do not see very clearly at any distance—near, far, or in between. If you see a faded green Hyundai tooling around Marion or Horry counties, please keep your distance—my depth perception cannot be trusted much either. I can, however, see quite clearly in the close-up bath-room mirror without aid of any lenses while hunting down and plucking out the man-growth on my chin. Most of the time/ Just don't stand too close to me in sunlight. I have been known to miss a few on a regular basis.

All of this lensing about was endured in order to stave off the inevitable bifocals for just a bit longer. But at fifty-five the dreaded day arrived when I heard: "Ms. Miller, I think you're going to need bifocals now." I am convinced that there was just a hint of a smirk hidden under that thirty-something optician's attempt at a sympathetic expression. No matter. I knew the day was coming anyway. What I did not yet know was how very difficult it would be to traverse stairs while wearing them. The same spunky optician assured me that transitional lenses would be a practical and attractive choice for someone of "your age and occupation." I still don't know if that was a compliment or an awkward faux pas. Either way, it stung.

Not only would I have "invisible" bifocals, I would also have a third option in the lenses. They call it computer screen focus option, or something like that. Oh joy—the stairs would become an insurmountable object for about a month longer. I was okay at home where I could "feel" my way down each level (of lenses and stairs), but in public it was an entirely different matter. I also had a bit of trouble locating that "computer focus" area while attempting to write coherently. I remember doing quite a bit of nodding up and down and muttering rather unkind words under my breath while writing the most ridiculous messes and developing some bodacious headaches while I was at it.

Of course, as time passed so did my triple blurred vision. I became rather adept at stairs. Unfortunately, the unkind words still slip out occasionally and I still can't make out even familiar faces from an embarrassingly close range. I find myself waving frantically at complete strangers and snubbing friends and family members. So, if I should stumble into your path one day at the grocery store and I give no indication of seeing you or knowing you, please forgive me. On the other side, should you see a stranger waving frantically at you from a slight distance, just wave back. By the time I get close enough to you to realize we are not best friends or even acquaintances, my red-faced embarrassment will be so worth the wait, I promise.

Transitional lenses have been conquered, but I'm almost ready to give up the near/far contact lenses and go back to the reading glasses dance. At least I'll be able to see something?

While we're on the subject of transitions, visual and otherwise, I thought I'd give you a quick overview on the newlywed status.

One would think that the transition from widow to wed would be a walk in the park or perhaps roll in the hay. But no. Not only is the transition from one back to two being traversed, we are also traveling from city to country and attempting to squeeze my lonely years of cluttered collecting into a smaller, more streamlined space. This process is not unlike trying to decide which one of eight adorable kittens to bring home, and not nearly as much fun.

Of course change is inevitable. While we breathe, we continue to morph—eyesight, or lack thereof, being just one example. I am just having a bit of difficulty making all the morphing manageable. Did I mention that we are also transitioning from work life to semiretirement and that one nearly thirty-year-old "child" is temporarily joining us on this journey as he also transitions from military to civilian life? What great fun for all of us. Said no one, ever.

There is also the clerical and decidedly unromantic matter of name and address changes—cards, accounts, banking, post office, email, online—aauuugghhh! Where, oh where has the wedded bliss gone? Oh, it's still around—just taking a back seat some days to the stress patrol that insists on calling shotgun, navigator, backseat and driver positions, all at once. And yet, there is still hope. As always, it comes from His word (thanks so much, publishers of large print editions).

"For God so loved the world that he gave his one and only Son, that whoever believes in him shall not perish but have eternal life. For God did not send his Son into the world to condemn the world, but to save the world through him" (John 3:16–17).

Very rarely will anyone die for a righteous person, though for a good person someone might possibly dare to die. But God demonstrates his own love for us in this: While we were still sinners, Christ died for us (Rom. 5:7–8).

And these words bring me to at least one glorious visionary conclusion. In its most perfect state, love is blind. God does not see our imperfections. He loves us unconditionally. Transitional lenses are not required, needed, or desired. Not even during life's many transitions, do-overs, and make-overs. He sees us as we are where we are. And still loves us. All we must do is believe it and follow Him.

# Refining Moments

*September 2015*

*M*ost of the time when the word "refined" gets mentioned my tiny little mind leaps almost immediately to one of my favorite things: sugar. The more refined it is, the more valuable it becomes for baking and other sweet pursuits. The less worthy options tend to be full of lumps and clumps, and, though easier on the pocketbook, they are not much favored or sought-after options unless and until the clumps and lumps are smooshed out or pounded into oblivion. Kind of like a quick and/or cheap makeover.

Once I can get myself off the sugar rush, the next thing that pops into my thought-challenged brain is precious metals, like gold and silver. And quickly after that comes a story I remember being told recently by a young man during a bible study about a missionary watching a metalsmith refine gold in a faraway country and how he learned a most valuable lesson during the process.

You may have heard this one before, but it was impressive to me—especially since the teller of the tale was still in high school and surrounded by folks quite a bit older (and likely thinking we were so much wiser). The metalsmith was heating the gold and skimming off the dross, over and over again—at very high temperatures until someone in the group asked how he knew it was time to stop the process and use the gold. The metalsmith, continuing his refining process, simply said he knew the metal was ready when he could clearly see his reflection in the material. At that point there would be no more "yuck" to muddy the metal. It would be refined effectively for good use. Sound familiar? Consider these:

"In all this you greatly rejoice, though now for a little while you may have had to suffer grief in all kinds of trials. These have come so that the proven genuineness of your faith—of greater value than gold, which perishes even though refined by fire—may result in praise, glory and honor when Jesus Christ is revealed" (1 Pet. 1:6–7).

"See, I have refined you, though not as silver; I have tested you in the furnace of affliction" (Isa. 48:10).

"For you, God tested us; you refined us like silver" (Ps. 66:18).

There are of course more references to be found, but these bring home the point about refining moments in our lives fairly clearly, don't they? It hurts, but it's necessary for our Maker to see His reflection in our unworthy little selves. Mirrors can be frightening things for some of us, but His reflection is never so, though we are often war-weary and scarred beyond our own recognition as the refining process continues.

Sorrow and grief may bring us to our knees, but when we are able to stand again we are changed, refined by what we were certain would surely kill us. Only it doesn't. It stays with us, of course, unlike the dross that gets lifted away in the gold process. We have these brains that retain memories. But that's okay too, unless we allow the heat of that furnace to burn us beyond recognition or disorient us so much that we cannot come back from it. We can get lost in the loss for so long that we lose our way completely. Fortunately we have others here to count on for new directions or to remind us that our refinement is not yet complete and we must keep seeking our way.

And it's not just those ginormous refining moments that help to purify us for effective use in this world. Oh no. Refining can take place within our choices every day. We have arguments, disagreements with others that require us to make a choice—we can be the offender or the offended and seek the refinement of forgiveness and being forgiven. Refining moments can happen when we succeed or fail in large or small efforts. A bully and a target can each endure refining moments when deciding to stop the behavior or not be crushed by it. As children, large and small, return to school this year, many will be faced with the decision on how to respond to bullying or how to stop being one. These moments refine.

Teams can win or lose, but the refinement comes in discovering how to handle each side of those scores. The same goes for their fans. Winning is exceptionally pleasant. Losing? Not so much. But there are refining moments for each outcome. They may not be life-changing, but they refine all the same, based on how winners and losers choose to handle each result. And, no, we all don't need a trophy to become useful and reflect our Maker. Winning and losing both aid in the development of sportsmanship—a reflection appealing to all.

Refining moments can come from experiencing life milestones—like graduations, college acceptance letters, passing a driving test (or not passing), a first date, a last dance, a move across town or across borders, landing a first job or retirement. All refine us.

Thrown stones refine us as well—the ones we toss and the ones that hit us. We can't please all of the people all of the time. We're really not meant to, I don't think. But boy can we throw some stones when we feel rejected or unjustly accused or disliked. It's not supposed to matter in the grand scheme of this life. Our purpose here really isn't about like or dislike—it's about love and how we show it—how we give it and receive it. Refining moments occur quite often within the realm of like and love. Just ask Facebook users and viewers. No, let's not.

I love to laugh almost as much as I love sugar again (there was a time during that nasty bug attack that sugar was totally disgusting to me—talk about refining moments), but I suppose it isn't within the laughter that refinement happens. Wrinkles may appear, but that's surely not refinement. Again, we get a hint of all that from reading scripture:

"Sorrow is better than laughter, for sadness has a refining influence on us" (Eccles. 7:3, NLT).

I guess laughter is akin to the pursuit of happy. It is fleeting at best and all about how we feel at the moment. It does not stay with us for long, so it can't do much refining. Pursuing happy leads to nowhere good usually—and it doesn't aid in our refining moments. In fact it may serve to block them and turn us cold and incapable of refinement. Shoot. I really love a good snorting laugh—the kind when the tears run down your leg sometimes. And laughter is enjoyable—it leads us away from stress, so that can't be a bad thing—it just doesn't refine, especially not the snorting variety, I guess).

To refine is to bring to a fine or a pure state, free from impurities—according to a fairly reliable dictionary definition. Refining has synonyms that help clarify its meaning too: civilizing, cultivating, elevating, focusing, honing, improving, perfecting, polishing, sharpening, and, of course, clarifying. Some of those words sound a little bit painful and I guess that's the whole point. It ain't supposed to be a cake walk. Sorry. There I go with the sugar references again. But the end result of all these refining moments is surely worth it. When we finally begin to reflect His image, we can truly know joy. Sweet!

# The Hummingbirdens

*September 2016*

It wasn't until sometime last year that I saw my first hummingbird perched perfectly still on a tall, thin weed under the feeder by the front porch. Oh sure, I had witnessed plenty of hummers flitting and flying and sipping and diving. I just had never seen one sit still before. It was probably at that moment when my casual interest blossomed into joy at the antics and seemingly impossible natures of these tiny creatures.

Sure wish I had stayed in the blossoming love mode a little bit longer. It lasted the remainder of last season and the start of this year's first sightings. Then something began to change. Oh so slowly my joyful enthusiasm for these miraculous creatures transmogrified into annoyance, followed rather quickly by aggravation and an overwhelming desire to flick said beauty from its perch outside the dining room window. My sweet hummers had become The Hummingbirden.

Since this is makeover month, it seemed only appropriate to share this transformation with you—to plead my case against one of them in particular—with the hope that someone out there in she-ville can help reconfigure my beastly bird burden back into undying love and admiration. Or at the very least, give me a hint or two as to how to deal with this one very neurotic and aggressive hummingbirden.

Don't get me wrong. I still love the little acrobats. I can be counted on to dutifully clean and fill their feeders on a very regular basis. Because I am relatively height-challenged, this usually involves having sugar water drip down my arm and into my bra as I attempt to reach way up to the hook with a fully loaded feeder in hand. There's just this one that's making it miserable for the rest of us (me and the other hummers, and the husband by proximity to my aggravation). I've really never seen anything quite like it.

This one male hummer (well, of course he's male) has taken to guarding two feeders on the front porch as if his very life is at stake. And if he keeps it up much longer, his very life may well be in imminent danger, by way of my diminishing patience. He perches atop one feeder and with quick jerking motion tilts his long-beaked head in all directions like he's some kind of teensy tiny mutant owl. No other hummer can get close to either feeder without being dive-bombed by the little weirdo. Every now and then he'll take a quick sip from the feeder, only to return posthaste to his guard post.

His tiny head feathers stay ruffed up. He's developed some rather nasty tics and jerks. I can't tell if this is purposeful antics or a horrible side effect of his sinister soldiering. He has to be tired and, more importantly perhaps, he has to be very lonely. No other bird can get near either feeder. And now it seems as if none of them want to—they've nearly given up, leaving old guard bird mostly alone with his neurosis. Every now and then he leaves his perch position, only to return with lightning speed should any other hummer or wasp or bee come close to "his" feeders.

We even made a special trip to the hardware store (more than our usual twice a week journey) to purchase another feeder for the back deck in the hopes that the other eight to ten little humming burdens in the area might gain some sustenance without getting jumped and nearly speared by the one who shall not be named.

In the process of searching for help with this humming burden, we've found out some other fascinating things about these jewel-toned migratory tiny mites. For one thing, they cannot walk. They can perch and sip and hover and fly backwards, but they cannot take a walk. I guess the other stunt skills compensate for this one deficit. Besides, they would be "sitting ducks" for all kinds of harm if they were casually strolling around, considering they weigh about as much as two and a half paperclips.

Hummingbirds migrate over many hundreds of miles every year. The ruby-throated hummer is mostly seen in the Eastern United States, while other species can be found in the West. Some migrate as far north as Canada. And, contrary to legend, they do not hitch rides on the backs of geese. Their little hearts can beat over a thousand times a minute. They must eat nearly constantly to maintain their strength. Wouldn't that be fun? They usually lay two eggs at a time, each the size and shape of a navy bean or a very small jellybean.

But none of this helps to understand the behavior of this one particularly burdened hummer. He just seems so very unhealthy with his territorial turf war attitude. Surely he cannot be content. Surely he longs for companionship, or something other than solo-sipping. Evidently he does not. If what is read on the internet via googling can be trusted, he is not the only one to succumb to such behavior. Hummingbirds are terribly territorial. They fight. But, they don't usually harm each other. They just like to stake their claims on particular places. This one hummer just took it to extremes and is paying the price via loss of companionship (at least that's what my human brain thinks—he may be absolutely fine with it).

Perhaps another good question right now is this: What in the heck does this have to do with *She Magazine* in September; is there a point here anywhere? Well, sort of. Please allow me to attempt an explanation. Even though the Hummingbirdens have been particularly problematic this year, I still love to see them arrive each spring and worry about them as they leave town for even warmer climates in September. I'll worry especially about this one crazy guard bird. He may have to travel solo on his migratory journey this year. I will try to remember him a bit more fondly after he leaves here (while secretly hoping he finds another perching place next year).

Sometimes in our haste to protect what is ours, we can get a little bit too militant in our duties. Protection for safety's sake is one thing, but when it turns into a neurotic mess and we are unable to find any calm within the storm of what we perceive needs guarding, we lose more than battles—we can lose our sense of self and community in favor of being right. Such is the nature of this hummingbirden. It tends to be our burden as well. And for some reason, I seem to be craving something very sweet right now. Sure hope I don't have to fight for that last cookie in the jar. And I especially hope I can stop giving human traits to animals and birds and stuffed toys—and possibly crayons. May the Hand that crafted the hummingbird rest on our shoulders, a reminder to stop fighting over our feeders and instead practice

1 Thessalonians 5:16–18.

October

**Hidden Treasures**
**Dancing in the Rain**
**Nothing Could Define Her**
**Victorious Secrets**
**Pumpkin Chunkin'**
**Thelma & Louise**

*S*urvivors were celebrated in October, primarily breast cancer survivors, but many others were included. Basically, we focused on our ta-tas and all things pumpkin and cinnamon scented.

# Hidden Treasures

*October 2008*

According to the American Cancer Society website (www. cancer.org), one of two men and one of three women will get cancer in their lifetime. We will know the victories and the defeats very intimately. The experiences will linger on our souls and be etched permanently in our memories. But, scattered along the trail of cancer, there are treasures often hidden from view. When the daily fog of a cancer walk is lifted, these jewels can often be found shimmering softly in the sunshine of our minds.

When my husband was first diagnosed with squamous cell carcinoma in December 2004, our first task was to learn how to spell it and pronounce it. Not so easy. Little did we know that it would be only the first in a long and difficult list of big, scary, ugly words we were to learn in the school of cancer. I had my first glimpse of how things were going to go when the ENT surgeon gave me the news in the hospital, and concluded her clinical pronouncement by inquiring whether we had any children and stating that we were headed for one very tough year. My initial reaction was a fervent wish that she be strangled by her own stethoscope before the day was over. Now, as life would have it, I look back on our experiences with her and realize that she gave us our very first hidden treasure—honesty. I still don't like her very much, but she always gave us an honest assessment of how things were going or not going, and she never let any "warm fuzzies" muddy her messages. She also was the only medical person that encouraged us to go ahead and move south because life is too short to always do the safest things. I should mention that this surgeon has a bit of a maverick reputation back home in Maryland—no matter, she's still a treasure.

When it came time for radiation treatments and chemotherapy marathons (you can't know how very long three hours can be until you are hooked up to a slow-drip IV or are watching one plop-plop its way through your loved one's vein), we were introduced to another set of hidden treasures. They took the forms of oncology nurses and radiation technicians. Unlike most of the doctors we encountered, these gems readily shared every little tidbit of knowledge they had gained over their years in the field—practical, serviceable treasures on how to find comfort in very uncomfortable situations. Trust me, you probably don't want all the details here. But, should you find yourself dealing with a cancer diagnosis, pay very close attention to your direct-care givers. They may hide their wings under their scrub uniforms, but you can be sure they are there.

Once we made our move south and my husband finished his chemotherapy sessions here, we had a few weeks of glorious freedom from it all. Though the man I married nearly twenty-five years earlier looked and acted nothing like the "cancer man", love still resided between us. He went from weighing a robust 265 pounds, including the retired firefighter's must-have bushy mustache and fierce appetite, to a shadowy 158 pound shell of a man who could no longer eat or drink by mouth without choking. Love became permanently wedged there in our vows—in sickness and in health, for better or worse, for richer or poorer. So there's another hidden treasure dug up from the depths of illness—abiding love. It seems that cancer can work this way, as a bridge to building love, or it can become a dark chasm. We found the bridge.

When he could no longer breathe because of the fluids rapidly building around his lungs, we ended up, briefly, in the local hospital, where he was subjected to all manner of personal indignity. I held up his body so the orderly could wash him. Because he could no longer stand, he was weighed in a harness above the bed (why this was important, I will never fathom). In the midst of this mess, came yet another hidden treasure. The attending physician's goal was to keep my husband alive, which is his oath. When he ordered yet another round of invasive respiratory therapy, I asked if the pain would be worth his effort to endure it. The physician did not respond, but I could see that the respiratory therapist, standing just behind the doctor, was quietly shaking his head no. I then refused the order and asked that my husband be moved to hospice care as soon as possible. After the doctor left, I thanked the therapist through tears for his help. He did not have to give me that sign. It could have cost him at least a reprimand or at most his job. There was the treasure, hidden within the trial: Human compassion, one for another, without counting the cost.

Hospice, of course, is a very well=known treasure. There are not enough words to describe its beauty in the mirror of impending death. Unlike a hospital, which is designed to preserve and prolong life, hospice offers the treasure of quiet rest and peaceful leavings. What I did not expect to find, however, was the treasure of witnessing our daughter cradling and stroking her father's hair in much the same way he did her when they met for the first time in a delivery room. The joy of knowing there was a full and rich circle enclosing their lives will remain with me always. She also kept his lips moistened with glycerin swabs, which also brought to mind the day he had to take the call from elementary school alerting us that his daughter had consumed an entire tube of cherry flavored lip balm. The facts that she was not in pre-K but in fourth grade, and that this was not by any stretch the first call from school that year may give a more accurate picture of how that call was received. This now humorous memory helped a little as we shared the sad duty of watching her dad and my husband literally breathe his last breath, peacefully and quietly, while the rest of the world kept right on moving.

The neighbors we had met only a few weeks before he died descended on our home with mounds of food and words of care and concern, the likes of which we had never seen. A lasting friendship grew from this hospitality. A new family was included in our circle of life—all treasures of the highest quality. An old friend and coworker chose to send a card every month for an entire year—just so I would know she had not forgotten that grief lingered long after death..

There is also the treasure we found hidden in the words our son spoke at his father's memorial. This young man, suffering his own private pains, stood before a gathering of nearly two hundred people and clearly shared the words he had written on crumpled sheets of notepaper. The end of his speech, for me, marked the beginning of his adult life when he said: "So, I do not worry about the man I will become one day, because I am, after all, my father's son." His words received a sustained ovation and my son began to live, in that moment, outside the shadow of his father's life and into his own future.

Then there's the sisterhood—brought closer by cancer. There are five of us. One has survived breast cancer and another skin cancer. We are all so grateful that we have stopped sniping at each other—well, mostly. And one sister does not let more than a few days go by without calling her baby sister (that would be me) to hear firsthand how she is surviving in widow world.

Cancer may take away many things, but it cannot remove love and friendship—unless we let it. So, if you are worried about saying or doing the right thing when someone you know is fighting or even losing the battle, don't be. You may just be the treasure they need to find. Just start glowing so they can find you. And, if cancer should visit your life one day, or it is sitting now in your living room, I encourage you to find a shovel and start digging for the treasures all around you. If it is too difficult to dig right now, simply find a Bible and begin reading. Romans 5:3–5 might be a good start, or perhaps Philippians 4:6–8.

# Dancing in the Rain

*October 2011*

Survivors just have a special way about them, don't they? What is it, I wonder, that makes one person dance in the rain while another chooses to cover her ears and shut out the happy noise? Is there a special gene for it? Can you buy it or copy it? I have had the privilege to write about some wonderfully gifted survivors on this journey—brave, courageous, determined individuals who dance to the music that they hear, joyfully answering their personal storms with a beautifully executed Viennese waltz, saucy samba, or even a wild Watusi.

The word "survivor" is mentioned often (about forty times) in the Old Testament NIV, and is usually preceded by the words "there were no…" or "destroy the…." The word is mentioned only once in the New Testament—Book of Revelation 11:12–14. And those survivors were terrified. Hmmm. Think maybe God is giving us a hint? Maybe it's not enough just to survive. Evidently, He expects us to thrive, and perhaps even learn to shag across the dance floor while the storms rage all around us. That's probably why we can find the word *joy* in the Bible about 242 times—six times for every one time we see *survivor*. It's a clue for living, perhaps.

In writing about survivors (of cancer, adversity, tragedy, loss) I have been amazed by their universal abilities to dance in the rain, to weather their storms. Last year, I sat in awe and deep admiration of a young woman who had only just begun her breast cancer journey and was genuinely more concerned about how it was affecting her family, her friends, and her church community than what had happened and was about to continue happening to her. She sailed through her storm and continues to be a beacon of light. She is a true survivor, dancing (and singing) in the rain.

I watched (unfortunately from a distance) my own sister commit to everything she had to do in order to survive her own diagnosis. She loved her blonde wig—the one she chose to wear as her hair fell out in clumps—and misses wearing it now that her own hair, dark and curly, has begun to reappear. She has survived to enjoy being wildly loved by ten grandchildren. She leaves most of the dancing to them though. Hers was a more private journey—just like her life—but she managed to pass along some expert moves to her brother-in-law when it was his turn to dance in the rain. He opted for a clown wig, but to each his own.

My late husband (her brother-in-law) survived long enough to tap to the tune of hope. He watched funny movies and wore his clown wig and outrageous hats. His motto was always to find the humor in the storm—even in the loud thunderclaps of weight loss from a radiated mouth that zapped all the saliva glands—boy, would he have loved a little internal shower. He danced through it all—the moves just kept getting slower. He had his last dance five years ago. And, just to be clear, it was figurative dancing for him only. When it came to actual dancing, he never met a backache or sore knee he didn't like.

Another woman I wrote about in April is now looking for ways to boost others on their journeys—to give back to God what He has so generously given to her by caring for her friends in need. What a gift. Another woman I have not had the privilege yet to write about is a cancer survivor and widow who chose to become a foster parent as one way of giving someone else a chance like the one God has given to her. She'll soon be an adoptive mother to that precious child. Looks like God has returned the favor to her and I . can't wait to see her next dance move.

I lost a friend to cancer years ago, but she never lost her hope. Instead she left a legacy for her family and friends of exactly how to dance in the rain, even when the floods start coming. And, speaking of floods, what about Noah, for goodness sake? A rank amateur had nothing but faith and managed to do a better boat-building job than a bunch of experts did on the Titanic. Now, *that's* dancing in the rain—the storms of criticism and disbelief (and being called a lunatic) must have been incredibly intense.

Maybe that's the lesson we can take away from these dancers in the rain. It isn't so much about surviving as it is about having faith through the storm—letting Christ lift us up and carry us when we can't dance on our own. It isn't enough just to survive, we need to find a way to thrive, to learn new dance steps and maybe teach a few to others along the way.

And, the irony of receiving my annual mammogram notice in the mail on the very day I was attempting to write about cancer survivors certainly did not go unnoticed. Thank you, Lord, for your clever sense of timing and humor. I will attempt to look forward to the opportunity to—uh—squeeze that appointment into my schedule. Since the directive has come with such impeccable timing, it seems appropriate to offer a few words of advice from the Susan G. Komen for the Cure foundation. They call it "facts for life"—screening can save lives.

- Have a mammogram every year starting at age forty if you are at average risk.

- Have a clinical breast exam at least every three years starting at age twenty, and every year starting at age forty.

- If you are at a higher risk, ask your doctor which screening tests are right for you.

In between, dance like no one is looking. It's not, after all, about just surviving the storms. It's about learning to dance in the rain and live every day of your life. No rhythm? Two left feet? No matter. Just keep on dancing. God orchestrated our universe but He gives us the ability to write our own music and dance our own tunes with the attitudes we keep. There's also an old saying that bears repeating once in a while. No Christ. No peace. Know Christ. Know peace. Tap into the tune of your faith.

# Nothing Could Define Her

*October 2014*

$S$he could not be placed conveniently in any one box. No way; not this girl. She made a habit of coloring outside the lines, usually with broken, paper-shredded crayons and stubby pencils. Her life was not ordered by tradition or swayed by the latest fads. She had a decidedly independent nature and defied anyone or anything to label her with any standard description. Not a liberal. Not a conservative. Not an optimist or pessimist. Not a Baptist or Catholic or agnostic or atheist. Really, nothing could define her. She would have none of it. Not, that is, until the cold, harsh reality of cancer entered her life. It was at precisely that moment her world changed in dramatic and, arguably, predictable fashion. There was really no escaping it, short of escaping the world altogether. And she would have none of that mess either.

She found herself quickly caught up in the defining and confining worlds of chemotherapy, surgical decisions, and white blood cell counts. Who knew that cancer had its very own vocabulary and its very own smell? People began to look at her differently. They treated her as if she might break into pieces with the wrong words spoken. (And, sometimes she did.) Great, yet more labels attached without permission and with what felt like super-stick gorilla glue; words like *pitiful, hopeless, sad*, and *terminal*.

And she wasn't even the one with the diagnosis. She was the wife, the caregiver, the mother of his children. And she would much too soon wear the widow label too. Like so many others who had gone before her and will, unfortunately, follow her, she did not wish to be defined by that label. But after surviving the crushing blow of a cancer label, widow was very alluring in its own depressing way. Even the Bible gives up many verses for and about widows. So, there she sat in her doom and gloom robe for quite some time. It was comfortable. It was easy. And it was deadly. Rather than being a true survivor, she was tip-toeing dangerously close to the edge of existence.

She had been given the poem about what cancer cannot do and she wallowed in it for a long while. But since she had no active faith, cancer could not steal from her what she did not possess. There was nothing to take. She wouldn't wear the label, remember? Oh no. Not her. But then someone came along beside her and led her where she had refused before to go. She bulked. She resisted. She finally went along out of sheer exhaustion and a little bit of guilt, for this person had been quite kind in general (while being specifically quite annoying). And, in case you haven't already guessed, that she was me. Some labels and defining things no longer irritate.

October is the month we celebrate survivors, and that is a richly good thing. There are survivors of all kinds in this life. Some survive illness. Some survive a loved one's loss. Some survive the stress of war. Some survive first grade and learn to love school after all. Some survive betrayal. Some survive the trauma of a charred holiday meal. But it is in the tentative footsteps toward survival that the real work begins. If we are paying close attention, it is often in the midst of the trial that the miracle begins to be revealed, well before survival is even imaginable. I believe this is true for all people—but some of us come to these revelation miracles kicking and screaming.

We recently (this "we" stuff is awesome, by the way) had the opportunity to visit Iron Hill Baptist Church in NC and listen to a group called "Noah's Faith." They uniquely blend their voices in song, from Southern Gospel to Contemporary Christian and back again,

One song was particularly beautiful and served to provide the "germ" for this article (no, it's not a virus kind of germ—if it were, I would sneeze it all over my children and anyone in need nearby). It is called "Send the Rain." The lyrics were written by Aaron Butler, lead singer and former pastor of The Harvest Church. Based on his sermon message, God speaks through him in multiple ways. Thanks again for the invite, Dale and Sherry.

Mercy Me sings a similarly themed song in "Bring the Rain." The refrain is a wonderful message during this survivors' month. It is really for all of us—survivors of many things, great and small. May we know and share the peace that comes from this kind of rain and from being beautifully defined by our faith.

"Bring me joy; bring me peace.
Bring the chance to be free.
Bring me anything that brings You glory.
And I know there'll be days
When this life brings me pain
But if that's what it takes to praise You,
Jesus, bring the rain."

I have four sisters. Two of them have survived breast cancer and two remain breast cancer-free. It will be left to me, evidently, to break the tie. Well, whoop dee doo. Yet another perk of being the youngest of five, I suppose. No matter. Whichever way the tie breaks—cancer or no cancer—there will come that still quiet moment before the next storm that nearly begs God to bring the rain, so "she" and I can continue to be defined more clearly as a child of His kingdom.

*(Unfortunately, another sister effectively broke the sister tie on cancer. She succumbed to pancreatic cancer less than one month from diagnosis in 2017. Her story can be found in January 2018 essay.)*

# Victorious Secrets

*October 2015*

*I* know. At first glance this is probably not the most politically correct (or, as the very cool people say, "PC") title for this month's topic, but please look again. It's not about sexy bra choices; it's about victorious people—and their secrets. Most, if not all, of the cancer survivors' stories I have ever had the privilege to read, or write about, or live nearby, share similar secrets– quite victorious secrets. They have learned how to go to battle with a formidable foe and come out the other side, physically altered perhaps and with scars to prove where they've been, but ultimately in triumph and victory. Sometimes it takes a giant problem, or a tiny rogue cell, to bring about ginormous success in living life well (no pun intended).

But how do they do it? How do people claim this victory over life-altering circumstances and diagnoses? Things like breast cancer or other heart-weakening experiences can take horribly devastating tolls on mere mortals like us. For pity's sake, I can't even face down a new roll of saran wrap without having a meltdown when I can't find the starting edge. I will pick and pull at that sucker until it's nearly in shreds—like it has been attacked by a bevy of nearsighted and somewhat nervous buzzards. Then Mr. Calm comes into the kitchen and quietly shows me the error of my ways, and the cut end of the wrap roll. That really gets on what's left of my last nerve. And it has next to nothing to do with the subject of victorious secrets. Obviously, I don't have any—I have just seen what others with greater gifts have made of the lousy hands they have been dealt.

They have taken a lowly one-of-a-kind deal and turned it into four aces or a royal straight flush. They know when to hold 'em. Know when to fold 'em. Know when to walk away. Know when to run. Never mind, and with apologies to Mr. Rogers. Victorious secrets are not, after all, about cards or karma or catchy country songs. The secrets of victorious people, I suspect, are hidden within their responses to life's various storms. So I took a little mental journey to see if I could maybe discover what they share in common. I didn't have to travel very far to find cancer fighters and survivors in recent memory, and within close proximity to my heart: Sisters and brothers by blood, marriage, friendship or faith. And they share at least three things:

1. They have been to war. Being victorious implies that you have been in a fight of some sort. A battle has been waged. Sometimes that battle happens all around them and sometimes it happens within them—and sometimes it happens in both places simultaneously. There is, after all, no victory without first a fight. They persevere through it all, knowing somehow that there will come a day when peace reigns. One day.

2. They have known the agony of defeat. Yes, they have felt defeated. There have been days (or weeks, months) when up is down and down is up and victory is nowhere near. And it is indeed agonizing to live in those days. But it is in those very days that character is sculpted from the ruins of life as they used to know it. And the character that develops from defeat beautifully produces the third shared thing.

3. They choose victory instead. Victory often is a choice. It isn't like a scoreboard tally. There are no numbers or stats involved. There is no country to win over, except the one within the heart. Victorious people have hope in a new day. They may be forever physically changed or made weaker, but the hope in victory gives them a new life to live.

The traits victorious people share then are really not so secret after all. They develop perseverance through storms of battle. They build character from the muscles earned in defeat. And they have hope for today and tomorrow, whatever it may bring. Victims, on the other hand, do not persevere. They do not construct character. And they have lost hope. If any of this sounds vaguely familiar, it's probably because you know all this already. We have only to open His Word and the "secrets" pop right out at us. Consider Romans 5:1–5 or 1 Corinthians 15:54–55 or 1 John 5:3–4 or James 1:2–4 or the following, Psalm 27:5:

"For in the time of trouble He shall hide me in His pavilion; In the secret place of His tabernacle He shall hide me; He shall set me high upon a rock."

We all have examples in our lives of people with victorious secrets. I have been blessed with quite a few. Now, how does one put a number to "quite a few" anyway? I think it's more than several and a bit less than many. Maybe. Regardless of the actual numbering, here are a few:

Barbara Maffett. I first met Barbara while writing her love story for a February She several years ago. Her husband had lost his battle with cancer and she shared their wonderful marriage partnership. Not long after that, Barbara was faced with her own deadly diagnosis: ovarian cancer. She was given a prognosis of perhaps a year. This battle would be waged without her husband by her side. Defeated? Yes—but only temporarily. She just celebrated her third-year anniversary of remission. Barbara is victorious. And she lives her life in joy and thanksgiving.

Betty Stephens. She is my husband's aunt and a breast cancer survivor. As she told me one time, she's had many body parts removed or replaced. But that doesn't stop her. I can't think of much that could. Betty has known the defeat of burying her husband, siblings, and a grandchild. She still, in her eighties, drives the tobacco trucks to the barn for her son. And hope truly defines her every move. Now that I think about it, all of my husband's aunts share this kind of hope. Evidently, there is something in the air they breathe out here.

Sheila Kelley. A transplant from New England to South Carolina a number of years ago, Sheila still drops off most of the "r's" in her sentences. We first met at church and my name is Maaati, according to her. She saw her late husband through a long and difficult terminal illness and misses him still every day. Especially now. She has been recently diagnosed with brain cancer. Her son has come south to care for her while she is in treatment and she will tell anyone who will listen (and it is difficult *not* to listen to Sheila) that she is claiming victory over cancer through her savior, Jesus Christ.

I count it a privilege to have crossed paths with these women and others like them. They embody life lived in victory and proclaim their faith boldly, offering living testimony to the victorious secrets of perseverance, character, and hope. And I'm fairly certain they can face down a new roll of saran wrap without losing their beautiful victorious secrets, quite unlike my sorry self.

# Pumpkin Chunkin'

*October 2016*

*L*ong ago I declared fall to be my favorite season of the year. Winter, spring, and summer have never given me the same thrill, but falling leaves and pumpkin sightings and chills in the air? Oh, yes, please. It also helped that I loved school and crisp apples and the county fair. And sweaters and long pants and boots. Favorite colors? Earth tones, of course—the hues that appear on the landscape just before the winter claims them with frost and cold and too little light.

And then it happened. I visited my neighborhood grocery store and began to rethink this favored seasonal preference. Oh, who am I kidding? I no longer *have* a neighborhood grocery—it is now a carefully planned and timed trek toward the sights and sounds of Mullins or Loris or faraway Marion or Conway. Gone are the days when I could just pop on over to the very nearby Food Mart for that one item I forgot. On the other hand, I can't complain about the birds, bunnies, deer families, and turkey gangs that inhabit life on a dirt road out in the country. Wait. I forgot the snakes. And those dang gnats. Never mind.

This recent rethinking of fall as favored was initiated by the pumpkin spiced explosion of flavor and scent overkill in nearly every aisle of the store. Don't get me wrong now; I do enjoy a pumpkin pie and an occasional (ha!) pumpkin crumble muffin or cookie. I even have been known to indulge in the purchase of pumpkin scented (more precisely a combination of clove, nutmeg, and allspice with a hint of buttery vanilla) candles to light the darker evenings. But the pumpkin flavored and/or scented cereal and pasta and bacon and oatmeal and frozen waffles and cleaning supplies and air fresheners, and yes, even personal tissues, is just too much.

As if the shelves and displays and freezer sections didn't do enough pumpkin pushing, the check-out line was yet another gauntlet of pumpkin bombardment. Nearly every magazine cover included a pumpkin design or dessert photo—the only exception being those gossip rags (the ones I disdain and shake my head at, while secretly hoping the person in front of me checks out slowly enough for me to read all of the tawdry and juicy headlines without the risk of losing my salvation).

I'd love to attend a pumpkin-chunking event right about now, and hurl those orange orbs into, well, orbit. I know I am offending a certain number of folks here—the pumpkin flavor lovers who cannot wait for the first sightings to appear on grocery shelves and big box stores. Please forgive me. I was with you; believe me, up until this season approached, I too could not wait to find them. It's just too much pumpkin. And too much of a good thing, it turns out, really is not a good thing at all. Even if it happens in the best season of the year.

A quick google check brought back, again, an overabundance of references to pumpkin recipes—from cheesecake to muffins to bread to pie to scones and soups. There were links to pumpkin restaurants and even a movie starring Christina Ricci, aptly titled "Pumpkin." We have pumpkin latte and pumpkin creamers. We even have microbrewery pumpkin ale. There's the meme floating around social media about pumpkin Xanax, for those with, uh, seasonal anxiety. Really, stop it.

I also discovered that I may be suffering from a relatively rare problem. It's called cucurbitophobia—fear of pumpkins. Evidently it just started this year. I've been okay with the pumpkin parade in fall until now. But this season, I have succumbed to the fear (or it may be more of a loathing). This fear can likely be related to their vast overabundance this time of year. Perhaps it is a vast right field conspiracy. The largest ever recorded pumpkin weighed in at a whopping 2,323.7 pounds.

That's a whole latte pumpkin, my friends. And it's the stuff of nightmares. Fortunately, it was grown way over there in Germany. We may be safe for another season or two—until they learn how to swim.

So what's the big deal? Why so pouty about it all? I'm not really sure. Maybe I'm just tired of excess, overkill, blight, the permeating sameness of life after some fifty years of loving autumn. (I'm a little fuzzy on the first ten or so years, probably due to older sisters scaring the dickens out of me and stealing all my candy at Halloween.) I can only guess what you're thinking right about now: "Oh brother, here she goes on another weird mind trip." It's either buckle up or turn the page quickly and get out of here.

No, wait. I can turn this orange orb thing around. Surely, there is something good to be said about all this pumpkin-flavored mania. We'll just focus on the positive side of pumpkins and preserve the favored and well-flavored season that is autumn.

Let's see. Well, there's much good to be had by consuming pumpkins. They are loaded with antioxidants, vitamin A, carotenes. And they're relatively low in calories, until the pumpkin spice patrol joins in with sugar, cream, more sugar, and various forms of added fats. They are quite versatile players in the kitchen. Even their seeds are edible. And they make great holders for dips or hearty soups.

We can find great joys in painting them, stenciling them, carving them—scooping out their guts and sticking lighted candles inside that drip hot wax. Some of the greatest joys though can be found in the finding of them. Who doesn't like a trip to the pumpkin patch, especially if there's hot cider involved?

I even located a heretofore unknown to me quote from Henry David Thoreau:

"I would rather sit on a pumpkin and have it all to myself than be crowded on a velvet cushion."

Solitary pumpkin sitting can be rather wonderful, if said pumpkin is big enough to accommodate the seat of the sitter. And it's not about selfishness; it's about the joy of solitude.

And we are still tuning in (or setting our DVRs) to see if Linus will find the Great Pumpkin. We enthusiastically introduce the hunt to a new generation of children. Tradition reigns? I guess sometimes it does. Fall is for pumpkins, right up to and including Thanksgiving (with October getting the greatest push—which, with today's marketing calendars, means we start seeing pumpkin stuff in August). And I will survive my little phobia. As a peace offering to pumpkin spice aficionados, may I leave you with one of my favorite old pumpkin poems?

Five little pumpkins sitting on a gate
The first one said: "My, it's getting late."
The second one said: "There are witches in the air."
The third one said: "But we don't care."
The fourth one said: "Let's run. Let's run."
The fifth one said: "Isn't Halloween fun?"
Then woooo went the wind.
And out went the lights.
And five little pumpkins rolled out of sight.
(Yay, they're gone.)

# Thelma & Louise

*I* have a sneaking suspicion that most men affectionately and/or proudly name a few of their body parts. And I have encountered a few women with the same tendency—to name their own. So I figured that this would be a pretty good month to announce the naming of a couple of mine, in an effort to take better care of them (namely via regular self-exams and mammograms).

Based on their current looks, however, it would be difficult to name them anything that even remotely suggests loveliness. I am very tempted to just go with Flopsy and Droopy. But that would not encourage me to take better care of them. No, I'd likely just keep hoisting them into a torturous underwire home and hope for the best. They've been hovering around my waist for what seems like years now—or, to clarify, the waist I used to have. That thing has turned into an amoeba-like creature and now oozes over a much wider expanse, from hip to hip. Child-bearing hips are great when you are of child-bearing age. Afterwards they just make it difficult to find pants to fit over them stylishly. The hourglass has been shattered, and time has run out—all over me.

Please believe me when I say I am not attempting to make fun of the girls or ridicule them in any way (other than with the truth). They have been very good to me—not even a hint of cancerous growth. And they have fed my children—until they started teething anyway. I have seen firsthand what can happen when cancer invades. Two sisters have had breast cancer.

The first had a radical mastectomy and the second a less invasive lumpectomy. Another sister died suddenly last year, just three weeks after a pancreatic cancer diagnosis and one grueling round of chemotherapy. I watched my late husband disappear slowly and painfully from a different type of cancer. Too many loved ones have lost their battles or nearly died fighting them. Chemotherapy, radiation, and subsequent scan result waits are not for the faint-of-heart.

I've also had the privilege of reading and editing stories of cancer survivors for this magazine. Each one, in her unique way, represents a triumph of determination and deep faith. It is really their stories that have caused me to take a bit of a lighter look at such a serious subject. I guess it's my way of dealing with the procrastination that plagues me regarding breast health. After all, it's difficult to ignore something you have named and must carry with you wherever you go. Every survivor I have ever known has been pretty adamant that self-exams and mammograms are not to be put off or ignored. And their warnings deserve to be heeded.

So, we forge ahead with the naming thing. There are so many possibilities. We could start with a simple Dr. Seuss plan and name them Thing One and Thing Two. But, no, that just will not do. (Have you ever stopped to wonder why *no* and *do* don't rhyme, but *to* and *do* do?) The great comedy teams also come to mind—like Lucy and Ethel, or Laverne and Shirley, or a more modern *SNL* version, like Tina and Amy—or we could go with the recently rebooted *Will and Grace.* Or maybe a cartoon version would be appropriate, like *The Flintstones'* Wilma and Betty? Nope. Not feeling any of these yet.

I'd consider naming the girls after guys, to be more gender neutral—but Batman and Robin, or Chuck and Todd, or Bill and Phil, or even Simon and Garfunkel, just don't make beautiful music together for me.

Hey, how about Cagney and Lacey—now that's a decent possibility. After all, they wear holstered things most of the time—much like a well-armed police detective duo. But on second thought, I just can't seem to warm up to a law and order kind of theme. I get the feeling that perhaps my girls lean more toward the other side of the law. It's just a hunch on my part, of course.

And that brings us to the spoiler alert title of this article. I have decided to officially name the girls Thelma and Louise. Thelma is more suited to the left side of the duo—she's a bit larger than her companion on the right and has always been a bit droopier. The slightly more perky of the pair shall be Louise. In the movie, Thelma and Louise were portrayed by Susan Sarandon and Geena Davis—yet another good reason to decide on these names. My dear husband has a long term dislike for Susan Sarandon (and her politics), so I get to have a good giggle, unfortunately at his expense. But if I keep up this kind of behavior, the last laugh may be on me, eh? I'll chance it.

From this day forward, Thelma and Louise (aka "the girls") will be cared for with more loving attention. I will self-exam and get my mammograms on a much more regular basis. At my last "annual" visit this summer, I was informed that I had not been in the boob vice since 2013. There is no excuse for that kind of procrastination, so I will not even attempt to make one. Suffice it to say that I was somewhat embarrassed by the time gap—especially when I discovered that the technician knew some of my husband's extended family rather well. Oh, the horror of it all!

In fairness to Thelma and Louise, I have also decided to dress them more appropriately. The raggedy bras are out. No more frayed elastic for these ladies. The underwire bras with one bent wire poking through the material and jabbing Thelma in the cheek shall be gone. The ones with stretched out straps due to the constant overexertion of attempting to uphold their ends of the bargain will be trashed. There's nothing worse for Thelma or Louise when a wayward strap decides to descend from the shoulder and travel toward the elbow. Have you ever tried to reach the back of a buffet line when a strap has your arm trapped at a thirty-degree angle? There's just no getting to those hot shrimp in the corner of the tray.

I guess it's also time to bite the bullet (maybe I should rethink the *Cagney and Lacey* idea), and get another accurate bra fitting. It is amazing how much better one, or two, look and feel when they are properly and proportionately dressed. Thelma and Louise could end up defying gravity in a well-fitted bra—and effectively change the end of their movie while they are about it. Remember the over-the-cliff cliff hanger ending? My Thelma and Louise will keep pushing forward on the road ahead instead, as I remember to be grateful for what I have and even more for what I do not have.

Besides, we are encouraged to take care of our mortal bodies while we are using them—something that I must do a better job with, especially as this body continues its hopefully slow march to the finish line from sixty-three and counting. Please consider 1 Corinthians 3:16–17 and 6:19–20. I may rise on wings like eagles and not grow weary, per Isaiah, but not if my body is ignored and taken for granted. Thelma and Louise will be given my best effort to keep them from edging over the cliff. But, should that ultimately be their fate, should cancer invade, they will still be given the best care I can manage. Because, after all, there is hope in all circumstances—just read the survivor stories in the pages of this issue for firm evidence of faith, hope, and love (1 Cor. 13:7)—from within and from above.

November

**Talking Turkeys**
**The Domestic Glitch**
**Bibbidi-Bobbidi-Boo**
**Thanksforgivingness**
**Thanksgrieving**
**Sparkle & Shine**

*N*ovember was a time for gratitude in all things. It was also the month that celebrated local Extraordinary Women, both in the magazine and in an annual special event. Women were nominated by other readers and groups, then selected and celebrated. Of course, there were turkeys to talk about too.

# Talking Turkey

*November 2007*

*I*n over fifty years on this planet, I've seen my share of turkeys. It wasn't, however, until it became my turn to dress it, baste it, and present it as the main attraction on a certain Thursday in November that I became so intimately acquainted with what Benjamin Franklin wanted desperately to proclaim as our national bird. It did not go well.

When you consider just how much the turkey has become part of our American culture (at least in November), it's not too difficult to see how this bird might have rightfully posed on our currency. We consume an awful lot of it. There is wild turkey (both feathered and bottled), domesticated turkey, leftover turkey (which is really the whole reason for going through all that trouble in the first place), turkey croquettes, ground turkey, smoked turkey necks and collard greens, deep fried turkey, turducken (for the adventurous soul who can get a chicken inside a duck inside a turkey AND have each bird cooked to perfection), and even turkey carcass soup.

We gauge the grace of our aging by how much wattle we find on our own little turkey necks. We dance the turkey trot and tap our toes to "Turkey in the Straw." Don't tell the turkeys but we also enjoy practicing our aim at the local turkey shoots. Our gridiron glories are not complete without at least one controversial call at our Turkey Bowls. The old bird has even found its way into our conversations, as in: I feel like such a turkey or, stop acting like a turkey. These, among others, are not meant to be pleasant or positive descriptors.

On the fourth Thursday in November, for every group holding hands and saying grace around a Thanksgiving table, there are equal numbers of variations on turkey cooking, carving, condiments, and side dishes. And the hints for turkey perfection are seemingly endless. Some will say that basting every hour is imperative while others insist on a slathering of mayonnaise while the turkey "tans" to a golden-brown crust. Some cover the breast halfway through; others dunk the whole bird in a boiling oil bath (aka deep fried turkey and possible three-alarm fires). It was not uncommon in days gone by to stuff the bird cavity with a favorite dressing (or stuffing). Amazing grace kept us from the emergency rooms with that icky recipe. But some of us still insist on cramming the cavern with bread, cornbread, seasonings, oysters and sundry seasonings. Then, of course, there's the white meat/dark meat controversy and the clamoring to grab that tasty morsel of meat tucked just behind the thigh—if it were a crab, we'd call it the back fin.

Because our Irish family spent many, many Thanksgivings sharing turkey dinner with a wide array of cousins, aunts, uncles, and significant others at our grandparents' hotel, we never exchanged too many turkey tips. The meal was prepared ahead and served family style in the giant dining room. Being the youngest in our family, I never got the chance to graduate from the kiddy table seating arrangement—yet another side effect of being the baby. After their deaths, our families had to fend for ourselves for Thanksgiving gatherings, as the hotel was eventually sold and turned into a parking lot for downtown Frederick shoppers. But the memories still hold dear, except for the seating discriminations.

It wasn't until many years later that I was inundated with turkey cooking tips from all directions when it was finally my turn to host Thanksgiving supper for my own family. The horror ensued rather quickly, as I attempted to talk turkey like a professional while still very much a novice cook, at best. Things went smoothly at first (providing a very false sense of pride and knowledge). Let's just cut to the chase here—my first turkey bird offering looked quite lovely on our well-dressed table, until my husband began the carving ritual. As the knife slid through the perfectly browned outer skin into the juicy breast, the gasps and shrieks pierced my ears. These were not sounds of excitement and anticipation. These, instead, were sounds of horror—as the turkey blood ran out of its hiding place and proceeded to run across the lace tablecloth much like the prom scene from *Carrie*.

Fortunately for the gathered and terrified family, my still-proud husband proved once again to be pretty good in a crisis. He quickly gathered up the bloody bird, headed for the kitchen, and unceremoniously carved up that Thanksgiving bird like a skilled surgeon, stuck the bloody parts in the microwave and then returned to the table with well-cooked parts. I was much too busy running for the bathroom and sobbing my no-longer-proud eyes out. The moral of that story was never ever trust a semi frozen turkey to be fully thawed in time for the big show.

While you are busy gathering your Thanksgiving supplies and recipes, and polishing your good dishes in anticipation of the day or after the feast has been consumed and antacids passed around the table, please consider sharing the following prayer. It was sent to me from a friend far away who always seems to know exactly what I need and when I need it. Thankful I am for so much—friends, family, and of course well-cooked birds.

*May today there be peace within.*
*May we trust God that we are exactly where we are meant to be.*
*May we not forget the infinite possibilities that are born of faith.*
*May we use those gifts that we have received*
*And pass on the love that has been given to us.*
*May we be content knowing that we are children of God.*
*Let this knowledge settle into our bones*
*And allow our souls the freedom to sing, dance, praise, and love.*
*It is here for each and every one of us. Amen*
—Author unknown

At the end of the day, it's not the turkey or the trimmings or the beautiful centerpiece that matter anyway. It's the people gathered at our tables and in our memories that give us our fondest Thanksgivings. The tables may be housed in mansions or meadows or on the meanest of streets, but we can still find ways to connect outward and upward. May we also connect with each other on the everyday Thursdays of our lives too?

Here's a little turkey teaser to share around the Thanksgiving table this month: Can you name three consecutive days without using the words Sunday, Wednesday, and Thursday? Answer: *Yesterday, today, and tomorrow.*

One more for the road: What is the difference between turkeys and chickens? *Chickens celebrate Thanksgiving.*

# The Domestic Glitch:
# And Other Rare Birds

*November 2010*

A h yes, I remember it well—the very first time I saw the rare and elusive Domestic Glitch. It was cowering in the corner of my kitchen and looked suspiciously like a dust-covered wad of cat hair. But I was not fooled. The cat had been dead and gone for six whole months, so it simply could not have been her long-haired, snarly cast-offs. I can only conclude that it was the Domestic Glitch.

Okay, enough of that little fantasy, or they'll be carting me off to Crazy Town again. What I really mean to write about this month has next to nothing to do with sighting a Domestic Glitch. It does, however, relate to other rare birds—the kind of creatures flying all over this southern town I now call home.

I spent the first twenty years of my life in Frederick, Maryland, and another twenty-five years in southern Maryland—in a little-known area called Charlotte Hall, sandwiched between the Patuxent and Potomac Rivers, very near the mouth of the Chesapeake Bay. With the exception of relatively brief stopovers in West Virginia and Virginia for college and career beginnings, I have spent most of my life as a Marylander. My nests have mostly been feathered in that state. With close proximity to our nation's capital for all home addresses, the pace of life was rather hurried and temperamental (emphasis on the temper and mental parts).

Nearly all of the major events of life, up to 2006, took place in Maryland—births, deaths, weddings, graduations, promotions, celebrations, holiday gatherings, etc. And then came 2006 and an inexplicable move to Marion, South Carolina. To call that move a Domestic Glitch would be a gross understatement, at least initially. We had been here all of two months, and the only person I knew and loved (the reason for moving in the first place) up and died on me. As God would have it, however, I was exactly where He meant for me to be. And He slowly began to introduce me to a few very rare birds, indeed.

Neighbors who did not know us showered my family with southern care and attention. Two, in particular, simply covered us in love and piles of food. Rare birds? Coming from a place where making eye contact can be considered an act of aggression, I'd say yes, definitely these were rare birds. One of these rare birds has since become a treasured friend and sister. The other has given me space to fly on my own, but I know for sure she is always just a phone call or a short trek across the yard away. I hope she knows that path runs both ways. Some people come into your life for just a season, but the memory remains for a lifetime.

Four years ago I went back home to Maryland to celebrate my late husband's life and to bid him a final goodbye. I even entertained the thought of returning to my home state permanently. I had no real intention of making South Carolina my home. I didn't have a clue how to feather a southern nest. Y'all take it so very seriously here. Plantation shutters, seasonal plantings, window treatments, and the subtle differences between putty and khaki walls? Yikes! I feel a domestic glitch squawk rising up from my inner Maryland self.

But then God began to show me more rare birds. That neighbor who turned into a friend and sister allowed me to know her faith, her family, and her best friend. That lead to meeting her family and her friends and that lead to meeting both of their friends at what used to be a little café called A Wing and a Prayer. All of that ultimately, by grace through faith, lead me to Christ and those decisions indirectly lead me to the night of the ring-topped donut engagement. What an incredible flock of rare birds of faith.

He also lead me to the rare bird of volunteer work at the Marion Guardian ad Litem program, in the interest of abused and neglected children, which lead to knowing so many rare and exceptional volunteer birds and a county coordinator of amazing quality and character. Sometimes families have trouble feathering their nests. Children deserve a safe and permanent nest in which to grow and spread their wings, and there are many rare birds working to support them in Marion County and beyond (DSS, Trinity Behavioral Care, Pee Dee Mental Health, teachers, clergy, law enforcement, medical staff, judges, to name just a few).

And then there are the rare birds of everyday life in Marion, SC. There is the lady at the post office who always stops to give a mother tips on how to best send packages to her son in Afghanistan, no matter how long the line is in the lobby. There is the father and sons at Martin's Service Center that provide old-fashioned service in a world filled with only bottom-line concerns. Recently while preparing for another trek to Maryland, Old Betsy got the once-over at their garage and, finding nothing in need of repair or attention, they charged me nothing. Rare birds? Absolutely.

Then there's Food Lion. Because I'm rather indecisive, I tend to visit there often. Every time I walk through the door, I get a pleasant greeting. At first, my still-northern self had found all the nice-nice rather suspicious. Then I realized there is one in particular there who takes her job very seriously. She knows many of her customers by name (including yours truly). It isn't company policy that drives her to greet us. It is her genuine concern that we have a pleasant experience in her store. Thank you, rare bird. She tells me she reads *She Magazine* every month, so I surely hope she reads this one because she is one reason I choose to remain here, among the rare birds of Marion.

Along with these rare birds, there have been many sightings of the elusive Domestic Glitch on Oliver Street. I don't know yet how to feather a southern nest properly. Southern hospitality still escapes my northern grasp. I don't make effective use of the phone, which drives my southern friends loopy. Maybe that's why I can't yet grasp the concept. No matter. They work around my northern shortcomings on a regular basis. My northern family and friends (yes, I really do have a few) marvel at the southern transformation and have almost stopped asking me when I plan to return to the Maryland feathered nest. They seem to understand that I am where I am supposed to be, domestic glitches and all. I know for sure that God's plan for me is right here and right now. Birds of a feather flock together—especially those rare ones—peacocks, ostriches, chicken hawks, loons, cranes, kiwis, and a wallaby (not a bird, but still a very rare creature).

I may never quite reach domestic bliss, thanks to the glitches, but I remain quite content to feather this southern nest with all of the rare birds God has seen fit to allow me to know. For this I am grateful beyond words, and not just during the Thanksgiving month of November.

# Bibbidi-Bobbidi-Boo
## The Mess of Magical Thinking

*November 2011*

Do you believe in magic? Then come along with me. Sleeping Beauty awoke from a deadly slumber when Prince Charming gently brushed her lips with his own—that's magical. Cinderella had a pumpkin coach and wore glass slippers. Put them together and what have you got, besides a very bumpy ride? Bibbidi-bobbidi-boo! In other words, or more specifically other lyrics, "the world is full of zanies and fools who don't believe in sensible rules. They don't believe what sensible people say. Because these daft and dewy-eyed dopes keep building up impossible hopes, impossible things are happening every day!" Really, I wonder.

I used to believe in Santa Claus and the Tooth Fairy, too—the one that left a measly quarter under my pillow then magically offered my own children a whole dollar for the same sized toothies, thanks to inflation. My stuffed animals came to life while I slept so, of course, they had feelings. Not even one could be left alone on the floor at night—a freakish bedtime ritual sadly transferred to my daughter, who will likely share it with my yet-to-materialize grandchildren. We also have the magical habit of saying "excuse me" when we accidently bump into inanimate objects, like store mannequins.

The Wonderful World of Disney was the best thing on television—back in the "olden days," anyway. I can still see

Tinkerbelle flitting across the TV screen. She whacked every-thing with that tiny magic wand and sent fairy dust flying all over the place. Then Tinker fell.

The magic took a rather nasty spill. I went from imaginative play and creative thinking to the darker arts of—gasp—reality. That big fat jolly elf stopped tossing toys under the tree, and that rather hyperactive spring rabbit quit bringing colored and chocolate eggs. Wait. Have I become a total cynic? Me? The one who still cannot wait for Halloween and party themes and silly things? I think not. But I have learned a thing or three about the Bibbity Bobbity stuff. Imagination and creativity still have their place in this life. I just had to stop with the what-if kind of thinking and the if-only lists. You know—if only I could lose ten (okay, fifteen) pounds, I'd feel great. If only I had more time, I could really get so much more accomplished. What if I won a million dollars? What if I had been born first instead of last in my family? If only I could write the next great novel of the twenty-first century.

When my children turned toward adulthood, I had to give up much of my "childish" thinking. Alright, yes—one of them still gets really, really cute cuddly pjs and themed socks on hol-idays—but I have promised the other one that I'll never do it again, at least not to him. Last Christmas was the final straw, when I made him stand beside the tree in his new jammies. He had just returned from Afghanistan. What was I thinking? Magical moments aren't so magical anymore. These are the children who were raised under the magical parenting rules that proclaimed all children to be winners. Just show up. You'll get a trophy. Their end of school year awards programs lasted for three days.

And, speaking of school (back when I was still playing a grown-up with a real live career, I had the privilege of teaching freshman and academic probation students about college suc-cess skills and how to acquire them. I also taught career-plan-ning course (now, that was some magical thinking). There was a small textbook we used and I remember very fondly that it stressed one particular skill over most others. It was really quite simple, rather easy to acquire, and could be explained in three little words: Be here now.

In order to gain the gifts of today, one must be fully present (no pun intended). Live in the moment at hand and turn down the volume on "what if" and "if only" thinking and day-dreaming. It's not so magical, but it works. Attend to the task at hand instead of the noise in your head. When you are in a class or on the job or reading to a child or praying or listening to a friend, be fully present. In our current world of multi-tasking and ever-present electronic devices, this may sound like an impossible and undesirable process. But it is magical in its simplicity of design and quality of purpose.

Plans fail. Promises are broken. People die. We get rejected. Friends leave. We hear "cancer." A phone call rings in horrible news. Life as we know it slaps the happy right out of us on a fairly regular basis. To put it bluntly, reality bites. And yet, on rare occasions and in everyday moments it lifts us beyond ourselves to a place of faith—where there is hope, and, yes, Virginia, even miracles. It begins with God's grace and requires our choosing of it. By these two things we gain salvation.

I currently subscribe to a weekday online message called The Daily Creed. It's a wonderful lesson on God's word with a "be here now" application. Currently the teaching is on Ephesians. The following quote provided a powerful "ah-ha" moment for me:

"The truth of the matter is that God did not save you to fix your life and make you happy. Instead He saved you that He might extend His love and grace and mercy to you and make you a part of the work that He is seeking to accomplish through His Church."—Brad Bird

And God in his almighty wisdom still allows us the simple pleasures of Bibbity, Bobbity, and Boo. We just need to remember where to keep our faith and hope. His saving grace will provide the miracles. It is not magic. It is love. So, be here now.

# Thanksforgivingness

*November 2012*

First of all, I must lodge a complaint. It is not supposed to be November yet. This was the year I was going to have all my Christmas shopping completed by the end of October and, as usual, I have not even begun. It just cannot be November, but the calendar on the wall shows otherwise. Sometimes calendars and clocks are not our friends.

Fortunately, and for the sake of clearing away my rather bad mood, November is also the time to start remembering what I am thankful for each year. It's also a good time to work on the forgiveness stuff, or at least practice some well-timed forgetfulness. But who could forget that it's time to stuff ourselves with turkey and dressing and pumpkin pies and blueberry muffins and sweet potato biscuits and maybe even some Italian cream cake, if I can muster up the nerve to tackle it. Debbie Page makes the very best I have ever eaten and that recipe she generously shared still sits in my kitchen drawer, daring me to try it.

Both of my children have made plans to come home for Thanksgiving. Oh joy of my heart. They will get pancakes for breakfast and turkey cookies and pumpkin pie and get dragged all over Marion so I can share them with others. The only place Devin has requested is the farm so she can get more target practice. This is probably a good time to share with Mr. Willoughby the BB gun story—the one that involves sibling rivalry and extended "time outs"—before they get here.

If they survive the shooting excursion, they'll get to meet the newest family member for the first time. He lives in the

218

backyard and has gained ten pounds every three weeks since he arrived in August. They should be able to throw a saddle on him and ride around town by the time they get here. Considering the list of fun-filled activities I'm planning, it's really not any wonder that they haven't been here since last Christmas, huh?

One of my very best friends from Maryland may be moving to Greenville, SC in the future. Yay! It's still three hours away from here, but it's at least in the same state and doesn't include the dreaded Capital Beltway excursion in Maryland. We lost touch with each other for a while after the cancer deaths of her dad and my husband in the same month six years ago. But we have joyfully reconnected and I can't wait to have her physically closer as well as emotionally connected. Her children used to bake cookies with me on Christmas Eve, for goodness sake.

I can't wait to enjoy real instead of virtual coffee breaks together after their move.

I saw my mother make what will probably be her last move with graceful determination. Some of it comes from her generation, but the bigger part comes from a steadfast regard for her daughters, and a greater understanding and acceptance of what lies ahead. Thanks, Mom.

I attended several funerals this year and am grateful for their gifts. Now I know that may sound a bit odd, but the ones I witnessed were truly celebrations of lives well-lived and the joy in knowing that loved ones, though departed, were truly resting in blissful peace was evident even through the tears shed by friends and family.

I began a business start-up class in Marion to learn if or when to open that cupcake/dessert/flying pig/stationary/gift basket shop. I also hope to learn about effective decision-making and narrowing down of wild ideas. Pigs do fly but sometimes they stink up the place too. Evidently, it pays to be discerning. We'll see how it turns out. At this writing, we've only just begun but I'm already thankful for the opportunity.

A lovely lady gifted me with a tin box filled with cupcake recipes by way of encouraging me to take a leap of faith and open that shop. Thanks, Marie. I'm not sure it will happen but my hips and I are having loads (literally) of fun trying out those recipes in the meantime.

I'm still engaged to a wonderful man who has taught me how to put up siding, dig holes, mix and pour concrete, install ceiling planks, drive nails, pull nails, stack wood, and share my garage with big hulking power tools. And I have taught him that northerners can also pitch a pretty good fit. Think wood, nails, hammer, bad aim, and poorly timed laughter.

I am grateful beyond words for another engaged couple who took time they did not have out of their stress-filled work/school schedules to meet my sister and her husband when they traveled to Charleston on vacation. Carrie and Lucas, you are amazing.

Good and true friends are still around, despite my ridiculous aversion to regular phone conversation (for which I am evidently forgiven). And I have almost completely stopped classifying them as southern or northern. It is amazing how similar they are anyway—except of course for the push/mash and ill/mad conflicts, bless their hearts.

Speaking of southern/northern, three times in just one week I have been told that I now speak with a slight yet noticeable southern drawl. This news came from both the southern and northern hemispheres of my life and I am well-pleased, y'all.

I am grateful for elastic-waist pants and stretchy fabrics and heeled shoes that give the illusion of longer legs because I am also very, very grateful for flour, sugar, and butter concoctions I can't seem to stop baking. Oh, and figs—I am so grateful for figs. They make wonderful jam and baby boy dog Levi was found under a farm fig tree.

Levi, the adopted four-legged stepbrother mentioned earlier has taken up huge space in my heart. He is also much huger than I expected him to be. His best trick is "sit." Actually, it's his only trick, but he does it very well. Unfortunately, I can't get him to stop biting my hand in anticipation of getting treats whenever he sits, jumps, leaps, runs, or chases his doggy siblings around the yard or through the house on those rare occasions when he makes it through the back door. Forgiveness and forgetfulness come in mighty handy these days. I am so grateful he is with us. This sentiment is not, however, shared with his step-siblings that are terrified he might stay and are not the least bit forgiving of his presence in their terrier-tory.

I am even grateful this month for the palmetto bugs. Their scurrying shell-like bodies with hinged appendages make me very aware that I am indeed still agile enough to jump around and scream at the same time I'm blindly swatting them into oblivion. I can even forgive them for playing dead until I reach down to toss them in the trash can, at which time they spring to life and I, once again, discover my youthful agility—so far, anyway.

All things considered, even the lack of gift-buying progress, I am grateful for November's Thanksforgivingness. In fact, it might just be time to let go of some of those Christmas gifting traditions anyway. I've recently heard about some wonderful alternatives like making charitable donations. It spreads the love and eliminates the wrapping paper and bows. It also helps turn the focus toward Thanksforgivingness for yet another month of the year. That can't be wrong, can it?

# *Thanksgrieving*

*November 2014*

Every Thanksgiving holiday we try to share what we are most thankful for during the past year. The operative word in that sentence, by the way, is TRY. Some years we do better than others. And some years there is a definite lack of trying. Oh, we're always thankful for many things but the eloquence with which we convey that thanks waxes and wanes much like the phases of the moon. It might have something to do with the presentation efforts, or lack thereof. My adult children and their accompanying guests tend to groan loudly when I pull out the thanking stones and the stamped cards that say "I am thankful for..." along with the ever-popular gratitude tree.

Oddly enough, we did a really good job during those few years when it was difficult to remember even the meaning of thankfulness—when losses and hard changes were much easier to identify. Mostly though we repeat the same old stuff—which, in and of itself, is not a bad thing. We continue to be blessed by fairly good health, good friends, and good senses of humor. The humor thing comes in very handy when said children decide to make fun of mom's well-worn Thanksgiving crafts. Hmmpff. The turkey hands just never get too old for me. And the gobbler-head cookies always get devoured well before we turn the calendar page to December.

When abundance overflows, we have a difficult time locating the thankful words. It is during those years when the groaning far outweighs the gratitude that we have really shared the most thankfulness. When there are hard times all around and a seemingly dry well of blessings, we can find at least something for which to be thankful. Why is that? Are we so consumed by our gifts that we just can't put them into words or is it that the counting of blessings is more easily accomplished when there are only a very few of them, or others in our lives are experiencing horrendous losses?

For example, I find myself giving thanks over and over again this month for the gift of a reasonably healthy husband (we don't count the knees anymore, or the gaseous digestive tract). I am especially thankful for him now because of the recent sudden death of a thirty-nine-year-old father of two beautiful little girls. He was the husband of a former coworker who is now left without the love of her life and must deal with the seemingly impossible task of grieving while parenting.

Fortunately, she is surrounded by faith, family, and friends who have enveloped her and her girls in a protective bubble of love and support. Their community (in Fluvanna County, Virginia) raised over $25,000 in less than a day through a website called gofundme.com and she has been gifted with nightly meals into 2015, thanks to an online program called TakeThemAMeal.com. I find myself being thankful now even for the Internet—the thing that sucks up too much of my "free" time in pursuit of connectivity and projects and news and writing resources and other superfluous stuff. It was, after all, through the accessibility of the worldwide web that both the funds and the food were provided to the family. So, thank you, Internet—and thank you, Fluvanna County for showing us how a community can respond in the worst of times by providing the best of practical supportive measures.

But this much-too-young grieving wife and mother is left to face a holiday season without the man God chose as her partner and father of her children. I still remember the day of their wedding when the minister addressed the crowd of happy witnesses and shared his thoughts on how he determines which couples standing before him will share stronger unions. It is not the two who gaze longingly into each other's eyes. It is those who instead look together in the same direction toward

God, putting His love first. And this couple was surely of that strong variety.

So what now? How does the one remaining move forward with a thankful heart? Perhaps she does not attempt to even fathom the answer to that question just yet. Perhaps she will be thankful just to make it through the season, the day, and the next hour. But thankful she will be. There is just something about the depth of grief that allows us to soldier on in spite of our natural desire to fall into an even deeper black hole. Or maybe it is the witnessing of others' grief that allows us to truly see our own blessings. I really don't know.

All I know right now is that this young woman is grieving even while she is surrounded by so many who love her and care for her. And it is beyond sad to know that her loss gives us such great reason to be thankful for our own lives. As we are taught, there is no promise of a tomorrow or even a next hour. The importance of that lesson sometimes gets lost in our daily little messes. It too often takes, unfortunately, the sudden shattering of our life windows to bring us to our knees—in prayer for others and for ourselves.

From personal experience (that all of us have had or will have), I can share that there is always a gift to be found in the grieving. For me, it was found in the freedom to pursue faith when all else had miserably failed. But my spouse was not taken so suddenly, and not so young—nor were my children such little ones. What can possibly be the reason for this kind of grief? Perhaps it is to turn us in His direction, to know without a doubt that there is a reason—somewhere. It may not even be known in our lifetime, or theirs. But we always have the choice to accept in thankfulness or deny in bitterness everything we receive and everyone we lose.

Of course there is that song lyric that tells us "only the good die young." Even Dr. Seuss gave us some help toward Thanks-grieving when he penned the words "Don't cry because it's over; smile because it happened." But I suppose the very best help, as usual, comes from scripture. Certainly, she already knows it—but sometimes the journey of grief takes its good old time getting us to the place where we can live what we already know is true. Thanks-grieving is a difficult dance step to learn—especially when you feel as if you are always moving backwards and teetering on very high heels, much like Ginger Rogers. But the tune is, for all of us, so very familiar—whether it is loss of loved one, or job, or health, or wealth, or way.

'And will she succeed? Oh yes, she will indeed. It is 98.75 percent guaranteed.' But how? Perhaps, when we can allow ourselves to be guided by the Living Word toward grace and peace, we find that thanks-grieving is possible and, arguably, necessary. So may our grieving always move us toward thanksgiving, even when it seems impossible for such a thing to happen? Perhaps it can start with some of these: Romans 5:1–5, Romans 8:28, Jeremiah 29:11, Psalm 94:18–19, James 1:2–5, and, especially for Amanda, Psalm 68:4–6.

# Sparkle & Glow

*November 2016*

Some extraordinary women sparkle. Some glow. And we all know some of each, don't we? And probably even a few that don't do either. No sparkle. No glow. Maybe just some glittery bits, tossed about willy-nilly. It's usually easier to pick out the sparklers though because they, well, they sparkle aplenty. They are also known as extraverts. According to extensive and mostly trusted research on personality types, the extravert gains energy from others. They sparkle when surrounded by people, energized by what is outside them. They almost literally plug in to those around them in order to fire up their sparkle.

Katherine Briggs and Isabel Briggs-Myers (a mother/daughter team of psychologists), aided by a strong foundation of research from Dr. Carl Jung, determined that there are basically sixteen distinct personality types. Any Psychology 101 course will give you the data on which they built their long-lasting and often cited type analysis. Do ESFJ, ESTJ, ENFJ, ENTJ, ESFP, ESTP, ENFP, and ENTP sound familiar?

Those who glow, on the other hand, tend to gain energy from inside them—it is an internal flame rather than an external shimmer. Both are equally extraordinary in their own ways, while sparklers (extraverts) tend to have an easier time gaining and maintaining their sparkle—there are many more of them in society—as any inner glow person can tell you. Inner glowers tend to be less talkative, quieter (unless you could hear the volume of noise going on inside their heads, that is—I know this to be true, being myself a glowworm). For their "types," simply replace the "E" with an "I" from the list above. Simple enough—and oh so fascinating to only weirdos like me, I suspect.

But the extravert and introvert, or the sparkle and glow aspects are only one portion of the "equation" that makes up our unique personalities—and none of us fit precisely into any one of the sixteen types. We each have our own specially blended recipe. But, for the purpose of discussing extraordinary women, we'll keep it at the sparkle and glow distinctions for now.

November marks the much-anticipated month for celebration of Extraordinary Women—some that glow softly from within and some that sparkle beautifully from outside. All are extraordinary in their own ways. And, after the arrival of Hurricane Matthew in early October, each woman (or man) reading this magazine is an extraordinary being, whether nominated earlier in the year or not.

Therefore, we interrupt this sparkle and glow thing to bring you a much different "message." After many months of bemoaning the country life on Green Acres—as in distance to grocery stores, snakes in the kitchen, and such—I have come to realize that it is a most wonderful place to be. When you are at risk of losing something, you tend to appreciate it all the more—slithers and everything.

Right now, today, it is time for me to be thankful. We can't wait until that one day, the fourth Thursday in November, to be grateful and count our blessings. Nope. Not now. So many people have lost so much. And it's not just the things and precious mementos. It is the loss of safe haven, of a harbor in the storm that must be so devastating. I am able to write to you from a very thankful nest—one with drinkable and flushable water, and electric power, after only four days of darkness. We only had one day of being "trapped" on the dirt road when the branch water rose high enough to block our only drivable exit. Just one day—twenty-four hours.

When we were able to get out, we saw exactly how fortunate we are. The ride down Route 917 became a nightmare of flooded homes and ever-rising waters. Days later, our neighbors in Nichols and Fair Bluff and Fork Retch and many other places saw their homes literally floating away. Others had trees blown onto and into their roofs. Electric poles and wires wrapped around those trees and snaked to the ground, carrying all forms of communication down with them. The roads in Mullins and Marion resembled a toddler's dinner tray after a first-time forage into eating spaghetti and broccoli. Snarled and tangled messes of wires and phone lines littered, and in many cases, closed the roads.

I have never before seen the underbellies of huge old trees. I hope never to see that again. It was an obscene view—like something we are never supposed to gaze upon. The sheer nakedness and splayed out desperation of those living things was horrific. Animals and pets of all kinds were lost in the storm. There was just so much chaos, so much undefinable loss.

And then the heroes began to emerge—those extraordinary people who risk life and limb to save others, to restore order, to reconnect us to "normal life." They surely sparkle and glow from without and from within. They are the first responders, the police officers, the linemen, the elected officials trying to recreate order in our lives. They are all extraordinary. And they are not alone in their efforts.

Every person who checked on a neighbor, who offered their home for haven, who wielded a chainsaw or maintained contact with those who were alone, those who navigated boats on waters that overflowed beyond anyone's memory—they too are extraordinary. You know who you are. You may sparkle or you may glow, but you are indeed extraordinary.

To those who found it necessary to complain—you are forgiven by those who had it much worse. That's just the way things are, once you have lived through a nightmare. Differences of opinion and personality fall away and are washed clean by the sheer gratitude of having air to breathe, a dry change of clothes, and a warm meal. The Carolinas are strong and will be stronger still after Matthew is a fading memory. I, for one, am so grateful to be a resident here.

By the time this magazine is published in November, there will be so many more reasons to be thankful for more than the usual turkey and dressing and gravy and pecan pie. I pray that those who lost their homes will have begun the rebuild or restore process. I pray that moving on efforts are being made with thankful hearts. We can all do our parts to help in those efforts—whether it is lending a hand or offering space in our homes or providing needed supplies or a dinner out or an encouraging word from His Word.

We can all find ways to sparkle and glow like the extraordinary people who are being celebrated this month. From my very thankful nest, I pray for peace within and without the storms of this life. And I thank God for every little piece of joy that has yet to be found, the little sparkles and glows just waiting to be discovered.

And coffee–I thank our God for warm, delicious coffee. And smart phones that can be charged in a truck without wasting gas. And for air fresheners that mask the odor escaping from a too-long silent refrigerator. And I thank God for you and yours—friends, family, neighbors, and strangers.

*Praise God from whom all blessings flow.*
*Praise Him all creatures here below.*
*Praise Him above ye heavenly hosts.*
*Praise Father, Son, and Holy Ghost.*

# Winter Season in the She Shed

**Gifts Differing, Resolutions & Love Stories**

*She extends a helping hand to the poor and opens her arms to the needy. She has no fear of winter for her household, for everyone has warm clothes.*

—Proverbs 31:20–21 (NLT)

December

**Gifts Differing**
**The Christmas Witch**
**Into the River & Out of the Woods**
**Santa-cipation**
**A Very Married Christmas**
**Gift Wrapped Words**

*C*hristmas was fully celebrated each December issue, and gifts of all kinds were on topic—usually of the nonmaterial kind. The issue was always highly anticipated, or Santa-cipated, if you will.

# Gifts Differing

December 2007

When I wath thelebrating my thickth Christmath, all I really wanted was my two front teeth. As a great fan of corn on the cob, I just knew that if I didn't see some new white bumps emerging from my vacant upper gums for Christmas, I'd be doomed to sit and wait another summer while Mom carefully cut off those juicy kernels meant only to be slathered with butter and gnawed off the cob in a left to right typewriter motion. When the kernels are cut from the cob with a knife, all the fun gets cut off too. And I don't care what anyone else says, it's just not natural to chew around the cob. Besides, if you eat around instead of by row, you lose the opportunity to say ding every time you reach the end and slide back over to begin again. Eating around the cob is for thithies.

As I careened through my teen Christmas years, all I really wanted was to be left alone, please—unless, of course, the phone rang and it was for me (the phone attached permanently to the wall by a long, curly cord, with a rotary dial and a party line. Oh, and maybe bell bottom pants and a mini skirt and a few more Beatles records. (Yes, records—the flat discs with a little hole in its middle that spun round and round and played music while grabbing up every stray ball of fluff in the air so that one had to gently and carefully pluck the fur balls off its diamond head needle before playing another song.) That's where the being left alone gift wish came in—all I really desired back then was to sway to the music, dance around, and sing along using a hairbrush as makeshift microphone and dream of one day marrying one of those British mop headed musicians. I also desired never to be caught at a red light on a hill while attempting to look oh so cool in that stick-shifted VW bug handed down from my oldest sister.

During my twenties, the Christmas wish lists consisted mostly of cash requests—to pay the rent, to make car and insurance payments, to pay the credit card bill that I should not have even had except that plastic was so much more convenient (until the bill arrived). When one leans toward service careers, debt always seems to become you. I also wished for a diamond during one or two of those years—or at least a promise of life-long love and commitment. Oh stop judging. I wasn't that far removed from the influences of Ward and June Cleaver, you know. Blame them and their perfect little TV lives—burning bras and being a career gal were also popular themes in my twenties—talk about your opposing forces.

The thirties were spent trying desperately to make the holidays for my own children joyful, meaningful, and full of Norman Rockwell memories while purposefully attempting to avoid the pull of Teddy Ruxpin and Cabbage Patch doll and Teenage Mutant Ninja Turtles mania. My little darlings settled for handed down power wheels and the occasional advertising hypes. They, of course, will tell you that their lives were forever scarred by not having the latest and greatest toys. I have learned to ignore their bleating about easy bake ovens and nerf guns deprivation.

Then along came the forties, with their own special little wish lists. Had it not been for those few remaining shreds of decency, I'm sure that I would have put antidepressants near the top of each yearly list, along with a sharp axe and a little dynamite to rid myself of certain annoying acquaintances (bosses, husband, children, friends of children, family, friends of family, etc.). Truly, all around me were lucky to have survived the conflagration of menopause and teenage rebellions sparking and arcing under the same volatile roof. Christmas? Bah! Humbug! Phooey! Who cares what the tree looks like? Make your own darned cookies if you want them so badly. And, no, you may not take the car tonight to go "caroling" with your friends. Do you think that I'm a total idiot parent? (Don't answer that one.)

Fortunately, the fifties arrived in the Saint Nick of time. There was a renewed sense of awe and wonder with Decembers (also, there was not a single teenager stirring about in the house.). I began to wish for more global gifts like peace on earth, good will toward all, and please, Lord, let there be no more trips to the local mall. Then came that one horrible Christmas when cancer was the gift received, followed the next year by a hopeful remission. And, most terribly, last Christmas, when the wish was to please, somehow, just let us make it through the holiday together without that man we all missed so much. And, we did. I am still grateful for the receipt of that gift and the promise that came with it as 2007 unfolded.

Now, what about this year? What do I really and truly want for Christmas? That's easy. All I wish for is to recognize and use the gifts already received and live quietly in the grace of gifts yet to come—the many gifts of joy and understanding and peace and comfort and fellowship and love that arrived the moment life truly began again. I wish it for all of us. For inspiration in that quest, I looked to Romans 12:6 "Having then gifts differing according to the grace that is given to us, whether prophecy, let us prophesy according to the proportion of faith." I also found guidance in 1 Corinthians 12:4–7, 1 Corinthians 7:7, and 1 Peter 4:10.

And, if it's not too much to ask, I hear that Paul McCartney is singing a newly single tune, so I guess I'd also like to revisit that Christmas wish of my sixteenth year. Oh, and thanks for those front teeth. If I find a whitener in my stocking that might help peel back the years, I'd appreciate that, too.

# The Christmas Witch

*December 2008*

As I was searching for inspiration for the merry best-Christmas-ever issue and turning over all the memory stones in my head, I poked around a little in the rubble of the article written last year. It mentioned many sad truths and happy rememberings of Christmas Past and great hope for finding and using our differing gifts.

This season I find myself at a crossroad—joyful in faith, yet somewhat concerned for what I have, or have not, done with it this year. In the search for meaning and understanding, I perhaps have been sinking too deeply in the quagmire of questing for knowledge. When we dig deeply we really can pull out the plums, but we can also get hopelessly stuck in the pie. Don't get me wrong, it's a wonderful pie in which to be stuck, but the operative word here is "stuck." Am I just a little too busy trying to grasp the meanings and not active enough in the doings? Am I, as usual, missing the theme of this Christmas issue? Probably.

Okay, where were we? Right, we're choosing the very best Christmas memory ever. This is a most difficult task. I remember parts of many Christmas seasons. I remember being fearful that Santa might catch me awake, thus spoiling any hope of finding Chatty Cathy or Betsy Wetsy under the tinsel-laden tree. I recall wishing I could be one of Santa's helpers so I could rightfully snack on the gingerbread cookie lounging on that plate by the tree. Then there was the year I was finally old enough to attend Midnight Mass. The combination of burning incense and eggnog-breathed, over-perfumed parishioners, and too many cookie raids from the tin in the kitchen earlier in the day brought forth a rather violent reaction in the car on the way back home. As a teenager, I felt compelled to express my displeasure at not getting clothes from stores one particularly moody Christmas morning (and what I would give now for a hand knit sweater or Mom-made dress). That year signaled the unfortunate birth of the Christmas Witch.

Let's fast forward to the year my husband surprised me with an exercise bike shortly after the birth of our second child in fifteen months. I cried for hours. What was he thinking? Turns out he was thinking only of me. After I stopped shrieking and sobbing, he reminded me that all I had complained about for the past three months was how fat and flabby I had become. He also reminded me that each time I whined about it, he confirmed how beautiful I was to him, just the way I was (fat and flabby, let's be real). He loved all of me. That, unfortunately, was quite the load to carry. It only took me another seven months and three thousand miles on that stupid bike to almost forgive him for gifting me the think I said I wanted but truly hoped I didn't need. An ungrateful and grudge holding witch was I. What a prize wife.

Of course, this was the same husband who decided earlier in our marriage to go Christmas shopping with his firefighting buddy twenty-four hours before the actual day arrived. The gifts received that year included a sweater vest that looked very much like the fuzzy maroon material that covered toilet tanks back in the seventies. Was I gracious about it? I was indeed, if you consider it gracious to run out of the room laughing hysterically and swearing I would never, ever be caught dead wearing that thing in public or in private. There was no attitude of gratitude on that Christmas Day. I could have instead been thankful that he had survived a particularly nasty series of fires in DC that year. But no, I was focused on the ugliness of that toilet tank sweater gift purchased at the last minute and probably between hearty hoists at the local pub. Cheers? I think not.

Then there was the Christmas I wanted to channel my mother and bake wonderful cut-out cookies for my precious little children. Okay, I also wanted to eat those little bells and trees and gingerbread men, but let's not dwell on my sugar addiction right now. Let's just say that, instead of a Hallmark memory moment for my littles, they instead cringe to this day when I bring out a rolling pin. The flashbacks of thrown dough and spewed expletives hurled by their otherwise sweet mother are still much too vivid. They also tell me the smell of a Christmas Cookie scented candle still brings on nightmares. Go figure.

Speaking of horrible dreams, has anyone besides me experienced that recurring Christmas morning waking terror? You know, it's the one where you wake up that morning only to discover that you have not decorated the tree or stuffed the stockings or wrapped the gifts or made the breakfast casserole or baked the cookies or set out the plate for Santa or tucked special treasures under the pillows of your sleeping angels, and now everyone is staring at you in horror and disbelief as they accuse you of singlehandedly, and with malice aforethought, accomplishing the task of totally wrecking Christmas for everyone, forever? Then you wake up in a cold sweat only to realize it is December 5, not 25, and you still have time to get it all done. The sad truth is that I continued to have this same dream many years after my sleeping angels awakened and transformed into surly teenagers and even adults with their own homes.

So here we are at the end of our time together and I still haven't managed to complete the task of describing the best Christmas ever. The witch kept getting in the way. Maybe it's time to ditch her and reach forward in the hope of creating new memories. Perhaps it is the Christmas yet to come that will be the best one ever. Maybe each December twenty-fifth brings us a new kind of wonderful—one where we remember its true meaning. Perhaps it is in the doing and sharing that the real gifts and lasting memories appear. Having faith is one thing; living it and sharing it is quite another thing. So I will still go to the kitchen this Christmas, but, Lord, please help me to stop flinging dough and start building instead a humble pie using only the fruit of the Spirit: love, joy, peace, patience, kindness, goodness, faithfulness, gentleness, and self-control. Better double up on the portions for that last ingredient too. As for the Christmas Witch, may God shout to her soul and pierce her heart with His words. May He linger with her over breakfast each morning and gently guide her to sleep each night. And may His presence be all the gift she ever needs.

# Into the River and Out of the Woods

*December 2010*

A few years ago I wrote about a wonderful Saturday afternoon spent paddling down (or was that up?) the Lumber River to the Little Pee Dee with a fun-loving group of guys and gals from church. Talk about gifts differing. Let's just say there were varying degrees of paddle savvy displayed on that lovely warm day. My paddle partner and I, for example, came to shore about an hour after the lead canoe (show-offs) landed at the destination point and, yes, we all had started at the same time and place. Our team managed to ram the pilings on our way in. Fortunately, the deck about remained intact. Can't quite say the same for our dignity, but it was still a wonderful afternoon of fun and fellowship surrounded by the stunning evidence of God's creation. There's just something about a river's glistening glow, framed by blue skies and brilliant sunshine—and frantic paddling.

On a more recent Sunday afternoon in November, some of that same group gathered once again on the shores of the Little Pee Dee, but this time they were minus canoes and paddles. Their differing gifts were still very much in evidence. Some new friends had been added and some old friends joined in as well. We gathered at the river but for a very different purpose. One little member of the group had decided that the second Sunday in November would be a perfectly lovely day for a dunking, for a public expression of faith, for letting go of the past and pressing on to a future dedicated to living in His light and joy to the Word. (Consider Philippians 3:12–14.)

The obvious question on the minds of the gathered group was something like this: Did it have to happen in the middle of November after a serious cold snap had made the river waters dangerously chilly? Evidently, it was in His timing alone. As the pastor shared a few thoughts on the meaning of baptism, the dunkee, decked out in overalls over tights, sweatshirt over thermals over T-shirt, and Crocs with woolly socks, had a chance to view those surrounding her (those facing the river and forming a tight wall against any possibility of escape) in the bright light of an afternoon sun.

Her boss was there with her grandson and a family friend, having left their own Sunday services early—a service being ministered by another grandson—so she could witness the dunking of her employee and friend and sister in faith. The dunkee's closest friends were there—those who gather together in good times and bad and everything in between—those three who gathered the night before to celebrate this occasion over pizza and salad and scrumptious desserts. One of those three was largely responsible for the event even taking place—the one who refused to let a sister wallow in self-pity and grief and self-doubt.

There were members of a new family standing beside those who brought her here—a family of believers that welcomed a new sister without hesitation and with great humor and love, from Revelation Ministries. The paddlers stood together too, along with those who also shared in the paddling through God's Word in self-confrontation classes at Mullins First Baptist Church. All had a part in bringing thie dunkee to this place along the river on this particular day.

And there was her beloved one waiting with a camera to capture the moment of impact and a towel to capture the drippings and to wrap her in the warmth of love—the kind of love that accepts a person as they are and where they are and waits patiently for Christ to show her the way, while living his own life by way of example. Thank you Lord for such a gift as these fine people placed exactly when and where they were (and are still) needed.

She placed the rocks of old remembrance in the pocket of her overalls—the rocks of unforgiveness, lack of faith, anger, resentments, excuses, comparisons—and walked into the nearly freezing waters of the Little Pee Dee River with her pastor. The rocks and the old life were left in the river's bed and she waded out of the waters and into the life meant to be led and into the waiting arms of one good man and the rejoicing of her new family and her old friends and fellow paddlers.

As you have likely surmised, the one who died to self and was raised to new life was me. Logical thinking is not my strong suit. Decision-making does not come easily and this one was surely no exception. But I am not too goofy to grasp the lessons learned by this public profession of faith and believer's baptism on a November afternoon in and out of a very chilly river. Do not hesitate in your faith decisions. Boldly go—even if you freeze your Crocs off.

Perhaps the larger point at the end of this 2010 year is that it happened at all and was witnessed by people I treasure so dearly in this new life. The greater joy may have been to have my children and family on the riverbank as well, but it is my hope that they will continue to see how Christ has changed mom and sister and daughter and aunt into a person who walks by faith—surely stumbling along the way, but leaving the weighty stones of the past in the river of life. In this season of giving, when we celebrate the birth of our Lord and Savior, may we find joy in new beginnings and emerge from our past into the light of a new life. It's not really the dunking that matters so much. We can figuratively wade into the river and come out of the woods by faith in a journey with our Savior.

Today is always a gift. That's why it's called the present. May the New Year bring you peace and joy and love and warmer waters. Merry Christmas!

# Santa-Cipation

*December 2013*

> *"Well," said Pooh, "what I like best—" and then he had
> to stop and think. Because although Eating Honey was
> a very good thing to do, there was a moment just before
> you began to eat it which was better than when you
> were, but he didn't know what it was called.*

—Winnie the Pooh/A. A. Milne

There's really not much point in going any further (but we both know I will). Winnie the Pooh has nailed the description of sweet anticipation. He just couldn't come up with the exact word for it. Now the end of our calendar year brings with it great anticipation—whether for Santa or for a New Year. Some of us can't get enough of 2013 and some of us are quite anxious for 2014 to begin.

As a child I remember loving Christmas Eve probably a little bit more than Christmas Day—and of course we're talking about the Santa thing—but not entirely. Growing up Catholic, we had a keen sense of what Christmas was all about—the Blessed Virgin Mother, of course. Seriously, we did celebrate the birth of our Savior, but when I was little (and probably not so little, if I'm honest about it); Santa also played a big jolly, jiggly part in our December calendar.

I mean, what else is an Advent calendar for if not to breathlessly await the day we get to open up the December 24 door and rejoice that Christmas Day is only one more day away? What I missed was the true meaning of that calendar—waiting on the day a child is born that is Christ the King. Now I know better. Much better. But let's reminisce for just a little while.

I remember lying in bed, wearing my new Christmas Eve jammies, trying to will myself to sleep—because I knew for sure Santa wouldn't come down the chimney if I remained awake. He would know my mind was still active, even if my eyes were squeezed shut. I also knew I could not get out of bed. This was especially painful on the years I snuck a second ginger ale before lights out. I also know now that this was a parental tactic to keep us abed while "Santa" delivered gifts. I know this because I used the very same guerilla warfare on my own two precious tykes years later. Evidently, they did not succumb so easily to the dreaded reindeer attack and Santa warning stories. I must have been quite the little wimpy kid. Perhaps it was the four older sisters' threats.

Christmas brings many Santa-cipation memories—like waiting to see what's lurking at the bottom of the stocking and hoping that big bulge isn't just an orange again. But it's not just at Christmas that we can experience that sweet moment of anticipation, like Pooh right before he dips his paw in the honeypot and raises it, dripping with sweetness, to his lips. (Wait. Do bears have lips? Oh bother.)

There are the moments right before the curtain rises and actors wait for their cues. There are the waiting moments right after the National Anthem is sung, and right before the whistle blows, for athletes. For dessert lovers, there is that moment of blissful waiting, as the fork or spoon, laden with goodness, sweeps toward the tongue—or maybe it's the unwrapping of a chocolate kiss or candy cane. For artists, it is perhaps the moment right before the brush taps the canvas. For the unemployed, it could be the wait just before opening the envelope or answering the phone—for the one that says, "Yes, you're hired." For book lovers, it is the turning of that first page to begin a new story, or for writers it may be that blank page waiting for its first word. For young love, it may be the moment just before that first kiss (and it is the same for old love too—I can assure you).

And sometimes it is in the waiting moments that we find, not the sweetness of Santa-cipation at Christmas, but we discover that sanctification is on the way. As we work toward walking in His way, we sometimes fall or take steps backward, but the goal remains and keeps us moving in the direction of His light—that place in time, somewhere along the broken road, that gives us hope for tomorrow.

"Wait on the Lord; be of good courage, And He shall strengthen your heart; Wait, I say, on the Lord!" (Ps. 27:14).

In the NKJV Bible, there are 144 references to *wait*. Most are found in Job, Psalms, Proverbs, and Isaiah. Fewer than forty are in the New Testament. What does that mean?

Are we not waiting so much anymore? I don't think so. We continue to wait now for His second arrival—but perhaps the emphasis has shifted from simply waiting on the Lord to doing for the Lord.

"But those who wait on the Lord Shall renew their strength; they shall mount up with wings like eagles, they shall run and not be weary, they shall walk and not faint" (Isa. 40:31).

Absolutely! And in the New Testament we also find what we are to do while we are waiting on the Lord. It's not just about anticipating desserts or games or plays or finished canvasses, or first kisses, or even anticipating His return.

We are to "go therefore and make disciples of all the nations, baptizing them in the name of the Father and of the Son and of the Holy Spirit, teaching them to observe all things that I have commanded you; and lo, I am with you always, even to the end of the age" (Matt. 28:19–20). Amen.

There is, believe it or not, another Pooh quote that seems to fit here perfectly, so we'll start and finish with the bear's words, knowing full well that it is God's Word we follow. Could it be that the author of Pooh's life had a divine inspiration as guide? It may seem that way.

"You can't stay in your corner of the Forest waiting for others to come to you. You have to go to them sometimes" (Winnie the Pooh, A. A. Milne).

May we all have a Merry Christmas and peace-filled New Year, as we wait upon the Lord.

# A Very Married Christmas

*December 2014*

*I* am learning quite a bit in this new and temporarily part-time country life (which will become fulltime just as soon as he can pry my cold, dead fingers from the weekly trash pickup truck). For example, I have learned that the Food Lion is no longer a mile away from home. It is now thirty minutes away, in any direction. So planning is important to survival. Lists must be made in advance and strictly adhered to, so as not to run out of the precious Dew nectar or any other zero calorie deliciousness. Hence I've begun "making a list and checking it twice," leaving it on the counter and turning around to retrieve it, not "laughing all the way."

I am learning that Nabs are not made by Nabisco, as my city-dweller brain had so wrongly concluded. They are made by a guy named Lance, who also makes other interesting concoctions that are unfortunately not sold at my not-so-local-any-more favorite big-box store (the one with the bullseye logo). Fortunately though, they are available just about everywhere else—which is a very good thing since they are consumed in rather vast quantities on a very regular basis. And not by me.

I am learning that holiday meals always include rice in the country, and not the northern mashed potatoes my fully grown children have come to expect. Last year was a bit of a disaster regarding this rule, especially after one child drove all the way from Maryland for mashed potatoes and gravy, only to be met with rice and what her traveling companion thought was mashed potatoes. After topping them with gravy and sending a spoonful to her unsuspecting mouth, she discovered that the "taters" were actually soft, warm potato salad—a family recipe that does not go with gravy. Ever. Sadly, she will not be joining us again this year.

A very married Christmas must now include all three side items so as to please both north and south. The gravy will be optional, but will not include gizzards or innards of any kind. Nor will the stuffing include hearts or livers. Sorry. I can only do so much so soon with such changes. I just hope Santa won't be confused this year about our dual citizenship in Marion and Horry counties. "Hanging the stockings by the chimney with care" will not be possible now, as we have no chimney. I wonder if the back deck will do. I wonder if the wild dogs will scare him off. I wonder if the black bears in the backwoods will be drawn to the scent of sugar cookies and "visions of sugarplums dance in their heads" as they maul their way into the side door.

Yep. I am learning a lot about a very married life in the country. It is quite similar to married life in the "city," only it's closer to the beach and much darker at night. It is, however, no less real. In fact, it is quite enjoyable and offers many good-to-follow examples of successful and sustaining married life. Case in point: we recently attended a sixtieth birthday celebration for one Rendel Mincey (the man with a huge heart and a practical joker's wit) given by his wife and family.

Mr. Willoughby had been invited to participate as a roaster—a role, I have come to learn, he is quite well-suited to play. My first reaction, of course, was to whine loudly and long that I would know no one and have to sit all alone in a corner sucking my city thumb while everyone else enjoyed great fun and togetherness at the Pleasant View Baptist Church fellowship hall because they surely have known each other forever.

As usual, I was wrong on several counts. First, I actually knew a few of the partygoers. Okay, four out of over a hundred is not bad for a city slicker transplant from the north surrounded by folks who mostly grew up around each other and see each other on a regular basis, and still seem to genuinely appreciate each other. Second, I really enjoyed the celebration and only sucked my thumb once when a little glob of icing fell on it. Or maybe twice—when Mr. Willoughby decided to tell one of the stories that I had asked him not to share. The ride home was just a little bit frostier than the weather outside the truck. Fortunately, I am also learning forgiveness. Besides, it was a rather amusing story—if you dislike rabbits.

So, what does this have to do with a very married Christmas? Well, it points my stubborn self to the receiving of gifts in the most unlikely places. Attending that birthday celebration "over the river and through the woods" taught me that there are examples of successful marriages and wonderfully gifted and talented people right in my own new backyard and it made me begin to feel like I just might fit into this new place after all. We may not share much (or any) history, but we certainly share at least a few things in common—faith, family, and a great appreciation for laughter. I hope their Christmas will be very merry indeed. I know my very married one will be, as long as there will be mashed potatoes alongside the rice on the table, and a certain stuffed Roaster sitting beside me.

Maybe this move from city to country is part of those major adjustments discussed during a recent (and difficult) study of experiencing God. I have certainly experienced a crisis of belief over it. But, if it brings us into closer loving relationship with our God, how can it not be the right action in faith? Perhaps I should also consider adding those innards to the stuffing this year. Or maybe we'll have some rabbit stew and invite a certain sixty-year-old and his lovely wife over to share it with us during the New Year. Or maybe we'll just invite them to join us at one of the fast-food places in Conway for another pleasant-view stroll down memory lane.

Wishing you and yours a very merry Christmas!

# *Gift Wrapped Words*

*December 2017*

It never ceases to amaze me the power that words can have over us. What is it, really, that makes us nearly swoon when hearing "I love you" or "You are beautiful"? Okay, I have seldom heard that second one, but I'm pretty sure it would be swoon worthy to the ears. Of course, the other end of the word spectrum can have an equally devastating effect—those words spoken in anger or bitterness or jealousy. It makes me cringe just thinking about the giving and receiving of those word bombs. Are they gifts? Not a chance—unless they spur us to positive action or change (or retreat).

In this December season of giving, our words can become the greatest of gifts—if only we would just speak them or write them out and send them. We are so very busy gathering our thoughts and our to-do lists and our shopping and decorating chores that our thoughts can get lost amid the hustle and bustle of preparation for this joyous season. The tree must be trimmed. The menu must be created. The wrappings must be perfect. Blah, blah, blah—it makes me tired just typing this stuff. And sometimes those beautiful words don't ever get wrapped up in a sentence that anyone ever hears or reads.

Of course, words without action to follow can be quite hollow and bereft of meaning. We can speak of our faith, for example, or that we will surely pray for you, but if we don't follow by doing the actual thing we talk about, there's a resounding thud at the end of our sweetly spoken words. It's that thud that can get us in serious trouble. The thud of silence

251

after "let's get together over the holidays" is spoken and not achieved leaves the hearer disappointed or disgruntled or possibly delighted (depends on the temperament, I suppose).

How many people do we need to thank this season for being our friend, our confidante, our nonjudgmental ear? How many spouses need to hear just what they mean to us? How many children crave our attention and conversation with undistracted fervor? Is there a parent or sibling or neighbor out there, just waiting to hear our voice—even if it's just to say, "Merry Christmas," or, "See you soon"? And when we toss out the well-worn "how are you?" maybe we ought to actually wait for the answer and follow up with another question or two.

In this month of giving and joy, I will have the privilege of sharing a writing lesson with a group of (hopefully) eager fourth graders. We will be talking about gifts and talents and how we see ourselves as writers or not. This should prove to be quite interesting, as there are more boys in the class than girls and, if memory serves, the boys are generally not too keen on the written word thing. We'll see what happens. I know I'm excited. I pray they will be at least mildly amused or enthused. The gnome hat and lighted Christmas bulb necklace ought to help, don't you think? Sometimes my general enthusiasm for words, words, words can be a bit off-putting (as in good golly, this *is so* boring). Anyway, prayers appreciated.

I know that letter writing, for example, is not a universally accepted form of communication. The written word has taken a back seat (like in the wheel well or trunk) to the quickness and ease of texting and clicking and picture posting. And, so we're clear, I do not always agree that a picture is worth a thousand words—especially if it has been air brushed or cropped or altered in many ways. Snapchat and Instagram are great fun though. I don't use either, but I love to see the results during my old person Facebook newsfeed scrolls. Alas, I have also succumbed to the easy text communication process. And don't get me anywhere near a phone unless it's an emergency. Written words, people—only written, typed, or texted words, please.

An old-fashioned stamped envelope sitting in the mailbox is one of the greatest gifts, especially if it is not of the billing or advertisement variety. I'm thinking of the card or personal letter or birthday greeting kind of envelope. I don't even care if there's no message inside except a quick "Love, So and So." The time taken to choose a card, write a note, stamp, address and mail it (really, just figuring out the open hours at the post office is a feat of major proportion), is a gift so precious and so rare these days.

I used to be a prolific letter writer—back when I could find a pen and paper without forgetting what I was looking for as I searched from room to room, then stopped for a quick cookie break in the kitchen, then lost my glasses back in the den, then decided a text would be quicker—if only I could locate my cell phone and my dang glasses. So I'm also guilty of letting go of gift wrapped words too. But I'm determined to get back to it this coming year. Writing a letter a week should be a good start (and likely all the budget will allow since postage stamps will continue rising in price—they are already moving quickly to the half-dollar level).

Personal emails count too. There's great joy when one arrives overflowing with chatty news and updates from friends and family—and no need for a stamp either. Unfortunately, emails can be problematic if you send them to someone who does not have the same joy of receiving. This brings me to a horrible memory, but "talking" about it seems to help. When my husband and I were dating, I did not realize that he had a dislike for email communication and a complete disregard for my opposing view on the same subject. We had one of our worst, uh, discussions when he did not find it necessary to respond to my message in a timely fashion (as in days went by and I got madder by the minute). We've since worked through this jungle of emotion by being married and able to sit for long periods in the same room or same vehicle and not utter a single solitary word to each other (yes, I'm still a little miffed).

I suppose gift wrapped words are only as wonderful as the person receiving them believes them to be. I love writing them and receiving them. some people do not. Though that same some person always wants my help in finishing a crossword puzzle. Go figure. I guess the beauty of gift wrapped words (as in cards and letters and long lovely emails) is in the eye of the receiver. This is probably true of my other somewhat annoying habit of giving gifts to others that I would love to have myself, isn't it? Perhaps I should reconsider the stationary set for that person who shall not be named. No. Not when he's already decided that "we" need an exercise bike. Bah. Humbug.

Meanwhile, may the gift wrapped words of Christmas cheer be with you and yours throughout the year.

January

**J is for Joy**
**Loading the Resolver**
**The Biggest Loser**
**Kicking against the Pricks**
**The Selfie Shirt**
**The Hard Way**

*T*he beginning of a new calendar year included all kinds of resolutions and a focus on health and well-being. Exercise was a key topic, as was a promise to self for greater joys ahead.

# J is for Joy

*January 2008*

It seems like every New Year begins the same way. January ushers in a brand new set of resolves we seldom keep. According to a recent Research Publications, Inc. newsletter, we tend to share many similar resolutions. They say that our most popular New Year's goals are as follows:

Lose weight (because we keep on finding it?)

Get organized (because the only thing we can't lose is weight?)

Quit smoking (good luck on doing both weight and nicotine loss?)

Get or change jobs (because we need to pay for the food and smokes?)

Spend more time with family (a good excuse for more eating?)

Learn something new (like how to quit smoking and overeating?)

Eliminate or reduce debt (because we can't stop spending on food and smokes?)

Volunteer (less time for smoking and eating?)

These sound pretty familiar, don't they? We've been there and done that—and probably need to do some of those over and over again. I'm not sure how statistically accurate the list is, either, as I find it difficult to believe that exercising or getting fit was nowhere to be found on that list. From personal experience, I can say without hesitation that a life without exercise, at the very least, is a serious mood crusher. The lack of it also causes upper arms to slap one in the face repeatedly while attempting to wave at friends or hail a taxi or, god forbid, erase a blackboard. Besides, how will I face our aerobics instructor next session without mentioning this omission? Let's just agree to add exercise to the list of common resolutions and save me from the punishment of bouncing on those dreaded giant exercise balls for a whole class.

Deadlines being what they are, I was knee-deep in Christmas wrapping paper, cookie dough, and memories of stolen snowmen (that's a sad little tale for another day) while crafting these words, so I needed to make out my 2008 resolutions list in a big hurry or Santa might just skip over me this year. I needed quick inspiration and fast typing to meet the December writing cutoff. It occurred to me that there are seven letters in the word January and there are seven days in each week, so why not just come up with seven words to live by for 2008? It sure beats trotting out the old list from last year—the one created from the year before that. No wonder we all share so many of the same goals—we keep repeating them New Year after New Year. It really gets old, doesn't it? Anyway, here's my 2008 resolution word list:

*J* is for joy.

I will find joy in every day. It will be there, hidden like a treasure, inside the trials.

*A* is for attitude.

Old joke: What did the snail say when it caught a ride on the turtle's back? "Wheeee!" Attitude changes everything (or it might be perspective, but I needed an *A* word).

*N* is for nourishment.

All parts need it—mind, body, spirit. Books and puzzles for the mind, five food groups and water for the body, prayer and devotion for the spirit.

*U* is for understanding.

Differences are many—opinions, perspective, values, religion, and politics—the list is practically endless. Agreement isn't necessary or even possible, but there can always be understanding.

*A* is for altitude.

Regret looks back. Fear looks not. Faith looks up—always up. It is the best natural high altitude.

*R* is for relationships.

Create them. Nurture them. Renew them. Start with Jesus.

*Y* is for yes.

Is there any more powerful word to make a day sing? So, yes I can. Yes to life. Yes to faith and fellowship and yes, even, to chocolate chip cookies at least once in a while.

There you have it. My resolutions are joy, attitude, nourishment, understanding, altitude, relationships, and yes. Now here's a New Year challenge for you: Devise your own set of seven-word resolutions—the words you will choose to live by this New Year 2008. I don't presume to know or suggest what you might resolve to do or undo this year. I only know that, at least for me, limiting it to seven short words can be a good start in the up-word direction. Make sure to share them with trusted family and friends who will keep you accountable.

Happy New Year to you and yours! (Psst—that's a seven word sentence.)

# Loading the Resolver

*January 2013*

*O*h, be still, my heart! It's that time of year, once again, when we get to choose our New Year resolutions and then begin the painful countdown to how many days it takes us to feel guilty about not keeping them. Maybe it's just me, but at fifty-eight I'm starting to get rather cranky about resolutions. Come to think of it, I'm getting rather cranky about most things.

Research from the fascinating (and headache-inducing) website, Statistic Brain (www.statisticbrain.com) , informs me that I am not alone. According to their information (verified by University of Scranton Journal of Clinical Psychology), the over-fifty crowd has only a 14 percent success rate in keeping resolutions past the six-month mark. Our younger counterparts (those in their twenties) have a 39 percent success rate. Brats. Perhaps we just die off at a faster rate. Surely we are at least as capable as those half our age. But if the numbers are to be believed, we cranky older folk are resolution challenged.

Then again, we can look to the logic of Mark Twain for possible explanation, and I quote: "New Year's Day now is the accepted time to make your regular annual good resolutions. Next week you can begin paving hell with them as usual." Ah yes, the pathway of good intentions generally leads directly there. Must be getting rather crowded in these dark days of winter resolution dissolution.

The same website mentioned above also listed the top ten resolutions for 2012, and they looked suspiciously familiar.

There really is nothing much new under the sun, now is there? Take a peek at the list and you'll likely find that your own list for 2013 (if you have one) shares many similar entries:

1. Lose weight.

2. Get organized.

3. Spend less. Save more.

4. Enjoy life.

5. Stay fit and healthy.

6. Learn something exciting.

7. Stop smoking.

8. Help others with their dreams.

9. Fall in love.

10. Spend more time with family.

These are all lovely goals, great for New Year attention and intentions, but there's not much of a wow factor in any of them, is there? We've likely been there and done that already (or, more accurately, tried to do that). Besides, behavioral psychologists will tell us that these goals are much too vague and unclear to be accomplished (How much weight loss and by when? Stay fit how and where? Spend how much time with family? Organize what/where/when?). We also tend not to gauge our progress effectively or give ourselves time limits and deadlines. The real deal killer, though, is our lack of self-control and self-regulation, they say. Oh, really? Guess they've never had difficulty staring down chocolate chip cookies or potato chips or (insert your own precious vice here). Anyone care to push the self-righteousness warning button here?

Perhaps Thomas Hardy had the New Year tradition nailed when he said: "The resolution to avoid an evil is seldom framed till the evil is so far advanced as to make avoidance impossible." Ouch. That hurt. Truths have a way of zinging us, don't they?

Alas, regardless of attitude or ability or motivation, it is that time of year to start loading our resolvers and aiming for lofty goals. January is, after all, a new beginning for each of us—a rebirth, a reawakening, and sometimes a decidedly revolting development. The first month of the year is named after the Roman god, Janus—god of beginnings and guard of doors/ entryways. He is always depicted with two faces—one looking forward and one looking backward—so as to capture the power of the future and the strength of the past all at the same time. Uh-huh, well, sorry Janus, you mythical thing—that sort of stuff has already been covered by the one true God.

Jonathan Edwards declared a resolution that seems like the best way to begin a new year or any new day, for that matter, when he said: "Resolution One: I will live for God. Resolution Two: If no one else does, I still will." Bingo! What a world this would be if we all resolved to copy down that one.

And, since imitation is the sincerest form of flattery, there's a particular woman of the Bible we could resolve to follow. Of course, there are many, but the one for this year may be Esther. She is described in Easton's 1897 Bible Dictionary as a "woman of deep piety, faith, courage, patriotism, and caution, combined with resolution; a dutiful daughter to her adopted father, docile and obedient to his counsels, and anxious to share the king's favor with him for the good of the Jewish people. There must have been a singular grace and charm in her aspect and manners, since 'she obtained favor in the sight of all them that looked upon her" (Esther 2:15).

Esther is definitely a woman to emulate. I'll never have her looks, but I can aspire to gain her traits. And if it's not too much trouble, I'd like her seven maids too. But for right now, it is time to fully load the resolver and aim to hit a higher target than the usual weight loss, health gains, and nicety-niceness goals. Perhaps with the counsel of the Holy Spirit, there will be fruit and those two plain as day commandments will be followed: Love God. Love others. So, here's the new list for 2013:

Matthew 22: 37–40

1 Corinthians 13: 2

Ephesians 2: 8–9
Galatians 5: 22–23

Yep, that ought to just about cover it. I'm still a little bit worried about those chocolate chip cookies and cupcakes though. Self-control might need more ripening time—and maybe patience too.

# The Biggest Loser

*A*h, January—the most wonderful time of the year for losers like me. Yep, that's right. Loser is not an ugly word, after all. Honest. Because I'm gonna lose the extra twelve pounds gained over the holidays. I'm gonna lose the bad attitude. I'm gonna lose these flabby muscles. I'm gonna lose my procrastination and exchange it for big check-offs on the wedding To-do list. I'm gonna lose my temper (no, really—I want to get rid of it—it's time to stop blaming the Irish heritage and take responsibility for it myself). I'm even gonna lose the spare tire that has taken up residence between my formerly fit waistline and what used to be a fairly perky chest.

Yes, thank you hormonal imbalance. Can't wait to lose you either. I've treasured your every precious gift—especially when I attempt to bend over to tie my shoes and discover that my arms have evidently shriveled to T. Rex proportions. Either that or the spare tire has invaded so much space that I can no longer even reach my knees, let alone my shoelaces. Velcro is starting to look quite appealing to me. (Note to self: lose the tendency toward old lady fashion sense before you start dragging your pocketbook everywhere with you and clutching it in your arthritic claws for fear someone will snatch it while you're distracted by the discovery of more rogue hairs jauntily springing from your chinny chin double chin.)

There's just something about the first month of the new year that brings with it such enthusiasm for losing things that we often get carried away on a cloud of hopefulness and determination that rather quickly fades into despair and self-recrimination when things don't get quite as lost as we had planned come February (or for some of us losers, come January 10). Oh, things get lost alright. But not the things we had planned on losing. Instead, we lose our keys, our glasses, our self-respect and very nearly our minds.

Talk about your great expectations. It's not unlike the annual Sunday school class Christmas fellowship that occurred just a few weeks ago. Each year, the Mullins First Baptist Church Just-As-I-Am class gathers at the Floyd home (thanks again) for an evening of fun and fellowship. We also play the ever-popular gift exchange game. You know, it's the one where each person brings a gift then is assigned a selection number that determines the order of choosing a gift to take home—only to have it ripped away by the next person in line. Usually the only person who leaves a big winner is the one lucky enough to draw number one because that person gets to make the first and the last choice in the game.

Not so this year. A certain unnamed mister was the lucky number one—but he too became the biggest loser when his boastful courage was felled by a spritely young girl with a certain "gift" for choosing the best present and defying anyone to take it from her. And no one would. Talk about your throw downs. Poor Shawn (oops) very nearly was left with a Clemson-colored wreath designed by his talented wife and meant only as a "gotcha" gift for an unsuspecting Gamecock fan.

The food shared that night was responsible for nearly half of the extra twelve pounds mentioned above. When master bakers attend the same party, you know you won't leave without a very satisfied sweet tooth. A good time was had by all, with the possible exception of those left with goofy green hats and a really swell fishing set. But even the losers came away with something— items well-suited for re-gifting next year.

Now, let's get back to the big loser thing. There's only one item on the list that I truly hope will be accomplished this new year. It's the loss of the bad attitude thing that matters most— and if that is taken care of, the rest of the items on the list should follow suit. I really want to be the biggest loser of bad attitude this year. It's amazing what happens when you decide to stop choosing it and wearing it like a stinking sack cloth. One thing I've discovered in my not-yet-golden years is that attitude defines altitude. In other words, when the attitude is bad, the height of spirit is quite low. Either that or the Spirit can't stand to be around a bad attitude and leaves for greener pastures until there are some changes made.

And what controls the attitude most? Weather? No. Events? No. People? No. Circumstance? No. Money? No. Health? No. I'll give you a little hint. It's the word of the year for 2013. Give up? It's *selfie* (and, in this case, not the photos so much as the focus).

This year I plan to lose the selfie attitude first. That ought to take care of at least 75 percent of the biggest-loser list for 2014, don't you think? Time to stop comparing selfie to all others and coming up short. It's time to push the selfie off the priority list and put others' needs in its place. It's time to stop looking at sugar and carbs as life-giving wonders and start thinking that way about fruits and veggies and nuts and berries instead. And it's definitely time to lose some of the selfie hours on the computer and seek out more active ways to stay connected to people.

So, that's it from over here in Biggest Loser land. 2014 is going to be the year of the Loser—loser of pounds, loser of flab, loser of spare tire, loser of bad attitude, loser of selfie. What is there to gain from all this losing? Oh, let's see—just everything. Check out Matthew 16:24–26, Mark 8:34–36, Luke 9:23–25 and Philippians 3:7–9 for a few priceless clues.

"But whatever were gains to me I now consider loss for the sake of Christ. What is more, I consider everything a loss because of the surpassing worth of knowing Christ Jesus my Lord, for whose sake I have lost all things. I consider them garbage, that I may gain Christ and be found in him, not having a righteousness of my own that comes from the law, but that which is through faith in Christ—the righteousness that comes from God on the basis of faith" (Phil. 3:7–9, NIV).

Here's hoping you and yours have the biggest loser year ever. When we lose self, we gain everything.

# Kicking against the Pricks

*January 2015*

*D*o you remember the childhood joy of knowing the answer to a question asked by your teacher and he or she actually calls on you because you were the only one in the room with your hand up—and waving it frantically—in the stifling classroom air? I do. I do. It was a most wonderful feeling—probably because it didn't often happen that I was the only one with my hand raised. I usually got beaten out instead by Little Miss/Mr. Knows-All-the-Answers-All-the-Time.

This glorious feeling reentered my mostly mundane (yet quite contented) life during a recent Sunday evening Bible study of the Book of Acts when our teacher asked if anyone knew the meaning of the phrase in 26:14, "kicking against the goads." I instantly took on the TV persona of Arnold Horshack in *Welcome Back, Kotter*. My hand shot up, followed by an embarrassingly loud "ooh, ooh, ooh, I know that one." Yeah, well, so much for mundane contentment and lack of prideful behavior. But I really did know the answer. I was sure of it. And I shared it joyfully (and probably with just a wee bit too much prideful enthusiasm).

As soon as I regained what was left of my composure, I shared that Jesus was asking Saul/Paul why he was continuing to so vehemently attempt to persecute Him while "kicking against the pricks"—like an ox continuing to want its own way while being goaded with a pointed stick in the correct direction. The phrase is an old one and comes from farmers who would use a sharp pointed stick to goad the oxen into the right

269

path—and they, like most of us, would kick against the pricking and continue to get a good goading. The word *prick* is used in the King James Version in place of *goad*. And in some translations of the verse, neither is used at all. In fact, an entire sentence is missing. This is a subject for another day though.

The phrase can first be found in Acts 9:5, when Luke describes the beginning of Saul's conversion experience. In 26:14, Paul is giving his testimony (a fine example of both meanings of the word) in court, while testifying to the power of salvation.

And he said, Who art thou, Lord? And the Lord said, I am Jesus whom thou persecutest: it is hard for thee to kick against the pricks (Acts 9:5).

Of course when I first read this passage, my mind drifted (no, I am not proud of this) to the more uh modern meaning of the word prick. Our slang vocabulary has given the word a decidedly distasteful flavoring, in that it is interchangeable with a certain male anatomy or describes a vulgar, mean-spirited person—as in "stop acting like such a prick."

Right about now, you may be asking yourself (if you've even gotten this far), Why in the world is she rambling on and on about this goad/prick thing? And what does it have to do with January? Excellent questions, both. I shall now attempt to prick your eyes with a sharply crafted explanation. Fingers crossed.

The first month of the year seems to always drag me kicking and screaming into making ridiculous resolutions for behavior modification and nutritionally balanced consumption. And, as usual, I begin the year with great expectations and lofty goals then rather quickly kick against them until my sweatpants and oatmeal and fruit of the Spirit living get all wadded up and land in a heap of disgust with myself for missing the mark yet again. This pricking usually begins about January 5. This year, however, I vow to start out differently by not kicking quite so quickly. Why? Because it is kicking against the pricks or goads that is a most "vain and perilous resistance."

When Paul finally stopped kicking against the pricks, some would say he became a different kind of prick himself. The Spirit effectively pricked his heart into conviction and conversion and Paul began his journey of goading (okay, persuading) others to follow suit. And, of course, there's that "thorn in the flesh" he wrote about at a different time altogether (2 Cor. 12:7). Could that thorn in his flesh have referred to his own kicking against the pricks? I guess it's possible, though not very likely.

Regardless, I have decided that it is time for putting a halt to my own kicking. It really does no good and it pretty much always hurts. Resistance to sound guidance has always been somewhat of a pattern for me. I'm told it comes from being the youngest in a family. We strive so hard to be independent, unique, and noticed by the rest of the herd that we often end up hurting ourselves in the process—to say nothing of the eye-rolling impatience from our litter mates. Yep, being the perpetual baby of a family calls for lots and lots of kicking.

January is as good a time as any to begin the transformation. For one thing, it's time to stop eating whatever I feel like eating just because it's there, and I'm feeling kind of hungry or bored or sad or excited or frustrated or sleepy. It's time to stop talking to food whenever I have something I need to mull over. And, speaking of time, I'll make much better use of it this year by tackling the procrastination problem head on instead of sweeping it under the bed while I'm busy avoiding actually getting anything done. This one goes hand in hand with the issue of decision-making skills—or lack thereof. If I'm deciding between chocolate and vanilla, I can usually be counted on to make a quick choice, but most everything else is relegated to never-never land. It's not that I can't make a decision; I just avoid them if at all possible. Heaven forbid I make one that bothers or disagrees with somebody else. Harmony at all cost is the ticket.

Fortunately there is always support to be found in biblical passages (yet another item on the to-do list for 2015—spend more time in communion with God and His word) for any concern or problem. And this resolve-to-do-better thing is no exception. In researching other references to pricks and goads, I came across a passage in Ecclesiastes that was very helpful, especially when considering that the word goad (synonymous with prick) is defined as "a pointed rod used to make an animal move forward." I definitely am in need of moving forward in many areas, hopefully while avoiding the painful kicking against the pricks this time around.

The words of the wise are as goads, and as nails fastened by the masters of assemblies, which are given from one shepherd (Eccles. 12:11).

Since the Bible is overflowing with wise words, perhaps a concerted effort to give it more time and attention should be at the top of the resolve list this year instead of being relegated to the bottom again. A good friend shared a great acronym for Bible recently: Basic Instructions before Leaving Earth. Yep, if one desires to move forward, it's time to stop kicking against the pricks.

# The Selfie Shirt
## Imperfect Reflections Meet Perfect Timing

*January 2016*

Near the end of 2015 I had the pleasure of meeting a young man named Jacob. Though our encounter was quite brief, he made a lasting impression during a rather difficult time. Jacob was wearing a "selfie shirt"—the words were printed in mirror image so that when he took a selfie, the image would transform correctly in the photo (in other words, the shirt was printed backwards). I thought it was very clever indeed, even though it took me a few minutes to actually comprehend the point. It was subtle, yet adorable, sort of like Jacob himself.

That T-shirt really got me to thinking (yes, dangerous territory) about our selfie-ness in general, and mine in particular—especially as we approach a brand new year with yet another chance to begin again and resolve to change what has not worked or needs to start working better. Reflecting on the year gone by is never a perfect image of what has actually transpired—mostly because the picture we see is imperfect. It's mirrored by our faulty eyesight.

Viewing our reflections in the mirror (literally and figuratively), doesn't really give us an accurate picture. Just like Jacob's selfie shirt imprint, we are seeing only a reflected view through the lenses of our own eyes—which is usually a bit on the self-focused side, leaning precariously toward upside down and backwards. Even the gift of a beautifully reflected sunrise or sunset on the glassy stillness of water, while impressive, is not quite what it appears to be.

And, speaking of lenses and eyeballs, I have begun to see my reflected image a bit more clearly lately—thanks to the gift of cataract surgery. Talk about your imperfect reflections. Vision restored to near 20/20 level, at least in one eye, has opened up a brand new world for me. Most of it is amazing. There is, however, the clear vision that now allows me to see all of the dust bunnies and most of the crumbs in the corners of nearly every surface at home. Oh Mylanta!

I cannot begin to describe the sheer embarrassment of seeing so clearly that I will never be a candidate for Housekeeper of the Year. And then I had the audacious stupidity of looking in a well-lit mirror. When I came to, and found myself on the cold (and dirty) bathroom floor, I realized that with every gift comes a burden There is now no sense in pretending I could ever again pass for a fifty-year-old, or even a sixty-year-old. The wrinkles are in accurate focus, as is the turkey wattle neck. We won't even discuss the frightening chin hairs and coffee-stained teeth. As if this were not enough, there is also the fact that one may not wear makeup for two weeks after surgery. No cover-up. No mascara. No eyeliner. Did I mention that a clown image appears when one wears only lipstick on a pasty-white wrinkled face?

Well, enough of that for now. The second cataract gets removed soon. No telling what that will reveal about the wrongness of my reflection. Let's just hope the halos get removed from night driving excursions. Right now, driving with a hand over the left eye helps dim the oncoming headlights, but it sure wreaks havoc with the depth perception. Don't be concerned though, I don't get out much after dark anymore. It's too hard to find my way back home. And I'm usually too busy hunting down dust bunnies and plucking chin hairs.

The selfie shirt encounter also served to renew my faith in God's perfect timing and His very clear instruction to work toward reflecting His image in this world. (Yes, I let my mind wander from a T-shirt to these more lofty thoughts—it's not easy living inside my head. Trust me.)

I met Jacob and his shirt when I embarked on a work journey that quickly turned out to be a bad fit for my limited skills. The very day I decided to pull the plug on what felt like an overflowing tubful of murky work water, I received a phone call from a friend in need that temporarily eliminated the anxiety of letting some very wonderful people down and replaced it with helping someone else in trouble. I'm pretty sure He also orchestrated the T-shirt thing too. His timing is always perfect. What an awesome Father—to teach a very helpful life lesson through a poorly reflected selfie image.

The very brief work excursion also served to put me in touch with a publication I had not seen before: *The Upper Room*. It is a series of nondenominational daily devotions, published bi-monthly and written by regular folks like us. It's simple and down-to-earth reflections on faith are filled with His grace. Again, His perfect timing trumped my imperfect self-reflection. There was an entry dated December 31 (yes, I cheated and read to the end—just as He knew I would) that brings home the imperfect reflections theme much better than I could. It was submitted by Mr. Robert Abel of Maryland.

Here's just a portion of what he wrote: "I am not a perfect reflection of Christ, but I find comfort in the knowledge that God doesn't expect me to be perfect but only to be as faithful as I can be. Even with our imperfections, God calls us to be faithful reflections of God's love."

We can always aim for the perfect reflection, but we will never achieve it this side of heaven. We are not designed to be perfect. Sometimes we come close. Sometimes we miss the mark entirely. Hopefully, we still reflect the light and let it shine in our ever-darkening world. See Matthew 5:16.

There is also another T-shirt to this New Year story. I encountered it while Christmas shopping just before deciding to put to rest what I thought was a good opportunity to do God's work. The emphasis on that sentence should be on "what I thought." Never, ever a good idea. My reflected image of self is not what God desires for me. We are to listen, instead, to the still small voice within us. His voice, reflected in what he reveals to us—and not in what we think we see or hear on our own. Stepping out ahead of God is a journey filled with potholes. Stepping out instead on His command is often the road less taken, yet brings us to a better destination. The shirt I saw while shopping in a nearby bookstore read simply: "I'm an English major. *You* do the math."

Duh! I love words. I believe it's a gift provided for His glory. He has mentioned nothing to me about numbers. There is surely a reason for this silence. But I did not listen. Shame on me. And a thousand apologies to those who counted on me to complete the tasks at hand. I pray they will have forgiveness for the results of my stepping out ahead of God's perfect timing, and for my very imperfect selfie reflection. And thanks for the inspiration, Jacob.

# The Hard Way

*January 2017*

*I* don't learn lessons well. I tend to start out on a good path then veer off into procrastination until the lessons get learned all too quickly, the hard way. In this New Year, I will attempt to do a better job of appreciating the lessons as they come to me from above. Trials are teachable moments, but only if we allow them to be. I have recently learned, again the hard way, that we don't always get a tomorrow.

My sister died in the early morning hour of November 17, 2016. She was sixty-nine years old, in otherwise reasonably good health, with a husband of over forty years, six children, two grandchildren (and a third on the way), four sisters—one of them her twin. In quick order, her family has endured Thanksgiving, Christmas, and a milestone wedding anniversary without her.

It was only three weeks before she died that the cancer diagnosis was made. She endured one massive round of chemo ten days ago—from which she never recovered. Two trips to the ER, admittance, intensive care, followed in blinding speed by her death. Pancreatic cancer rarely leaves survivors. She unfortunately was no exception. But having only three weeks? Horrific.

She was surrounded by her husband and six children, just as she would have desired it to be. Of five sisters, she was the most kindhearted, seeing only the good in others. She reflected God's light in many ways, as she walked on this earth.

When our oldest sister was being treated for breast cancer, she purchased six glass teardrop beads, one for each of us, and our mother, to wear in solidarity for our struggling sister. When I lost my husband to cancer, she chose a small smooth stone and carried it with her on her daily walks on the beach, bringing comforting prayers to me from far, far away. She did the same when I had my own life-threatening health problem ten years later. We had sixteen hours of drive time between us, and yet, she found a way to remain close by.

We used to take turns "babysitting" our mother while our two oldest sisters were scheduled out of town at the same time and needed backup. Either she or I would arrive first to stay with mom, and then the other would arrive later in the week to take the next shift. We usually had an overnight stay between us that always included a walk around the retirement village. Those were memory making times. And I am eternally grateful for them, especially now.

We shared some traits in common, as sisters tend to do. Unfortunately, I did not share much of her sweet spirit or abiding faith for most of our joint time in this life. She quietly volunteered for hospice. She worked many years at the public library in her adopted home of Rye, New Hampshire. She and her husband raised six outstanding children who are now left to navigate around the huge hole she has left in the tapestry of their lives. Her grandchildren will not have her with them for their own life markers.

She and our mother shared a deep love for the adventure of books. She was always assigned the task of suggesting a book for us to read in anticipation of our sisters trips—we've only had four. Yes, it's rather unheard of for a group of sisters to do a book study on the rare occasions of their togetherness. And now I don't know what will happen to those times. It remains to be seen. She was not the driving engine for those trips, but she was very much the sister that held them in highest regard.

As I remember, she was responsible for the very first trip we all shared together as mothers of children grown enough (finally) not to miss us too much for a long weekend. It was how she chose to spend an inheritance left to her by her husband's aunt (and that should speak volumes about her character, on several levels). All five of us gathered in Washington, DC on her "dime," and spent a few blissful days/nights touring our nation's capital and our shared history.

Two of us were still smokers then; relegated to the bathroom of a four-star hotel to puff away and laugh outrageously as one of us tumbled backwards into a blessedly empty tub after a supper of perhaps too much wine. She was still patient and kind and loving toward us, the wayward ones.

On a subsequent sisters trip our shared history took a huge hit when we took a guided tour of our hometown, only to realize that, collectively, none of us could answer all the questions about historic Frederick, Maryland—the home of all our childhoods, spanning five successive trips through elementary and high school in the same town. Good golly, how much we did not know—and probably worse, thought we knew and didn't. It made for a good memory though.

After the birth of their first child (on December 25), I was honored beyond words to have been chosen as her godmother. It was a first and only honor for me. I will always be grateful to both of them—and forever ashamed at my lack of care in that role. I hope my one and only godchild will forgive my trespasses, or lack thereof, as she has grown into such a beautifully amazing combination of both her parents—with nary a nudge or nurture from her largely absent godmother. The Bibbity Bobbity Boo I did not do.

I do remember each of my sister's six children from their early years. I even have a few treasured photos to prove the time spent. They were a wonderful bunch—then and now—but I have no real connection to them in their adult years. That is the thing I would change, if I could. But I have learned that we cannot go back—we can only go forward and promise ourselves that we will make a greater effort to stay connected—physically and emotionally.

My sister died, and I have no more time to cherish her presence in this life, only memories of the person she was here—from watching her go tight-lipped on the high school basketball court when finally someone annoyed her enough to get angry and play hard, to seeing her struggle while working for the local Selective Service Board and knowing many of the young men who were called up to serve in the Vietnam War. I remember her joy at finding her life mate and becoming a mother, her sincere interest in people—whether in a large gathering or one-on-one—she never missed a moment. Staying present is the best of gifts. She taught us all by her example. I can only hope that I have finally begun to learn the lessons and put them into practice in this New Year 2017.

February

**One is Enough**
**I Do Two**
**Tikkun Olam**
**Aphids, Dingoes and Ostriches**
**Let There Be Love**
**Love in the Sixties**

*I*t's no surprise that February was the love month issue. Love stories and weddings were featured, along with a focus on heart health from a physical perspective. Love is such a, well, lovely topic, isn't it?

# One is Enough

*February 2008*

*A*h, February. It is the month of Valentines and flowers and lace and candy hearts. It's the month of romantic, candlelit dinners and sweet nothings whispered in waiting ears and offerings of chocolate kisses and teddy bear hugs. It is the shortest and arguably sweetest month of every year and this time around we get a whole extra day to enjoy it—unless of course we don't enjoy that sort of thing. Some of us really don't like it one bit. If we describe ourselves as terminally single or recently separated or widowed (that would be me) or just plain lonely or simply fed up with the potential pressures of February 14th, we do not necessarily leap for joy at the thought of encountering Valentine's Day displays around every corner. Where does love go when it leaves us? Does it hover quietly above us for a time and then slowly fade away or does it vanish without a trace—in a heartbeat? Is it hiding from us or are we just unable to see it when it is right in front of us or beside us or behind us?

In the spirit of the upcoming heart-y days, I decided to venture into uncharted territory and ask my son (who is twenty-three years old and living with me temporarily by circumstance and not be preference) his opinion of my recent decision to consider developing a social life again. That's mom-speak for dating, for those who may not know. After he stopped hyperventilating and before I could redeem myself for even asking such a question of a young man still processing the grief of losing his dad to cancer two years earlier, I was smacked with his response. It took the form of a biting question to me: "Isn't one good man enough for you, Mom?" Whoa there. I should probably have seen that one coming.

After apologies all around and a quick retreat to our own quiet corners of the house, I had a few moments to reflect on his question. From his perspective, I did win the jackpot twenty-six years ago and should be nothing but grateful for that prize. And I am. However, when one experiences that level of commitment, it can make the loss of it feel like a cavernously gaping hole in what remains of a life. It can also make one long for a continuation of a paired existence over a solo one. With my son's response still ringing in my ears, I began to question if one is truly enough. Right now the answer is still yes and no. Can I live the rest of my life alone and still be grateful for that one love? Yes. Do I expect or desire to do so? No. Why? Because love remains long after the person who shared it is gone from this life. Love is still here. So, in one way, my son was absolutely correct in asking his question. One is definitely enough—and more than some of us experience in the whole of our lives. But, thanks to faith, it doesn't end there.

Without faith, though, we can only read about love and dream about it and wish that we had it when we don't. To frame my son's question a bit differently, how would I answer this: If we believe that God is love, is God, then, enough? The best answer is: "Yes, God is surely enough." But I am new to this and I'm not sure if I would be truth-telling by responding with an unequivocal yes to that question. It is, however, the goal of this life now. In all things, God is enough. Love is enough. There can be no wishy washy, middle of the road, or fence-sitting response. In the words of Nobel Prize winning American Author, Toni Morrison, "Love is or it ain't. Thin love ain't no love at all." (From her novel, *Beloved*.)

Of course, Ms. Morrison is alive and well and still writing wonderful words of art. But even around 400 BC man was pondering this love thing. It's nice to know we're not alone in our quests and/or confusions. Sophocles, the ancient Greek playwright, wrote this about love, "One word frees us of all the weight and pain of life; that word is love."

These words are especially helpful to us when we turn on our televisions or listen to our radios or read the newspaper, and are bombarded with horrific questions. How can a father throw his children from a bridge in order to punish their mother? Why do women methodically drown their babies, one at a time, allowing those yet to die to know what their fate will be? Why does another drive her car into a lake, leaving her toddlers strapped and trapped inside to slowly suffocate, alone and afraid? Why does a woman kill her husband, leaving their children parentless as she is arrested for her crime and ultimately sentenced to a life in prison? Why do addicts love their fixes so much more than themselves? Why do terrorists fly planes into skyscrapers or crash bomb-filled trucks into busy marketplaces? It is perhaps the complete absence of love. Love didn't fail them; they perhaps never knew it.

We can't imagine the horror of such acts or the hideous natures of the perpetrators. Or can we? Exactly how far removed are we from those who commit such crimes? Many are said to have done such things in the name of love. How many times have we, in our own lives, said or done or thought something ugly and still called it love for others? Guilty as charged, I'm afraid. And here is the real test: can we love those who trespass against us? Oh, that's the toughest one. Yet it is exactly what we are called by God to do.

Fortunately, even given all the horrors and losses and difficult decisions, love does remain. It is the only way we can survive this life. So, thanks son. I'm very glad that you answered my dating question with one of your own. It's not about finding love again; it's about knowing that love still remains and will always be enough—whether or not another person enters our story. In the end, love never fails to lift us back up when we falter. We have only to believe that One is enough.

# I Do Two

*February 2014*

If all goes as planned, this will be the last time I write about love and marriage from an unwed perspective. By the time 2015 rolls around, the subject may take on an entirely different meaning. In other words, I'm wondering if things will change dramatically by this time next year regarding my approach to love and marriage. I surely hope not. Right now I'm excited as all get out about it.

We two used to be halves of a long-married couple. We just weren't each other's halves. We are now about to embark on a new partnership in which we will be each other's other half. Neither of us has been half of a whole in over seven years. Both of us bring some rather well-worn habits and quirks to each other's lives. This is not unlike attempting to blend northern sarcasm with southern sass and not taking on casualties. So far, we've adjusted, but not yet on a permanent, no-looking-back basis. There are times we want to place each other in neat little boxes only to discover that neither of us fits very well or comfortably in confinement and both of us take great delight in punching the sides out of said compartments. He is much better at that, but then he has so much more experience with boxes, doesn't he?

Lately we've been spending a good bit of time hashing over the wedding plans and the marriage plans—these are two very distinct and nearly unconnected topics. And, as is the usual circumstance when it comes to wedding plans, the female half has been doing almost all of the hashing and rehashing (and over-hashing). All we need is some corned beef and we'll be all set, if we don't first choke on all the details. I had no idea that burlap and mason jars would be so complicated. It's a picnic, for goodness sake. I thought this would be so simple—baskets, blankets, fried chicken. Wrong.

Speaking of baskets, my future bonus son (a phrase I have willfully stolen from Nancy Grice's article a few months back— it's so much more descriptive than "step") has a very nasty habit of coming to my house with the goal of counting how many baskets I've added to the family since his last visit. He has even enlisted the aid of his up-to-now-lovely wife and my own dear children and almost-husband in the venture. They had a rousing game of "Guess How Many Baskets" during their Christmas visit this year. Very funny. If I shared that the winning guess was twenty-nine in just the kitchen area alone, would you think me an incurable basket case? Please don't answer.

Well, there I go getting off topic again. I believe we were discussing love and marriage this month, weren't we? Before the marriage begins, weddings usually happen. They involve careful planning and fun stuff like color choices and themes and guest lists and tasty menus. Marriages involve even more care and lots more difficult work. Unfortunately, one can be good at weddings and horrible at marriages. This is usually directly proportionate to the amount of time, energy, and prayer spent on each. Weddings and after parties usually last around three to four hours. They are events, after all. Marriages, unless we're talking Kardashians, last quite a bit longer and usually don't include guest lists and towering cakes. They do, however, require commitment and offer much greater rewards if successful.

But how do we find marital success—especially the second time around? I read somewhere recently that the key to a happy marriage involves just one word: forgiveness. Really, it can't possibly be that simple, can it? I mean, who goes first? Another source stated that the biggest problem in marriage today also can be summed up in one word: selfishness. The writer believed that "serving the kingdom of self" leads only to disaster in marriage (and most likely in life).

During my faraway youthful years, I fancied myself something of a liberal feminist. I didn't exactly burn my bra (it had too much important work to do), but I wasn't going to let any man lead me around or tell me what to do. I commanded my own destiny, and my ship ran aground on quite a few of my "maiden" voyages. And I spent a lot of time in a twenty-five-year marriage being angry and self-centered. Gaining age and experience and children and losing that spouse slowly to cancer, among other things, have helped me to redirect my course into slightly more conservative waters.

Given that brief history, you may understand why it took me by surprise when I found myself agreeing wholeheartedly with the Candace Cameron Bure suggestion that biblical submission is the key to a happy and long-lasting and God-centered marriage. She sure stirred up a hornet's nest of women-against-women controversy in January this year. Some media pundits literally spit out venom upon her suggestion that they may not exactly understand the biblical meaning of the word. They were too busy getting their panties in a wad about the submission thing. I admit it has taken me a while to grasp the concept of love, honor, and obey in a marriage vow. And I'm still hard at work on it, in anticipation of upcoming nuptials. (Have I mentioned June 22 lately?)

But the really important message is hidden deep within that firestorm "submit" word we find in 1 Peter and Ephesians and Colossians regarding wives submitting to their husbands. The Greek word, *hypotasso*, can be translated any number of ways, depending on the context in which it is used. Thayer's describes it this way: "a voluntary attitude of giving in, cooperating, assuming responsibility, and carrying a burden." It is, by definition, a choice—much like love is a choice.

We also spend a lot of time trying to understand the meaning of the word love. It can be found quite easily in 1 Corinthians 13. It is a verb. It requires action and commitment, whether we "feel" like it or not. But perhaps we should spend an equal amount of time remembering what love is not. It is not a feeling. Not an emotion. Love is not all soft and sweet and mellow. Sometimes it hurts to love. Sometimes it is hard as stone and sharp as a razor's edge (before shaving your winter's growth legs with it). But there is no fear in it, for we know that perfect love casts out fear—as in our Father's love for us.

Here's what I now know to be true in this life. Submission to another is not a bad thing. It is actually quite freeing. We have each been given the key to living in faith, hope, and love. It's all about the order of our allegiances: God first, then others, then self. So I think the person that wrote about selfishness being responsible for the death of marriages was absolutely right. Selflessness may just be what revives it. Aligning oneself under the command of another gives us the proper perspective. And that goes for life in general and certainly marriage in particular. A cord of three strands is not easily broken—God, husband, wife.

Just one more thing: Mr. Willoughby better not mess with my color choices or menu ideas for June 22 and he'll need to submit to a beard trim and maybe a dance or two. This submission stuff is a two way street, right? No? Fine then, I'll just keep working on it as we get closer and closer to I do two.

# Tikkun Olam

*February 2015*

No, I did not have my fingers on the wrong row when typing the title this month. Sometimes I do, but not this month. Honest. Tikkun olam is a Hebrew phrase I learned, and promptly forgot, a few years ago near the end of a study called *Our Hebrew Connection*. (Yes, Jesus was a Jew. And I was a recovering Catholic–mighty confusing stuff for a late-blooming Christ follower.) But recently I dusted off that workbook and started reading it again.

The phrase itself roughly translates to repairing that which is broken in our world. Whoa. Now that's a pretty tall order, especially given the current state of our world. The authors of the study ended the workbook with an introduction to tikkun olam and stated: "We can co-labor with God to bring wholeness and restoration to those in need."

This restoring and repairing can include, but is certainly not limited to, things like:

- Mending the broken-hearted

- Resting the weary

- Nesting the widows and orphans

- Giving beyond ease

- Daring to care for the least of these

- Easing the suffering of those in need

All these *ing*-ended words provide a clue to the underlying nature of tikkun olam. The heart of the matter is that we take action—start do-ing work that leads to some repairing, instead of just thinking or talking about "stuff." Mending what is broken in our homes can extend the usefulness of our things. Mending what is broken in our hearts may extend our lives and help us reach toward joy. Sounds like quite a good plan.

While researching further, however, I discovered a few dissenting views on the phrase definition. Go figure. Just when I think I've found an answer, more questions develop. There are those who believe that tikkun olam relates only to that which includes the law—to follow the commandments of God so that His work is eased. How presumptuous of us mere mortals to believe we can co-work with God Himself, the critics conclude. The truth is likely found somewhere in the middle between the two definitions.

I was tempted to drop this subject completely and focus instead on a truly important fashion subject: What not to wear after turning thirty. I found it while chasing after tikkun olam site definitions on the internet. Since I am just slightly over thirty, I thought it might be a sweet little diversion in the midst of the heavier topic of world restoration. Wrong again. It only created more confusion and wringing of hands.

I was fine with most of what was suggested. Graphic tees, mismatched socks, shiny pants and see-through anything are certainly wardrobe malfunctions beyond even the teenage years, let alone thirty. But then the next slide in the presentation nearly knocked me off my chair. Hoop earrings evidently are considered a serious fashion faux pas after age thirty. What? I love my hoops—small, medium, even large simply designed silver hoops. Besides, I can't wear much else, thanks to a terribly torn left earlobe hole. If I attempt to wear studs, that side dangles precariously from my lobe much like a bobble head dachshund perched in the back window of an Oldsmobile. I just can't do it. Well, that's not entirely true. I can do it. But I risk losing the left side of the pair every time I turn my head—or sneeze or nod in agreement or take a deep breath.

So then, we're back to tikkun olam. Even given the controversial nature of its definition(s), it is a much safer subject than hoop earrings and much more likely to produce something good. If we stick with the first meaning—the one that talks about serving God by seeing to the needs of others and aiding in their restoration—surely something wonderful can happen.

My heart for a long time has been with children and families in crisis. But then I allowed myself to get "burned out" and turned away from it. It's time to step back in the fire, even if only in a small way. And it probably won't be within the state or family court systems, either. But there is always some way to help actively that goes beyond just writing about it, isn't there?

In the annual *Kids Count Data Book*, states are ranked in four categories regarding the welfare of children: economic well-being, education, health, and family/community. Within each category are four subsets of criteria. Then each state is ranked on how well they are doing within these categories—the lower the ranking, the higher the well-being of children. Care to guess the ranking of South Carolina in the 2014 *Kids Count Data Book*? Out of fifty states, our rank is forty-five.

One statistic in particular just screamed off the page. Based on 2013 records, the study found that 72 percent of South Carolina fourth graders are not proficient in reading. The national figure is 66 percent. And both are improved scores. Of course the word *proficient* is not fully defined in these figured numbers. But maybe the tikkun olam key is here for me. Or maybe it's about getting the word spread about the numbers of children in foster care or kinship care—the hidden homeless in our communities—to help ease their burdens and encourage them to hope.

Regardless of where, when, and how we pursue it, there is always a way to help ease someone's burden or encourage their mending. The true heart of the matter every month of our lives, and without regard for our chronological age, can be found in Hebrew, Greek, Aramaic, English, and many other languages. Look to Deuteronomy 6:5–6 and Matthew 22:36–40 for just two examples.

And, just to be clear, no matter where tikkun olam takes us, I will most assuredly be wearing some inappropriate-for-my-age hoop earrings.

# Aphids, Dingoes, and Ostriches

*February 2016*

*A*h, February—the love month! It brings with it the sweetness of Valentine's Day chocolates, flowers, and mushy cards. Presidents are honored with a holiday (and retailers have an excuse for big sales). We turn our gnat-like attention to nurturing a happier, healthier heart, which in turn can conjure up the fourteenth day massacre, and dead-of-winter depression, and then the dreaded Jeremiah verses launch a guilt-laden assault on all that heart focus.

February may be the shortest month of the year, but it brings with it some pretty long days and dark nights. In a month of overflowing love, there always seems to come an undercurrent of what is not lovely. It's the age-old problem of dissatisfaction with what we think love is, instead of appreciation for the simplicity of its gift. Or maybe it's just me? Likely so.

One recent evening, I was spending a little too much time viewing Facebook videos of cuddly puppies and crazy cat antics when I came across one about a man who could predict answers to a series of questions without ever seeing the viewer in person (namely me). Okay, I'm game. It'll keep me from addressing the dirty dishes.

This video fella proceeded to ask me to come up with answers to his seemingly harmless and easy questions. If you want to play along, please don't read ahead. First, name a country that starts with the letter *A*, like Afghanistan or Algeria, but don't choose either of those. Think of your own. Once you have the country in mind, take the last letter of that word and come up with a bug that starts with that letter. Now, using the last letter of the bug word, name a jungle animal. With the last letter of the jungle animal, name a bird.

He then proceeded to tell me (on the video—I'm not *that* crazy) my answers to the bug, animal, and bird inquiries. He was exactly correct! If you played along and came up with the following answers, you, poor thing, have a similar mindset. The answers I gave were *ant, tiger,* and *robin* (or *raven*). Wow, huh? I was impressed. Don't ask me why he didn't also share the country I selected (Argentina, by the way). I guess it doesn't matter. I was stunned by his accuracy.

I think of myself as a relatively creative person, one who usually comes up with rather quirky answers for simple questions. Though it was a fun few minutes of idle time, I was slightly miffed that this guy could so easily deceive me (that Jeremiah 17:9 thing).

Now fast forward to a recent drive toward Conway from Ketchuptown with my mostly silent husband. I figured I could break the boredom by sharing the ant-tiger-robin game with him. Surely he would come up with those answers. He doesn't like to color outside the lines very often. He sees things most often in black and white (Mr. Logical Linear Thinker).

I proceeded to set up the game by telling him I could predict what his answers would be to a set of questions. Being a dramatic sort, I told him in hushed tones that I'd secretly write down the answers on a slip of paper, then fold it and place it between us as we drove along. And I did just that—only the slip of paper was a slightly used napkin. We were, after all, rolling along in a muddy-tired man truck. I began to set the trap, telling him to name a country that started with *A*, etc. Only he was not to give his answers out loud—just think of them in his head. This was rather difficult for him, as he tends to be a blurter.

I cannot begin to describe my shock and awe (and subsequent outrage) when the game was over and he shared his answers. Only one answer was even remotely close to the expected outcome. His country was *America*, which would have worked. But, no. He took a shortcut through Weirdville. His answer for bug was *aphid*. Are you kidding me? He picks an obscure sap sucker of a bug that reproduces without mating. Who chooses aphid over ant? Just wait—it gets worse.

The jungle animal he chose was *dingo*. Oh, come on. Dingoes don't even live in jungles. They live in Australia and are really partly domesticated dogs that tend to eat babies. Of all the animals he could possibly name, he comes up with dingo. By now I am seeing cross-eyed with aggravation. But he saved the very worst one (or best, depending on your perspective) for last.

His choice for a bird was *ostrich*. Oh. My. Gosh. The ostrich is a large flightless African bird that also, and in this case appropriately, defines a person who refuses to face reality. He couldn't come up with something simple, like maybe owl? No, he shoots for the moon of obscurity. Mr. Linear Thinker gives me *aphid*, *dingo*, and *ostrich*.

Needless to say, he totally obliterated the fun of the exercise. It's like he took a giant highlighter and outlined the wide chasm of our differences. I'm the one that's supposed to come up with the crazy, nut-bag answers. I was sure he would name the ant, tiger, and robin—just like 99 percent of those who took that video challenge before him—including me. What the heck happened?

I still don't have a clue. But there is one thing I do know pretty well. We are as different as night and day and likely to remain so for the duration. We stepped into marriage with our eyes wide open. Mostly. But in the last twelve months we have seen lots of sickness all around us, and in us. We each had hospital stays of the emergency kind. I am attempting to rebound from the resulting cognitive impairment and depression. He has retired from the work he loved/hated after nearly thirty years and is venturing into uncharted woodworking territory. I had cataracts removed while simultaneously attempting a new job, failing miserably. We are still learning to live together (after solitary confinement) in a place that is new to me and old for him. And my mother died the day after Christmas. Yay, us!

I don't share this to gain sympathy. It is what it is. It is life as we know it. The perfect, predictable life (or partner) simply does not exist. But the perfect loving God does. And He gives grace without limit. When we write His Word on the "tablet of our hearts" (our deceitful and desperately wicked, unknowable hearts), He gives abundantly and with surprising humor.

The man God gave me, the one who answers with *aphid*, *dingo*, and *ostrich*, of all things; the one who refuses to eat link meat or let me get away with bratty behavior; the one without a gall bladder that continues to have an ongoing gas problem—that irritating, stubborn man loves me better than I have ever been loved in my life. I hope to return the favor. We just won't be doing quizzes together anymore. Hope you enjoy a very happy healthy heart month.

# Let There Be Love

ebruary always brings with it a turn toward the affairs of the heart. It's the month we focus on all things heart related—whether it is "heart" as in caring for that most important muscle of our body and protecting it from disease and dysfunction, or "heart" as in love and romance and sweet valentines (and candy—oh yes, there must be chocolates—good for the heart, right?). Either way, it centers on love and how, with proper care and attention, we can live in it most fully.

While trolling around my tiny brain cavity for thoughts on February love (and marriage), the phrase "let there be love" abruptly tickled my left ear. I'm not exactly sure from whence that tickling thought originated, though I'm rather certain it was not through my usual spontaneous combustion of weird words and ideas.

Whatever the origin, I plugged the phrase into my electronic brain storage device (aka Google) and was immediately directed to not one, not two, but three song lyrics from three vastly different artists—Nat King Cole, the British group Oasis, and Christina Aguilera. Oh boy. Oh joy. I'm on to something here now. But wait, there are four. Simple Minds also put out a tune with the same title. Wow. Might be on to something here. Like maybe "let there be love" is about as original and mind-boggling a thought as "let there be donuts" or "let there be a parking space close by."

Turns out that all four songs of the same title have very different takes on the phrase, "let there be love." And isn't that the way of love, after all? We each take from and bring to love something just a wee bit different. Makes for an interesting life for us though, doesn't it? The language of love is often misinterpreted between those who desire to love each other most. As the theory goes, we give love in the way we desire to receive it—it just doesn't always work out that way.

As a second time married person, I have discovered once again that men generally see things in a more logical, yes/no or black/white way. Women tend to see the same things in a more emotional, maybe centered or grayish way. This is not rocket science. It is a simple matter of how we are wired for life. If there is a problem in marriage (or dating or engagement), each person brings a different perspective to the solution table. And that's perhaps why there are at least four versions of "Let there Be Love" floating around. We want so much to get it right.

Being much older this time around, and so grateful for that second chance at love, I just knew it would be different. Wrong. Or maybe I'm the only wrong one here, but that's so lonely. I need to have a partner in crime in this "let there be love" thing. It's scriptural—love your neighbor as yourself is, after all, the second greatest commandment. So why do I keep struggling? It's a question for professionals perhaps, or it could be that competitive stubbornness keeps begging for attention. Let's hope not.

Biblically, we have a solid foundation of what love is, if only we could fully understand the verses that speak of it so eloquently. It is, after all, a verb. Not a feeling. Our feelings often muddle the truth of love. 1 Corinthians 13:4–8 spell out what it is and is not. "Love suffers long and is kind; love does not envy; love does not parade itself, is not puffed up; does not behave rudely, does not seek its own, is not provoked, thinks no evil; does not rejoice in iniquity, but rejoices in the truth; bears all things, believes all things, hopes all things, endures all things. Love never fails".

The ultimate definition of agape love is found in 1 John 3:16. "By this we know love; that he laid down his life for us, and we ought to lay down our lives for the brothers" (ESV).

And yet, we still struggle with its meaning and execution—sometimes on an even hourly basis. (On a personal note, why has it taken me until right now to see the obvious-to-every-one-but-me connection between 1 John 3:16 and John 3:16? Evidently the blinders remain in place, as usual.)

Oh, yes, please, let there be love. Always. Now we're getting somewhere. Even in the most difficult times. Even when it hurts beyond comprehension. Even when it makes us angry. Even when we feel we don't receive it or can't give it. Let there be love. Marriage vows get bruised and tattered every day. We can do and say horrible, insensitive things to each other. The same goes for families and neighbors, coworkers and friends. We betray and are betrayed. Feelings are hurt. Grief overtakes us.

And yet we must continue to sing, let there be love. It is an action required of us all. Without it, we are nothing but crashing cymbals and banging gongs. The music of love must play on—different lyrics, different designs, different rhythms and rhymes. May we just keep singing, "Let there be love."

# Love in the Sixties

*February 2018*

No, it's not the decade—please no, not *that* again. Peace, love, and rock & roll have long since turned into creases, lumps, and extra rolls. I mean to talk of love when you're in your sixties—as in birth years (yes, as in old farts—sorry.) I'm turning sixty-four this year—but not till May though, so let's not rush it—and we've only been married for just under four years. Doesn't seem quite possible, does it? We've overheard the murmurings, as in, "How in the world did they manage to snag a partner when they were so old and snaggle-toothed already?" Oh, so very funny—our collective children are laugh riots (or so they think).

Together we've had plenty of practice at marriage though, my husband and I. Between us, we have over fifty years of experience—not including this marriage. Mistakes were made. But love endured for quite some time in our "old" marriages. What happened? One died and one quit. That's about the gist of it—with grief on all sides, regardless of the circumstances. And in consideration of the aforementioned laugh riot children, that's all there is to say about it.

But what in the world does an old people's marriage look like when it's still so young? You know the thing about "grow old along with me; the best is yet to be"? It takes on a bit of a different flavor when an already old person newly married sings it. We haven't had all that much time to really get to know each other—except that we sometimes know each other very, very well. For example, I thought I had cornered the market on sarcasm until I learned the hard way that he was already a stealth bomber. Little did I know that he had been practicing snarky retorts for quite some time before we met? Drat! He can read my many moods and respond like a ninja. Bless his heart.

But there is all that previously unshared space to navigate—"the early years" of our youth not shared. The younger marriages, the children born, the relatives, the family histories, the friendships—we have nothing to share in any of those areas. On top of that landmine, add the fact that we are from two distinctly different regions of the country. Geographically, we are both east coast, but that's where the similarities end. I push. He mashes. I eat dinner in the evening. He eats it at midday. Fortunately, we both like butter, eggs, grits and pepper. Breakfast is not a challenge for us. It is, however, the only meal that does not stir the pot of opposing palates.

We do have one thing in common though—both of us are the youngest of five siblings, and there's a set of twins in each of our sibling groups. And, as my oldest sister surmised, "this should be interesting—I wonder how long these two babies will survive before they realize that only one can be the center of attention at a time." Bless her heart.

We've also missed out on seeing each other physically at our best. Long gone are the bikini days for me. Two babies and an obsession with baking have taken their toll. His food baby is resting uncomfortably over his belt, while my child-bearing hips have expanded to easily birth a hippo. His gray hairs are distinguished of course, while mine are painted up on a near monthly basis now, as I desperately cling to brownish auburn with a constant showing of ugly roots around the edges of a vertically wrinkled brow. Neither of us can claim pearly whites. Our lips are disappearing into our chins (all three of them). Pretty soon the lids of our eyes will droop into a permanent twilight.

And the memory loss? Good heavens! We're like the old ladies' joke about not remembering why we went upstairs, or left the room, or ended up in the bathroom instead of the kitchen with our coffee mugs or found our glasses under the couch cushion again. Add hearing loss to the mix and you have a recipe for constant bickering. He can't hear me. I don't like to repeat things. He insists I do. Then I can't remember what I said in the first place. And he doesn't believe me. Auuuggggggghhhh!

There is that one thing we share that makes all of it worthwhile though. (Oh for pity's sake, not *that*—though "that" is doing just fine.) We share a common faith in a one true God. We might differ on some of the details, but it's the triune God—Father, Son, and Holy Spirit—that keeps us walking in nearly the same direction. We trip over rocks, and take swings at each other's discernment from time to time, but our shared focus is on the eternal. It is that alone that gives our marriage an ageless joy—whether four years or sixty-four years married.

I have had those few who have questioned what will happen in eternity, since we have each had other spouses before. Will we return to our original marriage? Will we stay in the new one? The easy answer is Luke 20:34–35. But the best answer, at least for me, is simply this: We won't care a fig about that when we are face to face with Him. Holy, holy, holy, Lord God Almighty! There will be no room there for toilet seat tiffs or toothpaste wars or whose turn it is to feed the dogs. Oh, glorious day! And, in a nod to my long ago Catholic upbringing, we'll try to practice this prayer while we are still here and enjoying our earthly marital bliss:

> *Lord, make me an instrument of your peace:*
> *Where there is hatred, let me sow love;*
> *Where there is injury, pardon;*
> *Where there is doubt, faith;*
> *Where there is despair, hope;*
> *Where there is darkness, light;*
> *Where there is sadness, joy.*
> *O divine Master, grant that I may not so much seek*
> *To be consoled as to console,*
> *To be understood as to understand,*
> *To be loved as to love.*
> *For it is in giving that we receive,*

*It is in pardoning that we are pardoned,*
*And it is in dying that we are born to eternal life.*
*Amen.*

We will work on loving each other in the here and now while keeping our focus on what is unseen and eternal, so we do not lose heart (2 Corinthians 4:16–18). And we surely don't spend a whole lot of time in front of a mirror or reminiscing about "the good old days"—except for the ones that involve our children. Their stories and memories are always welcomed. And we will all be sharing the great joy of a new baby in our collective family this spring, if only we could decide what our names will be. Contrary to others' suggestions, I will *not* be called the old gray mare. But Extra-Nana has a nice ring to it.

Peace, love, and sometimes rocky roads. Happy Heart Month to all y'all.

# Afterthoughts

*She Magazine* ended publication rather abruptly in 2018. Later issues were started but not completed to distribution. The discipline of writing a contributor's article every month and editing others' stories has faded from view. The loss continues to be felt, as I have struggled mightily to find another niche for what God would have me share. Evidently, the spirit is willing but the flesh is weak. Then the idea for this book became a reality and soon consumed my daily work until publication. But I trust this is not the end of a writing ministry, unless He tells me otherwise. Surely something hopeful will come of this book—if not for me, then maybe for others who read it. Maybe it's for you.

Much has happened since February 2018. In May, we were gifted with a beautiful baby girl grandchild. And I was gifted with two grandmothers who always include me as one of their own—thanks Diane and Gayle. Your generosity does not go without notice, ever. To be a grandparent, even if only by association, is a most wonderful thing—worth every sag and wrinkle of age. By the time this book is published she will be toddling through two and bringing multiple joys.

My son suffered many setbacks in his quest for a life after military service—from education, to housing, to sustaining employment, to recurring bouts with active alcoholism, PTSD, and loss of his Army family. Then he arrived at Hebron Colony Ministry, in Boone, NC. Two weeks later, we were overjoyed to hear him speak of Jesus as his savior. Time will tell how his life unfolds after his ten-week stay with the ministry, but he has been given what he has lacked until now—faith, hope, and love from an eternal source.

My daughter continues to amaze me. She has been so very loyal to her family (especially her "Marmie") and has matured into a giving, loving, person who is successful in her work and rich in friendships. Often she has been the mother and I the child. She carries with her a genuine love for others and a sense of humor that could make it on the comedy circuit, should she ever move in that direction. I cannot wait to see what God has in store for her, just around the corner.

My husband and I have enjoyed the benefits of house church with a small band of believers, and we are settling into a partnership built on faith and nurtured by love. It has made quite a difference in our walk, as we are active contributors instead of passive observers. Again, time will tell where we go from here—but the journey itself has been amazing so far. Our marriage continues to strengthen with each passing trial, much like a three corded knot, dipped in churning waters, and tossed out to dry in the noonday sun. Our knot has become quite strong, thanks to God. We are learning each day to live in contentment, whether the season is spring, summer, fall, or winter.

I will leave you with the copy of an unpublished essay, intended for the March 2018 issue of the magazine I so miss. It is musings on contentment—a great topic for endings, and for new beginnings.

# The Age of Contentment

*I* have been known to spend a lot of time worrying about things (and people and places and thoughts and possibilities and dreams and nightmares) I cannot control. I'm not anyone's example of a bubbly, optimistic person. I just don't have that happy-go-lucky gene in my personal pool. I can display some childlike wonder every now and then; a good clean joke or riddle or pun does send me into fits of giggles once in a while. A chocolate chip cookie fresh out of the oven can elicit squeals of delight. But that's about it on the giddy front for me. Large groups of people (and by that I mean any gathering over three humans and/or animals) exhaust me and I find the need to shelter in place much more than others—or at least that's my perspective. And we all know that our perspective is our reality.

Basically, I have spent most of my life, from childhood through the treacherously navigated adult phase, in an awkward state of mild to severe depression and/or anxiety. Perhaps it's just the perspective again, but I'm pretty sure it's a fairly accurate assessment. This world, after all, doesn't exactly glow with goodness and light—especially these days. I can get much too caught up in the way of the world. But I have been working on a better understanding of one simple word lately and it has begun to make all the difference. That word is *contentment*.

The *Oxford Dictionary* definition would have us believe that contentment is synonymous with happiness and satisfaction. A recent article on the subject of poverty opened my eyes to where we are in this country regarding earthly contentment, as compared to the world at large. And I quote: "If you have a place to live and food to eat every day, you are richer than 93 percent of the world population." Let that sink in for just a few moments.

I have spent far too many days complaining about living so far from a grocery store that I have often failed to notice that we have no troubles buying them or using a car that we own to get there and back with plenty of gas to spare. Am I content with my current age, looks, work, makeup, exercise routine, hairdo (and hair don't)? That's a no for each one. However, there is a true contentment outside of those areas, and inside us that supersedes even the most egregious failure in each one. And it is something to be learned.

Sometimes it helps to first figure out what something is not before coming to the definition or even recognition of what it is—contentment is very much like that, I think. If we know that contentment is not about a feeling or about simply being happy or satisfied, we get a little bit closer to what it is and how we can obtain it and maintain it. Or at the very least, strive for it. Being content is not so much about being happy where we are and with what we have—no, it's more an understanding of where we will end up, no matter the current circumstances of our lives here on earth—which are, of course, subject to change in the blink of an eye or the dreaded ring of a phone. As always, it helps to look to His Word:

"Let your conduct be without covetousness; be content with such things as you have. For He Himself has said, 'I will never leave you nor forsake you'" (Heb. 13:5, NKJV).

"The fear of the Lord leads to life; then one rests **content**, untouched by trouble" (Prov. 19:23 NIV).

This does not mean that we who fear the Lord will never be touched by trouble—it means, I think, that worldly trouble will not touch our fear of the Lord. We won't turn our backs on God because troubles come our way. We will live in awe of the Lord—whether troubles arrive or depart, or circle around us like hungry buzzards. To know contentment in this life is, perhaps, to understand the varied meanings of fear and love. Perfect love casts out fear and fear of the Lord leads to life.

Both fear, but one is positive and one is negative. There is no negative in God's love. Agape love—there is no fear there. Fear of the Lord is respectful submission, not oogy-boogy scary fright. In that way, then, we can be untouched by trouble—even when "trouble" comes. Fear of hell or death should not overtake love of God.

I spent a wonderful evening recently catching up with a very dear friend over supper at Margaret's in Mullins. She and her family have seen their share of heartbreak—they have endured a season that none of us desire, a time when whatever can go wrong does, and tragically so, with seemingly endless days of tears and sorrow. We have all been there, or will be there at some time in our lives. She struggles with understanding the meaning or purpose of all the pain, both physical and emotional, but is leaning on her faith—putting one tentative foot in front of the other, supporting her loved ones, returning to "normal" activities day by day, trusting that He will be there, is there, and was there, even during the height of the storm that is now slowly subsiding.

I believe that she is attempting mightily to live in contentment and not in what has been raging around her. It hurts every day, and it hurts those who love her to see how the recent storms have buffeted her. Hopefully, she will have many more days, mixed with joys and sorrows. But that is just how this life unfolds. With God all things are possible. Nothing is impossible, even when it seems to be. And it surely isn't happy all the time. In contentment, we find a way to breathe through all of it, knowing in faith that the ultimate end of sorrows is only the beginning of eternal joy.

So then, what is contentment? What does it mean to be content in all circumstances, whether young, vibrant and lovely or old, tired and wrung out? You know, it must have something to do with that peace that passes all understanding. It must be that biblical meaning of the word, and not the worldly one.

"Now godliness with contentment is great gain. For we brought nothing into this world, and it is certain we can carry nothing out. And having food and clothing, with these we shall be content. But those who desire to be rich fall into temptation and a snare, and into many foolish and harmful lusts which drown men in destruction and perdition. For the love of money is a root of all kinds of evil, for which some have strayed from the faith in their greediness, and pierced themselves through with many sorrows. But you, O man of God, flee these things and pursue righteousness, godliness, faith, love, patience, gentleness. Fight the good fight of faith, lay hold on eternal life, to which you were also called and have confessed the good confession in the presence of many witnesses"

(1 Timothy 6:6–12).

In seasons of grief, grace, and gratitude, contentment is to be found within; not from this world, but through Him. Hold on to your hope. In His love and tender mercies, I am humbled and very thankful to have shared some time with you.

Always choose joy.

(Especially when you don't feel like it)

# THE POWER OF Writing

Now it's your turn in the she shed. On the following pages you'll find some seasonal food for thought questions and a challenge to complete your own milestones chart for the seasons of your life. Hope you find these questions thought provoking as you consider your own seasoned contentment. Again, thank you so very much for choosing to read these essays from my personal journey of grief, grace, and abundant gratitude for His love and the opportunity to love others as we are called.

# Spring
## Food for Seasonal Thought

When have you experienced a new beginning?

What was it like?

What did you learn from it?

How important to you are birthdays, anniversaries, and other milestones?

If spring is your favorite season, why?

In your experience, has the bunny or the cross dominated your Easter celebrations?

Is there a bible verse that resonates spring for you?

In what ways does spring restore/renew your faith?

# Summer

## Food for Seasonal Thought

How have I worshipped the sun over the Son, the creation over the Creator?

Summer usually brings vacations, loosened schedules. How does that affect your walk of faith?

If summer is your favorite season, do you know why? Has it always been?

Does the heat of summer intensify your emotions?

Is patriotism important to you? How do you celebrate independence?

Are there verses that bring summer to mind for you?

Summer brings the ripest of fruits and delicious picnic celebrations. What's your favorite summer memory?

# Fall
## Food for Seasonal Thought

Cooler days, the rustle of leaves, pumpkin spice in the air–is this your favorite season? Shorter days, back-to-school, no more beach time–or is this your least favorite season?

It's a time for thanksgiving, gathering together, and preparation for Christmas—what are you favorite memories wrapped around the fall season? Or do you dread the thought of Halloween?

Education was mostly a positive experience for me, but not always for my children—does the memory of school days make you smile or cringe—or both?

Leaves changing color and dropping to the ground can be a great sign of hope—they let go in order to rest, renew, and regain their greenery later—in what ways has your life been a changing landscape?

Bible verses for the autumn of our lives—what comes to mind for you?

# Winter

## Food for Seasonal Thought

Ah, the gift of winter—hibernation time at its best, do you agree?

Do you remember hoping for snow days as a child? Even if school was a favorite place, the snow days held magic (or so we thought).

What has been your favorite Christmas gift—both given and received?

February is Heart Month—for lots of reasons. How do you celebrate Valentine's Day, or do you?

We are told that our hearts are deceitful and desperately wicked—who can even know them? Does the winter season seem to make this particularly true? In what ways does it or does it not?

# Milestones for All Seasons of Life

*To everything there is a season, and a time for every purpose under heaven.*

—Ecclesiastes 3:1

**C**hallenge: It's time to write out your own seasonal milestones and spiritual markers! If you have not yet reached the later seasons of your life, consider writing what you hope will happen in seasons not yet seen. And if writing just isn't your thing, simply spend some prayer time on the challenge or share your thoughts with a trusted friend. The seasonal notes that follow may help jog your milestone memories. I promise the journey of your seasons is worth it. Enjoy!

**Extra credit**: In which season are you most contented? Do you think your personality is defined or reflected by that season? What about your season of faith? Are you in spring, summer, fall, or winter? How can you find contentment in every season of your life?

### Spring—Birth to Twenty
Birth and toddlerhood
School years
Making friends
Graduations, proms, teenage angst
Faith of your family

### Summer—Twenty-One to Forty
Adulthood
First jobs/career moves
Serious relationships/marriage
Parenthood
Moving into new home/apt
Independence/responsibility
Letting go of family faith

### Fall—Forty-One to Sixty
Midlife crisis
Career success/change
Losing loved ones
Grandparenting
Financial goals
Wrinkles/gray hair/slowing down
Reconnection of faith

### Winter—Sixty and Beyond
Retirement
Health concerns
Renewal of hobby interests
Gifts of time to read and reflect
Ready for journey's end/comfort of faith

# Notes

CPSIA information can be obtained
at www.ICGtesting.com
Printed in the USA
LVHW070346160321
681579LV00023B/248